The Stars Will Still Be There

NICOLA NUTTALL

The Stars Will Still Be There

**What losing my daughter
taught me about
life, love and hope**

HarperElement

An imprint of HarperCollins*Publishers*

1 London Bridge Street

London SE1 9GF

www.harpercollins.co.uk

HarperCollins*Publishers*

Macken House, 39/40 Mayor Street Upper

Dublin 1, D01 C9W8, Ireland

First published by HarperElement 2024

This edition published 2025

1 3 5 7 9 10 8 6 4 2

All plate-section images are courtesy of the author, with the exception
of plate 5 (bottom), courtesy of Lorne Campbell/Guzelian

A catalogue record of this book is available from the British Library

ISBN 978-0-00-866800-6

Printed and bound in the UK using 100% renewable electricity at
CPI Group (UK) Ltd

This book contains FSC™ certified paper and other controlled
sources to ensure responsible forest management.

For more information visit: www.harpercollins.co.uk/green

This book is dedicated to Mark and Gracie for their unconditional love and patience, and for allowing me to share this story. And to Alice and Alfred so that one day they can read all about their legendary cousin; she loved you both so much.

'You see this smile, Betty …?
It's not really a smile.
It's the lid on a scream.'

Bet Lynch, *Coronation Street*, 15 May 1989

Prologue

August 2021

A girl steps out tentatively from the wings of the theatre. She's wearing a navy blue playsuit with bright white trainers bought especially for the occasion. Although she's nineteen now, it will be years before she doesn't get asked to prove her age in a bar.

The audience is restless; many have spent the afternoon drinking, so her arrival on stage draws some *boos* from the front row. This girl is not the national-treasure comedian they queued for hours in the rain to see.

She stands with the spotlight a flat halo at her feet and lifts her eyes from the cue cards in her hand to see two and a half thousand faces staring back at her.

She smiles, but if you look closely, you can see that her hands are shaking.

She lifts the microphone closer to her mouth; there's a howl of feedback. The auditorium quietens and she takes a deep breath.

'Let me tell you about my sister, Laura.'

2018

Plot Twist

October

The day that Laura came home from Chicago felt like Christmas, and that wasn't just because we'd had to get up at the crack of dawn to collect her from the airport.

I'd spent the previous night at the kitchen table making a huge '*Welcome Home, Laura*' sign from a flattened cardboard box and a rainbow of Sharpies.

'She'll not thank you for making a show of her with that,' Mark had said, leaning against the counter as he waited for the kettle to boil.

'I know.' I'd smiled at the thought of her expression.

The automatic doors opened and closed, releasing small clusters of dishevelled travellers into the arrivals hall. I scanned the features of each tired face until my eyes settled on the one I'd been waiting for. She was dragging a black suitcase behind her, a heavy rucksack on one shoulder, eyes slightly red from the overnight flight.

'Bloody knew you'd be standing there with a sign,' she said, as she hugged us hello.

'And I knew you'd be secretly disappointed if I wasn't.'

She'd picked up a hint of an accent along with her tan and seemed a different girl to the one we'd waved off ten weeks ago; somehow taller and newly exotic.

We took her for a celebratory breakfast of avocado on toast, and she told stories of her long working days cold-calling the residents of Illinois. Her job as an intern in the campaign office of the state governor had been to ascertain political allegiances and, assuming the person on the other end of the line was sympathetic to her candidate, check they would be voting in the imminent state elections. She had loved every single minute of it.

Once satisfied that we'd wiped our hands free of buttery toast crumbs, Laura passed her phone around the table, first to me, then her dad, Mark, and finally to her sister, Gracie. We swiped through photos of gleaming skyscrapers, a lake so big it looked like the sea, and selfies taken between new friends with good teeth.

It was the first time Laura had travelled alone, and as she annotated her pictures with unfamiliar names, places and funny stories, just for an instant my mouth filled with a sour tang. It tasted like sadness. We'd moved on to the next act and she would be having her adventures without me from now on.

Those last weeks of summer sank softly into autumn. We joined thousands of parents on the inevitable pre-university trip to IKEA, where we piled a wonky trolley with pillows, duvet, fairy lights and mugs, exchanged rueful looks with other parents at the checkout and wondered how so many reasonably priced things ended up costing such a lot of money.

I watched Laura meticulously boxing up her belongings, ready for her first term at King's College London where she would be studying International Relations, another step in her long-term plan for a career in the security services. Her excitement was contagious, but the thought of setting the table for three every night left me feeling hollow inside. I was two years from a completely empty nest and had no idea how I'd cope with no longer being needed.

'You should think about getting a lodger,' she said, securing the lid on a plastic crate containing towels and crockery. She sat back on her haunches and blew the hair out of eyes that were sometimes blue, sometimes green. 'Honestly, I really don't mind. I'd be quite happy to sleep in the spare room when I come home for holidays.'

Mark stacked the boxes in the boot of the car as I gave her bedroom one last look. It was completely bare now, blank walls dotted with the greasy memories of Blu-Tacked posters, empty drawers and naked metal coat hangers jangling in the wardrobe.

I cried when we left her, of course I did. She was all at once too small and too young to be alone in the big city, but Laura was ecstatic with the lush promise of freedom and couldn't wait to say her goodbyes. I'd braced myself for an initial period of radio silence as she threw herself into Freshers' Week, but she surprised me by phoning home every couple of days.

She once called me when we were both in the middle of preparing dinner – me frying chicken to make curry for three, she boiling pasta shapes for one in a kitchen shared with eight others, overlooking the Olympic Stadium in Stratford.

'Mum, I can't get this pasta sauce open and I'm too much of a feminist to ask one of the boys to do it for me.'

'You big dope … just tap the side of the lid on the floor, quite hard. It'll break the seal.' There was a silence in which she contemplated the fact that there were still things I knew that she didn't.

I heard the jar open, first with a click and then a gasp as the vacuum was released.

'How did you even know that?'

'You don't get to be 48 without learning the odd trick or two, my love,' I said, and she laughed at how delighted I was to still have something left to teach her.

Laura's course was taught within the Department of War Studies, right in the centre of the city, and a forty-minute tube ride each way from her halls of residence. The lecture halls were bursting with the loud and the confident; no warm flat vowels or familiar northern accents to be heard. It was a long way from the comfortable domesticity of the all-girls grammar school she'd attended for the last seven years. Laura had always yearned for the big city life, but I began to wonder if it was meeting her sky-high expectations.

Back up north, my brother Neil celebrated his birthday with a family dinner and Laura delighted us by coming home on the train. She seemed happy enough but I thought she looked tired.

'You sure you're OK?' I asked, tipping her face towards the light to get a better look at her eyes.

'I'm fine, Mum,' she said, pulling away. 'Think I might be starting with migraines, though; had a couple of quite bad ones recently.'

The rest of the family had their own opinions on what might be causing the headaches.

'Too much partying,' was my dad's contribution. 'Seriously, are you drinking too much? I know what you students are like with all that cheap alcohol.'

'It's London, Gramps, nothing's cheap.'

'Are you eating properly, Laura?' from my mum. 'Not just Pot Noodles, you know, but plenty of fresh fruit and veg?'

'Laura, could it be your glasses aren't strong enough? When did you last get your eyes checked?' Mark asked. Then, quietly, in the kitchen, as we scraped plates and stacked the dishwasher, he said, 'Do you think she's taking drugs, Nic? I might be well out of order but just have a look at her pupils. I'm sure they're bigger than normal.'

Before her trip home, Laura had registered with a new London GP and had mentioned the headaches. She also told him that one

Saturday evening she'd been sitting on her bed reading textbooks and the next moment had woken up to find herself on the floor, her face wet and bruised, with no idea of how she'd got there. The doctor didn't seem especially concerned with either the headaches or the floor incident, but suggested she monitor the situation and pop back if something similar happened again. Laura did as she was told and recorded the dates of subsequent headaches on a piece of scrap paper.

The day after Neil's birthday dinner we had the luxury of some unexpected time together as a family of four. As usual, it took far too long for the girls to get ready, and it was mid-afternoon before we finally arrived in Lytham St Annes. We ate panini and crisps at the Vinyl Café, sitting outside in the courtyard despite the cold, as naturally we'd brought Ziggy along – because what's a beach without a dog?

As we walked along the seafront later, the gunmetal sea reflected a thick layer of heavy grey cloud, then the low sun broke through and we were treated to the most spectacular sunset, the sky and sea flooded with an almost celestial golden glow.

The light was extraordinary, almost surreal – portentous and profound, as if the weather was a warning of something. It's easy to load events with significance after the fact, but, even at the time, we felt a little unnerved by the strange weight of that day.

The next morning, Laura woke with another headache. She was quiet and held her head stiffly, as if the slightest movement caused pain. I found her a couple of paracetamol which she swigged back with apple juice, but they didn't seem to make any difference.

'Don't go back today,' Gracie pleaded, as Mark brought Laura's bags down to the kitchen. 'Stay another night and see how you feel tomorrow. You can always get the train on Monday. We can have a movie night on the sofa.'

'I need to get back, Grace,' Laura replied flatly. 'I'm doing a presentation tomorrow.'

'Stop fussing, she'll be fine.' Mark picked up the car keys from the bowl on the dresser. 'Come on then, if you want to make this train.'

Just as the car pulled away, the radio started playing a song that my beloved Nanna used to sing to me as a child: 'Lulla Lulla Bye Bye'. Although I'd never heard the original before, I was instantly back in her living room: I felt the blast of the gas fire and the mossy bobble of her green three-piece suite.

Were you trying to tell me something, Nanna? Was it a warning, or has hindsight made a superstitious ghoul of me?

In the few short weeks that Laura had been living in London, she'd been typically productive: she'd signed up to train with St John Ambulance, secured a part-time job with Ladbrokes and applied to become an officer cadet with the University Royal Navy Unit.

She phoned home to tell me all about it. 'I've just been to get measured up for the uniform – it's really smart. We get taught to sail, there's all kinds of travelling and we even get paid. Can you believe that? Can't wait to start, they're all so nice. Need to pass the medical first, though.'

This was just a formality, as Laura had always been fit and healthy. Earlier in the year, and right in the middle of her A Levels, she'd completed her first marathon, just to prove she could. For years we'd taken part in the Race for Life and each time she got a little bit faster until, aged eleven, she finished the 5km race ahead of me. Laura was the third runner in. I ran the last mile, out of breath and teary, pointing to the little blonde girl just ahead and shouting proudly to anyone who would listen: 'Look at her! That's my girl, that's my daughter!'

By Monday the headache had passed, and on her way to lectures Laura called in at Boots Opticians for the eye test that would complete her Royal Navy medical.

She called me from a bus. 'Right, I don't want you freaking out.'

'Why am I going to freak out, Laura? What's happened?'

'So, I went for the eye test, and they weren't happy … said there was pressure behind my eyes, and I need to get it checked out at the eye hospital.'

'Hospital! What else did they say? Is this serious?'

'She asked if I had double vision and I said that I didn't, and she said that it looked like my optic discs were swollen and I needed to get myself to Moorfields Eye Hospital straight away. Apparently it looks like "papilledema", whatever that is.'

'And how are you feeling?'

'OK, just tired. It was weird, I couldn't keep my eyes open in that seminar.'

'That's not like you – you never sleep anywhere but bed.'

'I know, right? Really strange.'

As she spoke, I entered the unfamiliar letters of *papilledema* into my phone, guessing at the correct spelling. SERIOUS, PRESSURE, BRAIN, SWELLING flashed up on the first page of the results and my insides sloshed with a wave of ice-cold anxiety.

Laura waited an age to be seen at the eye hospital, undergoing a variety of tests, and heading back and forth between the waiting and examination rooms. When she finally saw a doctor, he said that nothing looked amiss with her eyes, but he would refer her to a neurologist, just to be on the safe side.

'He said it's nothing to worry about, so stop panicking.'

'Are you sure? Do you want me to come down?'

'Honestly, stop fussing, Mum. I'm fine.'

'OK, if you're absolutely sure. But you call me straight away if anything changes.'

'I will.'

'Promise me? And Dad says make sure you get a taxi back; we'll send you the money for it.'

She agreed, then completely ignored me and got the bus as usual.

Despite her reassurances, I still felt a cold unease deep in my gut. Every instinct told me to head down so I could see her with my own eyes, but Mark persuaded me to wait.

'The hospital said she's fine and she's feeling OK, so why do you need to rush down there? She's a big girl now, Nic, you've just got to let her get on with it.'

The next morning, I called her, but the phone rang out. I realised she could have been sitting in a lecture – of course, that would mean she couldn't answer – so I sent her a text and waited a couple of hours. No response. Foreboding traced an icy finger down my spine.

I tried her every ten minutes and so did Gracie, and then so did Mark. We left a stream of messages, each more anxious than the last, but she didn't pick up. I was becoming increasingly frantic; she had never felt so far away, and I was desperate for the reassurance of her voice.

It was early evening by the time she called back. Her phone had been on silent because she was in bed with a terrible headache, vomiting and feeling painfully sensitive to light.

In a quiet voice, she asked, 'Please can you come?'

For once in her life, Laura was asking for help.

Gracie was adamant she was coming too, a genuine concern for her sister mixed with the heady promise of an unscheduled day off school. I can't remember ever driving quite so fast, but we needed to make the last train and it would be tight. A ten-minute delay leaving Glasgow made all the difference and we boarded the train, giddy with relief to be a step closer to Laura.

The Central line to Stratford was still standing room only at almost 11 p.m. Gracie and I sent a semaphore of weak smiles back and forth across the Tube carriage, nervously reassuring each other that everything would be absolutely fine and that we were probably making a fuss about nothing. Mark had booked us into a Travelodge, so we dropped our bags then tried to hail a taxi. The roads were disappointingly empty, so instead we jogged slowly through silent streets that were slick with drizzle.

The student block was eerily quiet, just two security guards playing on their phones and the shabby detritus of Freshers' Week posters flapping on the noticeboard. Laura wasn't answering her phone so one of the bemused guards took us up in the lift, asking us to wait outside her flat while he checked it was OK to let us in.

The room was pitch-black and airless. It took a while for my eyes to adjust after the brightness of the corridor, but there was Laura, an indistinct shape, motionless on the bed. We carefully helped her to sit up; even the slightest head movement made her flinch with pain. She was clammy, a sheen of sweat on her pale face as she turned away to vomit sour yellow bile into a carrier bag. I knew that this was more than a migraine: something felt seriously wrong.

I helped her out of damp pyjamas and into sweatpants and a hoodie, her limbs uncooperative and heavy with sleep. Gracie ordered an Uber, and I crammed a few things into a bag, clumsy and flustered, with the frantic pulse of blood loud in my ears.

Down in reception, the security staff debated which was the nearest A&E before settling on Homerton, in Hackney. We staggered out to the taxi, Gracie and I holding Laura upright as she clutched the carrier bag and tried her hardest not to be sick in the car.

A&E was still pretty lively in the very early hours of a midweek morning, but Laura was quickly triaged and given a sick bowl. She kept her eyes tightly closed against the aggressive fluorescent lights and did her best to sleep against my shoulder. Gracie and I orchestrated a campaign of pleading looks and *help-me* eyes until a sympathetic nurse took pity on us, and we were moved to an empty bay where Laura could lie quietly before being assessed.

A doctor breezed in with a brisk swish of the blue privacy curtain, introduced herself as Amber, and fired off a series of questions: 'When did this start?' 'What are your symptoms?' 'How are you feeling now?' Laura seemed foggy and disorientated. I could tell she was downplaying how bad she felt. Sick of the hospital, she just craved sleep and a return to bed, so I filled in the gaps.

Amber took out a pen torch to look closely at Laura's pupils and asked her to follow its movement across her field of vision. 'Laura, can you hold your arms out for me, please, straight in front with your palms facing downwards? OK, now can you turn them upwards, please … and now keep your arms in front but close your eyes.'

Gracie and I watched intently, trying to second-guess the clues she might be looking for, studying her face for a tell of concern. I realised we were holding hands.

'Right, now I'm going to hold my hand out and I want you to push against it with yours, hard as you can … push, push, push … OK, that's good, now the other hand. OK, now hold your arms out for me again, I'm going to try to lift them up, and I want you to try to resist me.'

Amber's face remained impassive as she clicked a ballpoint pen and scribbled on a clipboard, then paused and exhaled heavily. She lifted her eyes and they met mine, which were waiting expectantly for some words of reassurance. She squeezed a straight-line smile from closed lips and slipped out of the cubicle, returning minutes later with a hospital porter.

'Just going to whizz you upstairs for a CT scan, Laura,' she said calmly. 'Won't take long – it's pretty quiet up there at this time of night.' The porter took the brakes off the bed and skilfully manoeuvred it out of the bay.

* * *

Laura was curled in a foetal position on the bed, facing the wall and trying to sleep when Amber drew back the curtain, more slowly this time.

'Have you got chairs?' she asked.

'Oh, yes, I'm sorry,' I replied, standing up in preparation to give them back. I assumed that she needed the ones in our cubicle for someone else, but she was just checking we had places to sit.

Amber crouched down on her haunches. 'I'm really sorry to have to tell you this, but Laura has a brain tumour. In fact, it looks as though there might be two.'

The words were like a wave in the sea that lifted me off my feet, unmooring me and sending me scrabbling for something solid to hold me up. It was almost surreal and I'm not sure that I didn't even half laugh. Maybe I'd exaggerated Laura's symptoms to the doctor; if I took back my words, would it change the diagnosis?

I can't remember what else we were told: my ears were too full of the seawater sounds of shock. But I gathered that Laura would be kept in overnight and taken for a further scan the following morning.

The tectonic plates had shifted; our world was never, ever going to be the same again. As the doctor left the room, there was a moment's silence.

'Plot twist,' said Laura dryly, in what was the understatement of the year.

I left Gracie holding Laura's hand as she drifted in and out of sleep, and allowed myself to be ushered into the small family room – two fabric chairs, fake flowers in a vase and a box of tissues on the table – to make the worst phone call imaginable.

Mark was fast asleep. It was 4 a.m. by now. Having maintained a relatively brave face in front of the girls, this was the point at which it all dissolved.

'Mark.' Deep breath. 'Laura's ... Laura's got a brain tumour.'

'What ... Nic?'

'I knew there was something was wrong. Why the fuck didn't I trust my instincts?!' A howl came from deep inside me. It sounded barely human. I folded in two, wracked with pain, my heart bleeding into the empty hollow that had opened up inside me. I had no idea what to do or what would happen next, and I was inconsolable. Mark was barely awake and was trying to make sense of my words with his sleep-soaked brain. He asked me questions I couldn't answer, and I broke my heart into little pieces and stuffed it down the phone line.

Another porter came to collect Laura and took her up to a ward, then we were sent home – or at least back to our hotel. By the time we arrived back at the Travelodge, many of the guests were leaving to start their day. Gracie and I shuffled down the corridor like traumatised survivors of some natural disaster: pale, sticky-eyed, trembling with nervous exhaustion. We attempted a few hours of sleep, stirring intermittently to cry and tighten our grip on each other. I woke in a strange bed and wondered where I was, everything normal for a glorious split second – the roller-coaster at the top of the slow climb before a swooping, stomach-turning gravity drop.

Nothing would ever be normal again.

I would have avoided making the next call forever if I could. My parents were all too familiar with grief and loss; and while the wounds of their trauma had healed over time, the skin was still paper thin. How could I put them through this again?

'Hiya Mum, sorry for ringing so early, you both OK? Is Dad there? Put me on speaker, you both need to hear this – I'm so sorry but it's really not good news.'

I pressed my forehead against the cool glass of the window, watching the buses on Stratford High Street full of normal people doing ordinary things.

'There's no easy way to say this – but Laura's got a brain tumour … more than one, they think. It looks really bad.'

Back in an Uber to Homerton, I held tightly to Gracie's hand, my knuckles sharp and white, terrified that, somehow, I might lose her too.

Laura had been admitted to a busy adult ward, mostly populated by older ladies in various stages of confusion. One lady was crying because she believed everyone hated her and kept leaving because she was Jewish. A very patient nurse explained that nobody hated her and those who had left had just got better and gone home. Another lady was convinced that someone had stolen her knickers.

To get a clearer picture of what we were dealing with, Laura was taken down for another scan, this time an MRI. Despite protesting that she was perfectly fine and able to walk, the porter insisted on a wheelchair. They were taking no risks now; the unexploded bomb in her head marked her as fragile and potentially unstable.

Morning rounds were in full swing when Laura was brought back to the ward. A new doctor stood by Laura's bed and explained to her attending students that brain tumours in someone so young and healthy were unusual and, having seen the scans, she was pretty sure that there must be a primary cancer somewhere in Laura's body that had spread undetected until it had finally blown its cover and metastasised into her brain.

This was the first time we had heard the word *cancer*. I looked for Laura's reaction, but her face was a blank. I didn't understand the coded language of diagnosis back then and I'd maintained a vague hope that this was just a benign and inconsequential growth; nothing we couldn't handle. Until that point, I don't think I'd even realised that brain tumours were cancerous. I felt slow, stupid, and completely out of my depth: I knew nothing.

Gracie and I sat at the side of Laura's bed and talked about everything other than the reason we were there. Talking about it would only make it real, and we weren't ready to admit that yet.

I went down to the hospital shop and bought family bags of sweets and a deck of cards to entertain the girls.

We were playing 'Heads Up', the game where you hold a phone to your forehead and the other players shout out clues until you guess the words on the screen. It was a film round and Gracie had just shouted: '… and Louise!' which was absolutely no help as we were trying to guess the civil rights film, *Selma*, when the curtain was slowly pulled back on its metal rail and two junior doctors appeared in the gap. They looked like they had just been pushed reluctantly on stage, their discomfort unmistakable.

Just when we thought things were as bleak as they could be, the MRI scan had shown eight tumours rather than two.

Now they needed a CT scan of Laura's whole body – rather than just the head – to search for this elusive primary. As we waited for Laura's turn in the machine, nobody mentioned the skeletal men and women unmistakably in the final stages of cancer who were being wheeled into the scanning area by cheery porters. But as soon as Laura was out of earshot, Gracie and I broke down, sobbing in each other's arms. We could only keep up the brave face for short periods and we saved those for when Laura was watching.

The next stage was a thorough fingertip examination of Laura's skin: two doctors searched for clues as if her very body had become a crime scene. As they scrutinised her planes and plateaus, we wandered the wide corridors up to the cafeteria and down to the shop. We'd already picked up the geography of the hospital, learning our route from the road map of abstract paintings and public health posters on the walls. Gracie dipped cold chips into a pool of ketchup as they closed up the canteen, and we tried to rub words of positivity together into a tiny smoulder of optimism.

For all its everyday challenges, parenting had been a breeze so far. I knew we'd been lucky and I regularly gave thanks to some unknown, benevolent dealer for this good hand of cards. We weren't rich or spectacularly talented, but we had what we needed, and the girls had grown up bright and happy. My skills as a mum would probably have put me mid-table in the championship. I wasn't Premier League-level fun, or tigerishly ambitious for them, but I covered the basics with enthusiasm: made sure the girls felt loved, that they did their homework and usually went to sleep with a story.

After eighteen years, I thought I'd earned my stripes, but in truth I had never even been tested. I was out of my depth and desperate for Mark to arrive; he seemed to be taking ages. I knew there would be lots to organise, and the traffic would be bad, but I could imagine his dread. Once he arrived, his life, too, would change forever.

Outside, small children with masks and Halloween buckets ranged like a picket line around the entrance to the hospital. Many of us dropped loose change into their buckets, hoping to buy some good karma for the people we loved. I rubbed my arms, hugging myself tightly against the chill of the evening as I watched the brand-new families leaving with precious, fresh babies snug in unfamiliar car seats. It seemed like only days before we had been bringing Laura home in a teddy bear snowsuit, and the memory was a tight squeeze around my throat.

Mark finally arrived and I cried with relief as he held me, tears soaking the shoulder of his woollen pullover. My relief was mixed with bitterness; I was angry because he had taken so long to get down, angry that he wasn't with us when we were given the news, and angry because in the days before the diagnosis he'd made me feel like I was overreacting and making a fuss. I knew that I was being unreasonable and cruel, but I wasn't in a very reasonable place.

I reconfigured my brave face and led Mark up to the ward. Laura was packing her bag, ready to be discharged, elated to see her dad. There was no reason to keep her in hospital for another night, but we'd need to return the next day for a breast scan, and again on Friday to talk to the doctors.

The four of us were together again and it was such a relief not to be the only adult: someone else would be able to ask the questions and take in the answers, and this felt like a great weight lifted. Now that we were reunited as a family, I had the overwhelming urge to get us all in the car and just drive far, far away from this unthinkable scenario. We could escape, leave the country, get new identities, and pretend this wasn't really happening. How far could we get with a tank of fuel and a boot full of denial? But this was real life, so I took my phone out and booked a hotel. I couldn't contemplate letting Laura out of my sight ever again, so I chose a family room where we could all be together in two double beds.

I felt compelled to tell everyone about Laura's diagnosis, to provide an explanation for the swollen eyes and the shell-shocked faces. Receptionists, complete strangers, couples on a mini-break having drinks in the bar, all living normal lives when the bottom had fallen out of ours.

I don't think I slept at all that night. How could I sleep when I couldn't trust the world anymore? My job as a mother had been to keep the girls safe, to help them avoid all of childhood's dangerous trapdoors, and feed them well so they would grow. I'd made sure they were vaccinated against childhood illnesses, cleaned grazed knees, sorted out inhalers and warned them about strangers. But I had been looking in the wrong direction all along: the menace had been on the inside, growing in Laura's brain. The phone call in the horror film was coming from upstairs.

*   *   *

Once we were finished at the hospital we went back to Laura's halls. Six weeks ago, we'd moved her in, dragged the boxes up in the lift, unpacked her shopping, and helped to make up her bed. Now we were faced with packing it up and bringing her home, boxing up frying pans and cereal bowls, all the things we'd bought that day in IKEA, a whole lifetime ago when our biggest worries had been how many mugs she might need.

Gracie and Mark took Laura back to the hotel so she could sleep, and I walked to a nearby shopping centre. I needed to find some means of regaining control and that meant a substantial notebook to write everything down in. I am one of those people who seeks emotional solace in fresh new stationery. I needed the soothing rhythm of cursive letters trailing ink across a smooth clean page.

I needed a *list*.

I also took the opportunity to call Leo, without worrying about Laura overhearing the conversation. Leonora was not only a close friend, but until recently she'd been married to my brother, Neil, and she was still very much part of our family.

Leo had been frantically doorstepping doctors in the hospital where she worked as an oncology sister, looking for advice and some kind of plan. I hung on her every word, hoping to hear that this was a problem with a solution, but a day spent grilling colleagues had only confirmed that this diagnosis was the worst kind of bad news.

That night we went out for tea. We must have looked like any other family in Jamie's Italian. Keeping the conversation light and tiptoeing around the elephant in the room, I could barely breathe for the terror that had expanded to fill my entire chest like insulation foam, but we still laughed and bickered, feigning a pantomime of normality over bowls of pasta and garlic bread.

'You should start a bucket list of brilliant things, but make sure you take me too,' Gracie said.

'I like your thinking, but just so you know, I've no plans to die just yet,' Laura replied.

Next morning we took an Uber back to Homerton. In the back, we were silent, suffocating, but in the passenger seat Mark began a long and animated monologue about the pros and cons of electric and diesel cars. It was the most I'd heard him speak since he'd arrived in London. He was much more comfortable discussing engines and mileage ranges; this was his safe space. The driver responded with bemused one-word answers.

We all reveal our fear in different ways.

The doctor explained that, despite extensive testing, no primary cancer had been detected. They still believed there was one, they just couldn't find it. It might even end up being categorised as a *cancer of an unknown primary*, depending on the outcome of any surgery. We were given a wedge of discharge paperwork to take home, the whole grim story down in black and white to be shared with a medical team we didn't have yet.

We found ourselves in a greasy spoon café around the corner from the hospital where the smell of fried food and noisy kids on half term added to my feeling of general queasiness. Laura needed to speak to the admin departments at King's College and notify Student Finance that she was having to leave university with immediate effect. We couldn't speak on her behalf: for reasons of data protection, they only wanted to hear it from Laura.

She explained again and again in a quiet voice: 'I'm just phoning to let you know that I'm probably going to have to leave university because I've got a brain tumour – a brain tumour, yes. No, no, I don't think I'm going to be coming back, I'll need to stay closer to home, thank you, that's very kind … is there anyone else I need to tell?'

Every time she said the words, it left me winded.

* * *

Saturday brought a constant stream of visitors to the house. They came to demonstrate their love with cards and little gifts: bed socks and hot water bottles – soft, warm presents for the sad, sick girl. Their intentions were kind, and Mark and I repeated the story again and again until it no longer felt like ours.

At one point I snuck outside and sat on the low garden wall with a mug of tea, staring dazedly into space and wondering how on earth we were going to get through this. Don't get me wrong – it was lovely to see the friends and family that came to visit but it was also exhausting, standing in the kitchen making endless cups of tea and soaking up sympathy. Sometimes, *we* even had to do the comforting. Most of the time I just wanted it to be the four of us; I didn't want to have to share Laura with other people. I was selfish and greedy, and I wanted all of her time. We spent our evenings watching old Disney films, snuggled under blankets on the sofa, and we went to the pub for tea. Nobody really felt like cooking anymore and I resented spending time in the kitchen when it was time away from Laura.

It was around then that the angel of death started to visit me. Sometimes she would just whisper in my ear, other times she'd take centre stage in feverish dreams or sidle into my peripheral vision when I was awake. She looked exactly like Siobhan Fahey from Shakespears Sister in the 'Stay' video – long dark hair, pale skin, PVC catsuit, and a great deal of eye makeup – murmuring unspeakable things and cackling like a cartoon villain as my eyes widened in horror.

I knew exactly what she was: the embodiment of my worst and darkest fears.

I was never much of an early riser, but now I was wide awake at 5 every morning. As soon as I floated close to the surface of consciousness, Siobhan would start tormenting me with a greatest-hits showreel of increasingly grotesque scenarios: I saw myself writing only three names on birthday cards; Gracie utterly bereft and suicidal; the unthinkable possibility of Christmas without Laura; and the inevitable disintegration of our family.

It would be impossible to get back to sleep and so, to banish the unwelcome visitor, I would quietly get dressed in the dark and head out for a run. I'd found that shuffling down the Leeds and Liverpool Canal before sunrise provided a perfect opportunity for the kind of ugly crying you can only really do in private.

Crying did actually help; noisy howls of pain in the early morning when the towpath was quiet, or in a muddy field filled with bemused cows. The worst tears were those that came at bedtime. I'd do my best to muffle them, let the tears just soak soundlessly into the pillowcase, but it was the runny nose that would give me away. Sometimes Mark would hear and try to comfort me with a pat on the leg or a squeeze of the shoulder. I think sometimes he knew I was sobbing into the sheets but ignored me for want of something helpful to say. Sometimes he was just asleep.

After the tears I would always feel a bit lighter – perhaps it was like bloodletting to 'rebalance the humours' – and I'd feel better able to face the day. I wondered why we talk about being 'reduced to tears', as if they make us less than we truly are, when aren't we enhanced or elevated in some way by their honesty?

It's difficult to maintain a brave face when your heart is broken, but I could see Gracie watching my reactions; she needed to feel there was still hope, and fear is deeply contagious. Running soon became a necessity. It helped me create some illusion of control and stability, dulling the sharp edges of rage and fear that often threatened to overwhelm me. By the time I returned home, the worst would be out of my system. I'd take a shower, dry my hair, and apply a full face of makeup before anyone else was awake. All I really wanted to do was hibernate in the safe cocoon of my bed and sleep until it was all over, but I needed the girls to have confidence in me, so I defined my eyes with liner and mascara, warmed my pallid skin with blusher and disguised the lines of worry with concealer. It felt important to maintain the charade that everything was going to be OK. As soon as I appeared without mascara, the girls would know they had something to worry about. My eyelashes were the equivalent of ravens to the Tower of London.

During one such run, a few days after we'd brought Laura home, I watched the sun rise, a slash of peach and gold against the inky October sky. My cheeks were nipped by the cold, and I couldn't feel my fingers, but the morning had been so clear and beautiful I couldn't help but feel a stirring of hope.

I kicked off my trainers in the porch and ran upstairs to check on Laura. Mark was already with her, and I could tell from his grim expression that something had happened. He waited for her to go to the bathroom before telling me.

'Looks like she's had another seizure in the night. She woke up and the sheets were all wet. Tried to strip the bed, bless her – slept in the spare room. She can't remember what happened. I think she's a bit confused.'

Laura came back into the room and Mark quickly changed the subject to breakfast. I busied myself sorting out fresh bedding, anything to distract from this creeping and ominous dread. She was starting to lose control, her own body had become frighteningly unpredictable and unreliable.

Leo used her contacts to secure us an appointment with a highly regarded neurosurgeon. We were squeezed in at the end of his evening clinic at a smart private hospital with leafy grounds and a car park with actual spaces and no ticket machine. Mr L was a substantial man with sandy hair and an appropriately grave expression. He looked young for a surgeon and struck me as someone who would favour mustard-coloured corduroy trousers and prefer rugby union to football. He seemed slightly alarmed as Laura, Mark, Gracie, Leo and I crammed into his stuffy consulting room, filling all the available chairs and settling on the examination bed like anxious crows in our most serious clothes.

After we'd introduced ourselves, Mr L asked Laura a series of questions that I couldn't keep from answering on her behalf. It was a knee-jerk reaction to protect her from having to say the words or think about what was actually happening.

'If Laura could answer, please, rather than you, Mrs Nuttall, that would be helpful.'

He offered to show us the scans from Homerton and the five of us gathered around his computer screen. I'd been keen to see them and had imagined myself scrutinising those images with a forensic detachment, but in reality, seeing my child's brain mapped out in greyscale knocked me for six.

The scan showed a vertical slice of brain, scattered with little points of light, and a squash-ball-sized mass just above her left eye socket. Mr L explained that this largest tumour was located in the inferior frontal region, which is the area responsible for speech and language skills, and although it wasn't quite pushing the brain out of position, it was exerting significant pressure within the skull, causing the seizures and headaches.

It was crystal clear how bad this news was. It felt like all the oxygen had been sucked from the room. I was immediately too hot, sweating and shaky in my smart coat.

He pointed out the dura, a leathery lining inside the skull that the tumour had worn gossamer-thin, almost to the point of transparency. It must have been growing there a while, rubbing and pushing and squeezing like a fat cuckoo in Laura's brain; how many tiny clues had we already missed, how much time had been wasted?

'Have you noticed any changes in Laura's personality recently?' Mr L asked.

We all looked at each other, wondering if someone else might have noticed a seismic shift that we'd missed, but there was a consensus of slow headshakes.

'No, not really, nothing to speak of.'

'Because I'm detecting what we call a "blunted affect" in Laura: she doesn't seem to be expressing her emotions in a normal way, her reactions are somewhat reduced. Is this something you recognise?'

There was a pause and a few suppressed smirks as we considered the idea that Laura's desert-dry sarcasm and occasional lack of compassion might be symptomatic of the location of her tumour. I thought of how she'd emptied her room with no sentimentality, leaving home with barely a backward glance, and almost laughed.

'To be honest, I think she's just always been like that. We thought Gracie was emotional enough for the both of them,' Mark replied.

If Mr L thought there was anything worthy of a smirk, he didn't show it; this was a sombre business. He explained that the tumour couldn't be removed in its entirety because that would risk damaging the healthy brain tissue, causing paralysis, a stroke or worse. Instead, he would 'de-bulk' it to remove the core of the tumour and release the pressure. This would probably need to be followed up with precision radiotherapy.

The scan showed multiple lesions, so metastasis from a primary tumour was still likely, but there was a small chance it could be a multifocal glioma – a cancer that originated in the brain. Later we found ourselves speculating as to what would be best in terms of outcome: a primary cancer still unidentified, or brain cancer. The news was only ever going to be bad, we just needed to establish exactly which flavour of bad. Like having to choose between being eaten by a tiger or a shark.

Surgery was scheduled for the following Wednesday. This seemed to be both too far away and far too soon.

Mark and the girls headed back to the car park while Leo lingered behind to walk with me. 'You OK?' she asked, putting her arm around my shoulders and pulling me into a half hug.

I nodded, but it was obvious I wasn't.

'This is good news, you know, Nic,' she said.

I stopped walking and looked at her, incredulous.

'How on earth can anything he said in there just now be considered good news?'

'At least he's prepared to operate on her. He must think it's worth doing, so that's got to be good thing.'

I hadn't even considered that it might be inoperable.

Leo was right, and I needed to do a better job of focusing on the positives, for everyone's sake.

From the moment Laura was diagnosed, a peculiar thing had happened: it stopped being *she* and became *we*. I'd be surprised to find myself saying, 'We're having a scan next week' – as if cancer had suddenly become a team sport. Obviously, it was only Laura having the treatment and enduring this whole horrible experience, but we were with her every single step of the way and this little verbal slip truly reflected our experience.

To be of most use to Laura, and to advocate on her behalf, I needed to improve my understanding. My knowledge of biology began and ended with photosynthesis and the C grade I scraped at O Level, but I needed to up my game and understand the language of doctors. If I couldn't grasp the technical terms, how could I ask the right questions and be sure Laura was getting the best treatment?

Once everyone had gone to bed and the house was quiet, I would sit at the kitchen table, open the laptop, and interrogate the internet until the early hours, learning the terms and rolling unfamiliar words around my mouth like marbles until I could say them with confidence. I joined Facebook groups and asked for advice, searching for stories of survivors who'd defied their own prognosis.

I scribbled down notes about freezing tumour tissue for immunotherapy, useful supplements, the benefits of cannabis and the pros and cons of a ketogenic diet without sugar or carbo-hydrates.

I was open to everything Dr Google suggested.

It was during one long dark night at the laptop that I set up an anonymous Twitter account to share my darkest thoughts with complete strangers: it felt safer that way. My emotions were too bleak and explosive to inflict on the people I loved and I was learning that *in real life* it was kinder to stick to anodyne responses, to swallow down the rage and not let it leak from my eyes as tears. It's not easy to look terror in the face; it could turn a person to stone. Instead, I poured my heart out in 280 characters as @shits-caredmum.

My first tweet was someone screaming into the abyss.

I always thought that being diagnosed with cancer would
be the worst thing imaginable, but it turns out I wasn't
even close. Finding out that my fantastic daughter
(18, first term at uni) has at least 8 brain tumours
trumps everything.

Laura was permanently starving, a side effect of the high-dose steroids necessary to reduce the swelling in her brain, and although I attempted to steer her towards healthier options, my home-baked, sugar-free, flavour-free cakes were not terribly popular.

Other than going out for essential food shopping, I avoided seeing people. I couldn't remember what I used to talk about. What did people say when we met by the tills in the supermarket? Did we talk about the weather, or current affairs? I had forgotten a time when the first question wasn't, 'How's your daughter?' But then I would swing erratically between not wanting to talk to anyone or even make eye contact, and flagging down complete strangers in the street to tell them what had happened. I felt uncomfortable with the awkward exchanges of sympathy and kindness but also furious when people didn't approach me to ask how Laura was. Impossible to please, I blazed with an internal rage, bitter and resentful of lives that hadn't also just gone into freefall.

Friends talked me into meeting for a drink, suggesting a change of scene might do me good. I conceded reluctantly, steeling myself for sympathetic looks and well-meant curiosity at the village pub. It was a rainy evening, and I picked up an umbrella, which, at the push of a button, would light up with tiny battery-powered stars. I hadn't used it in years and decided to myself that, if the lights still worked, everything would be OK.

This was the first of a thousand little deals I would make with the universe. I made bargains all the time – if we made it through those traffic lights or I won that game of solitaire, everything would be OK. Saluting magpies became very important, too. It was amazing how superstitious rational people could become when faced with something they had no control over.

The lights came on: one–nil to me.

A Shit-scared Mum

November

We had one last meeting with Mr L. A final opportunity to present him with the long list of questions my late-night research had generated, but each was met with a solemn shake of the head and a 'we just don't know yet'.

I knew that until he received the tumour histology report Mr L had no further information to share, but it didn't stop me asking, desperate to know everything, to find a clue, a glimmer, just something to go on.

'I've read about vaccines and how they can be made from tumour tissue, so will it be possible to save some and freeze it, so that maybe she could have some kind of immunotherapy treatment in the future? If we can afford it?'

Mr L looked surprised by the question. Mark looked slightly embarrassed that I was bringing it up at all; he thought my approach confrontational at best, aggressive at worst, but I was just desperate.

'We'll do our best.'

The surgeon's focus was on the immediate danger to Laura's life, and he needed to make sure we were fully aware of the risks involved in complex brain surgery. This was a dangerous and delicate business; the worst-case scenario was obviously death, but it could also cause a stroke, or irreversible damage to Laura's speech and language function. All operations have an element of risk, but there's a good reason why people use this one as shorthand for something particularly difficult: this really *was* brain surgery.

Laura's life was entirely dependent on the success of the operation, but we had no other options for consideration. A big clock was ticking.

Pre-op was scheduled for Monday, then an MRI scan on Tuesday to determine the location of the tumours and provide a roadmap for the surgical team, like workmen excavating a road for gas pipes who need to know precisely where to start digging with the JCB. Finally, a positron emission tomography (or PET) scan at St Mary's Hospital, for one last chance to try to spot a primary tumour. This required an empty stomach, so Laura was nil-by-mouth all day until immediately before the scan, when she had to drink a pint of water then lie completely still while the imaging machine worked its nuclear magic.

We sat in the hospital atrium and waited for it to be over, with no idea whether this final image would unlock the mystery of what was happening in Laura's body. We had run out of things to talk about; we just watched the tides of people arriving and leaving the hospital, clutching balloons, flowers and baby bumps. Cheerful, excited faces and those creased into masks of care and worry. Would I gamble my fears for theirs? In the Top Trumps of misery, we were looking pretty difficult to beat at that moment.

On the way back, we stopped off at an all-you-can-eat Chinese buffet for a quick tea. Laura was starving by now and both girls took full advantage, making lots of trips to the various food stations and returning with plates of glutinous sweet and sour chicken, brittle spring rolls and tiny cubes of red jelly decorated with improbable cream.

By the time we got home, we were alternating between a manic giddiness and the quiet realisation that the rest of our lives depended on what happened in the next twenty-four hours. Surgery was scheduled for 7:30 a.m. so alarms were set for 5:30 to make sure we were there in good time.

It was a very early start. Mark went to check Laura was awake and found her still in bed, staring up at the ceiling. He thought maybe she was having cold feet about the surgery, that perhaps she was scared. After all, this was a life-and-death business.

He sat on the bed and tenderly stroked her hair while she gazed into space. 'It's OK to be scared, Lulu, and if you want to cry that's OK too, but you're in good hands. He's a good guy, one of the top surgeons in the country. I know it's not easy but, come on, we need to get moving now.'

Leaving her in bed, he went downstairs to make breakfast.

Gracie was already in the kitchen. 'How come she's not up yet?'

'She's awake, but she's just having a minute.'

'A minute to do what?'

'I don't know … think? It's a big day for her.'

'She's in bed, thinking, when we need to leave in half an hour? I'm getting her up.'

Mark followed Gracie up the stairs. Laura hadn't moved. They tried to rouse her, but it became immediately and sickeningly obvious that she was completely unresponsive.

Mark shouted up to where I was getting dressed in our attic bedroom, and I knew instantly that something terrible was waiting for me downstairs. My stomach lurched with dread. I ran in to find him trying to shake Laura awake, her inert body moving like something lifeless. She was unconscious but with her eyes open – it was the most gut-wrenchingly horrific sight imaginable. I think I froze, momentarily paralysed by the appalling scene in front of me.

'Uh, oh,' whispered Siobhan. I caught a glimpse of her pale face, a sliver of black and white reflected in the dressing table mirror. 'I think this might be it.'

And then we were all shouting over each other, trying frantically to bring Laura back to us. Gracie was in tears; she had hold of her phone and was poised to call an ambulance, but Mark was hesitating. He knew that an emergency call would send a local ambulance and take us to our nearest A&E in Blackburn. Laura was first on the list for surgery in Salford, she needed this operation urgently. But there was a real danger we could lose an entire day stuck in a quicksand of admin, tests and procedures and miss the theatre slot completely.

Then the decision was made for us. Laura suddenly went into a full-body tonic-clonic seizure. Although she was still unconscious, she began to vomit violently, the Chinese buffet she'd enjoyed last night reappearing with a vengeance, a scene of utter carnage. It looked like she was being thrown around by an invisible giant, her body rendered completely rigid then shaken violently, contorted in the throes of a massive convulsion. It was like a scene from a horror film, quite literally terrifying.

Mark and I could do little more than try to keep her safe until it passed, as Gracie dialled 999 and pleaded for an ambulance.

We manhandled Laura into a rough approximation of the recovery position, acutely aware that she was now at critical risk of choking. Her limbs had become rigid and unyielding, her arms outstretched, her fingers clawing at an invisible monster. Gracie was doing her best to explain the situation to the operator, answering the flow chart of questions between heaving sobs. I could hear the faint voice ask to be put on speaker. Then, a louder voice: 'Right, Gracie, I need you to tell me when she breathes, so I want you to say *in* when you hear her take a breath and *out* when she breathes out, OK?'

'OK … *in* … Please don't die, Laura, please don't die … *out*. Oh, God, Laura. *In* … I'll do anything, just come back to me, please, Laura, wake up …'

'Gracie, are you still there? Has she stopped breathing?'

'Sorry … *out*.'

It was a whole new level of fear as we waited for that ambulance. Gracie snatched a magnetic torch from the side of the fridge and hurried down the drive to light the way for the emergency response vehicle, returning with two first-responders who huffed up the stairs, weighed down by bags of medical equipment and stiff green uniforms.

I launched into a summary of Laura's medical history while one ticked boxes and typed on his tablet, and the other helped us to wrestle her uncooperative limbs out of sodden pyjamas. He tapped around the pale skin of her inner arm to find a vein, tightening the tourniquet before sliding in a needle and connecting tubes up to an IV.

We were desperate to get her to Salford as quickly as possible, and frantic with worry that it wouldn't be in time to save her life.

Somewhere in the melee, Gracie had found a moment to call Leo, who rushed over to provide us with back-up. She arrived dressed in her uniform and ready for a shift at work, her eyes wide as she took in the horror of the scene: a war zone of bodily fluids, discarded clothing and the plastic detritus of the IV inserted to control the sickness.

Laura was wrapped in a red cellular blanket and secured into a wheelchair, which the paramedics manoeuvred carefully down the stairs, meanwhile an ambulance reversed slowly up the drive, waking the neighbours with its strobing blue lights. Eventually, Laura was safely buckled in and, although I did my best to persuade the driver to run us directly to Salford, they could only take us as far as Blackburn, sirens on and lights flashing, with Mark and Gracie following closely behind.

I held Laura's hand and spoke softly to her as we sped down the quiet streets and onto the motorway. She was drifting in and out of consciousness and I had no idea what was happening inside her brain. The deterioration had been so sudden; my worst fear was a bleed or some catastrophic event that might deny her the option of surgery entirely.

Laura couldn't respond to the emergency doctor's instructions to lift her leg, raise her eyelids, or squeeze his hand, and although we were getting the occasional mumbled word, she was only sporadically conscious. We begged her for a sign that she could hear and understand us, but she slipped away into unconsciousness, like an exhausted swimmer surrendering to the depths.

I couldn't understand how this had happened so quickly, when she'd been laughing and eating prawn toast less than twelve hours ago. I called Salford Royal to explain why we hadn't arrived and managed to speak directly to one of the neurosurgeons operating that morning. I babbled on, incoherent, but he was coolly reassuring.

'Mrs Nuttall, please don't panic. Just get her here as soon as possible and we'll do whatever needs to be done.'

Another ambulance was found to take us on to Salford. This time it was a white-knuckle ride of a journey, flying down the busy motorway to central Manchester just in time to catch the worst of rush hour traffic. We jumped from lane to lane to find the clearest route, speeding down the central reservation and weaving between the lines of cars.

Laura was fastened to a gurney, too unwell for a wheelchair now, and I sat on a pull-down seat opposite. Again, I explained Laura's diagnosis and described the events of the morning while the paramedic tapped details into his tablet. I gripped her limp hand tightly and tried to stop her inert body from sliding about as we careered around corners.

Finally at Salford Royal, the gurney was wheeled neatly into a small room off A&E and Laura's blood pressure, oxygen levels and temperature were taken for the fourth time that morning. Mark and Gracie arrived soon after, their journey through the snarled Manchester traffic slower without blue lights and sirens. Mr L swept in, dressed in green theatre scrubs and cap. He tried to get a response by flicking her arm sharply and using the cap of his pen to trace a line down the sole of her foot, but she was too deeply unconscious. His expression was grim, confirming what we already knew: Laura's life was hanging in the balance.

She was taken through to 'Majors' for assessment. The area buzzed with activity and industry, noisy with phone calls and the beeps and alarms of monitors. In the eye of this storm, we stood sentry around our Sleeping Beauty, making silent deals and promises to the world if only she would wake up.

We took turns trying to coax a reaction, hoping that it would be our voices that cut through and brought her back: 'Laura, can you hear me? Please can you just squeeze my hand if you can?'

'Hey, Laura, we're all here, you're safe … Can you just show me that you can hear us? Can you open your eyes, darling?'

'Laura … Laura, you're in the hospital and we just need to know if you can hear us. Please can you do anything at all for me? Wiggle your toes, squeeze my hand, blink, anything?'

Nothing.

I hadn't expected Neil, but my heart lifted at the sight of his familiar face across the room. I don't think I had ever needed a hug from my brother more. I wiped away tears as he moved to put his arms around Gracie and then Mark. He took in Laura's unconscious form, and I saw him try, and fail, to disguise the shock that flashed across his face. A career in the police had exposed him to tragic situations on a daily basis, but when it was family, well, that was different. I needed him to tell me that everything was going to be OK, even if it wasn't true.

I couldn't imagine how this day was going to end or what would be left of us when it did.

The porters took Laura for an emergency scan and Gracie and I found a drinks machine in the waiting room. It was already packed: mums and dads with small children on their knees, bigger kids being reprimanded for not sitting still, an older man holding a makeshift dressing to his wounded head and a couple of early morning anti-social drinkers. Slack faces watching the clock, yawning, impatient to be seen. I was unreasonably envious of those just waiting for an X-ray or a few stitches, parents whose children would be right as a rain in a day or two, people who had no reason to know just how lucky they were.

The scan showed no evidence of a haemorrhage, which was good news but it didn't explain the seizure, and, despite all our efforts, Laura was still unconscious. Mr L decided to have her prepared for the craniotomy but would hold off as long as he could in the hope that she might regain consciousness. As she couldn't sign the consent form, the surgeon did it on her behalf: standard procedure when the patient is incapacitated to this degree.

Leaving the hospital was the very last thing we wanted to do but Mr L was insistent; there was nowhere to wait, and it would be many hours before there was any news. We ended up in Nando's – numb, bewildered and reeling from the trauma of the morning. We stared blankly as a cheerful waitress handed out laminated A3 menus as if it could possibly matter whether we ate peri-peri wraps or halloumi salad while Laura was suspended in limbo, floating between life and death.

Gracie and I were washing our hands in the restroom when Mr L's name flashed up on my phone, causing my heart to drop like a lift. I knew it was too soon for this to be good news.

He told me that Laura's stats had deteriorated rapidly; waiting for her to wake was no longer an option and they were going ahead with the surgery now. We would only know the full outcome when – and if – Laura woke up.

Neil had to go back to work, Mark went home – ostensibly to let Ziggy out, but I knew it was because he couldn't bear the anxious wait for news. I couldn't leave; I needed to stay close. Gracie and I wandered aimlessly around a nearby shopping mall until she came up with the idea of seeking sanctuary in the cinema and taking advantage of the soft reclining seats that flattened out like beds. Exhausted by the day's trauma, we were grateful for a long film, a dark room, and the opportunity to sleep through all but the first ten minutes of *Peterloo*.

As we slept through the movie, Mr L was making an incision in Laura's scalp, then drilling, gutting and peeling the tumour away from her brain. Our battle was being fought in an operating theatre just a few miles away.

We woke up and stretched as the credits rolled, and immediately my phone rang. It had, of course, been clutched in my hand the entire time, with the ringtone set to maximum. Mr L sounded cautiously positive: the de-bulking had gone as well as could be expected and Laura was now in recovery. A decision had been made to keep her in an induced coma overnight, to reduce brain activity and keep the swelling down – the skull has very little spare space to allow for a swollen brain and an increase in pressure could cause oxygen deprivation, or even death. Laura was far from out of the woods, there was a significant risk of brain damage and loss of speech, but things would become clearer the following day when, if all went to plan, she would gradually be woken up.

Mark was already back in the hospital, waiting anxiously for us in the foyer. Mr L had allowed a quick visit up to Intensive Care to see Laura and we were grateful for the opportunity, even if she was fast asleep.

It was late, and the corridors were deathly quiet as we followed the signs up to ICU. Only two visitors were permitted in each room but the nurse in charge turned a blind eye and the three of us slipped in to see her.

Reverentially, we tiptoed through the ward, our eyes cast down, away from the quiet vigils taking place in a circle of low light around each bed. Every patient there was on the knife-edge of the seriously ill, every loved one a shadowy sentinel, whispering prayers and holding listless hands from a hard chair at the side of the bed.

Laura's room crackled with the static of pulsing monitors and soft lights. She looked so vulnerable, a thick plastic breathing tube in her mouth allowing the gasping mechanical ventilator to push air in and out of her lungs. Machines and wires tracked her heart rate, her blood pressure, oxygen saturation and the pressure inside her skull. Her very existence had been reduced to this series of neon digits on a monitor. She was heavily bandaged, but I could see bruises beginning to bloom under the skin. There were splashes of iodine on her surgical gown and her long, honey-coloured hair had been fashioned into a loose plait to keep it out of the way. I imagined a thoughtful nurse concentrating as she plaited the hair of this unconscious girl, holding out three long skeins as the surgeon prepared to cut through her scalp.

When Laura had needed her first ever operation – to insert grommets into little gluey ears – I'd held her hand as she slipped away under the anaesthetic. Watching her small six-year-old body fall into unconsciousness had felt horribly traumatic, like seeing the very life spirit drift out from her. I had sat in the hospital canteen with Mark and cried and cried until she came round. When she did eventually wake up, Laura had clamped her hands over her ears and complained that the world was now too loud. It had seemed so serious at the time, but now just tiny, inconsequential.

The beeps were reassuringly metronomic and the calm intensive-care angels promised to take good care of her, and that she was in safe hands.

Reluctantly, we left her to an artificial and dreamless sleep.

It was much busier and a lot less sinister up on ICU in the bright light of day. Laura had a specific nurse assigned to take care of her and I watched as she meticulously recorded observations in a thickening file that told the sad story of how a girl who had carefully planned out the next seven years of her life had ended up in this bed, in this room.

Gradually, the IV sedatives were reduced, then withdrawn completely. I watched and waited for some change in Laura's brain activity, scrutinising her face for the first signs of life. She was a deep-sea diver fighting her way back from the depths up to the light. The nurse said that she might be able to hear me, so I rambled on about nothing, hopeful that if she was on her way back, she might be able to follow my voice up to the surface.

Her eyelids flickered as if she was dreaming and I squeezed her hand – three short pulses to say *I love you*, like I'd done since she was tiny.

She returned the squeeze four times: *I love you too*.

It felt like I had been holding my breath for days.

'Laura, my darling,' I babbled, my eyes shining with tears. 'It's so wonderful to have you back! Sweetheart, you might find that you can't speak, but I don't want you to worry about that now, you're back with us and it all went fine and that's what counts, everything else will follow. Can I get you anything? Do you want to hear Gracie's voice? I know she's desperate to talk to you and I promised I'd call as soon as you came round.'

Laura nodded almost imperceptibly, then winced. Although the pain was muffled by morphine, it was plainly uncomfortable for her to move her head, newly soft and bruised, like damaged fruit.

Gracie picked up on the first ring.

'She's just waking up, but I think she's OK. You can talk to her – she wants to hear your voice, but she won't be able to reply. I'll put the phone near her ear.'

I could hear the bright euphoria of Gracie's voice as she prepared to launch into a monologue, but she was soon interrupted.

'Hey,' Laura croaked, her voice rusty after two days of silence and breathing tubes.

She was groggy and sore, but the signs were all good. As far as I could tell, she'd emerged unscathed and without any obvious damage to her brain. It felt like we had won.

As the day progressed, Laura got a little stronger: she asked for mint choc chip ice cream and managed to hold short conversations, despite feeling very tired. She had no memory of anything that came after the Chinese meal. I wished that I could say the same.

The medical team checked Laura's brain activity at regular intervals throughout the day. They had a list of questions, but the first one would always be the toughest.

'Laura, do you know where you are?'

This was the only question she ever got wrong. She was close, but her first response was always '… Stratford … Stretford … Stanford?'

Just a single slippery word that she was so close to catching but couldn't quite grasp. It took a couple of days for her to be able to pull it out of the air first time, but eventually she replied with confidence: 'Salford … I'm in Salford Hospital.'

Two days after the surgery she was disconnected from the last of the machines, and celebrated her new-found freedom with a shower and clean pyjamas. The dressing was removed to reveal a long scar – fifty-one stitches in total – neatly sutured and located discreetly behind her hairline. The dots and lines of purple felt-tip pen showed the surgeon's 'workings out', or maybe it was where the clamp had held her inert head in place. He'd only shaved a small strip of hair and we all agreed that they were the neatest stitches, so small they made me think of Beatrix Potter's *Tailor of Gloucester*. It all looked beautifully tidy on the outside; I just hoped that the inside had been equally straight-forward.

When a bed became available, Laura was transferred to a side room on the neuro ward, and, after much pleading, the ward sister gave permission for Gracie to stay with her overnight. They ate snacks I wouldn't approve of and watched Disney films on a laptop, shoulder to shoulder on the starched white sheets of Laura's hospital bed.

Laura had been bright and chatty on Saturday, her system still slightly numbed by the last vestiges of anaesthetic, but on Sunday, when we'd hoped to take her home, she crashed back down to earth. We sat around her bed as she slept the hard, deep sleep of the dead, hoping that this wasn't a bad sign, checking intermittently that she was still actually breathing.

Mr L thought it prudent for her to spend another night in hospital, which, although disappointing, also brought a degree of relief. I knew how close we'd come to losing her and felt fearful of bringing this fragile girl home. What would we do if something went wrong, or we messed up her care in some way? Once we had her home, we'd be on our own.

Next day, she was much brighter and was moved down the hierarchy of diminishing needs to a small six-bed ward, and then finally she was discharged.

We came home to find a keto lasagne on the doorstep. 'Let me know if there's anything I can do,' is the standard response rolled out in times of crisis. It's well-intentioned but means little. Good friends don't wait for an invitation – they make you a chilli or a curry in a Pyrex dish and leave it, still warm, on the doorstep. We had no energy for the small talk required to entertain visitors, but we were so grateful to come home and find homemade soup or cakes left next to the milk bottles.

Laura looked surprisingly well, despite the swelling and the bruising. A ladder of stitches began within the mass of her matted blonde hair, travelled horizontally high above her left eyebrow and curled downwards to finish in front of her left ear, like an upside-down fishhook or a question mark. The thought of her soft young skin being pulled back and away from her skull made my head swim and turned my legs liquid, so I tried not to think about it. We fussed around her, competing to tempt her with nice food and constantly checking she was warm enough. Laura smiled but didn't say much; she was pale and painfully delicate, a soldier still shell-shocked from the battle just fought. On Tuesday, I washed the hospital out of her hair with gentle baby shampoo, tentatively rinsing away the crusted blood, bone dust and other unimaginable substances spilled during surgery, the brackish water bloody and brown against the white shower tray.

Wednesday was the day I had been dreading.

We arrived at Salford Royal to be met by Mr L in a tiny side room with low staffroom chairs, and not enough space for us all to sit down. I felt the unmistakable electric chill of bad news in the air before he even spoke.

It was diffuse glioblastoma multiforme, the most aggressive kind of brain tumour.

It was incurable, and it would be fatal.

'Like a cancer?' asked Laura.

'Yes, exactly like a cancer,' replied Mr L, and I felt momentarily sorry for him, having to deliver such dreadful news.

It was the worst possible diagnosis, and my stomach dropped.

'So, what happens next?'

He explained to Laura that her care would now be transferred from Salford Royal to The Christie. Like most people in north-west England, I knew The Christie as the go-to hospital for complicated or difficult-to-treat cancers, and with its reputation for excellence and innovative care, it would be the best possible place for Laura to be treated. She would need full head radio-therapy; the more precise stereotactic option was no longer appro-priate as the tumours were too extensive and diffuse. This would be followed by a course of oral chemotherapy.

'So, will I be able to go back to university this year or will I need to wait 'til next year?' Laura asked.

There was a weighty and deeply uncomfortable silence. It was obvious to all of us that Laura hadn't grasped the devastating implications of her diagnosis.

Mr L looked beseechingly at me as if I might help him out with an answer, but I looked down and watched as fat tears splashed onto my hands.

'I'm sorry, Laura, but I'm afraid you won't be going back to university.'

Another silence while the news settled on us like snow.

'Do you have any questions you'd like to ask me?'

'Yes,' said Laura. 'Do you know that you're wearing your scrubs inside out?'

He was, too, and a burst of laughter bubbled up out of nowhere, like the pressure released from a shaken bottle of fizzy pop.

Mark and I followed Mr L out of the door, and I asked him the question that we couldn't avoid, despite not really wanting to hear the answer.

'How long do you think she's got?'

'Do you really want to know?'

We nodded.

'Well, obviously nobody *really* knows, but without treatment we're talking weeks or a few months. With treatment, maybe a year.'

I waited for a 'but' or a 'however' but it didn't come. That was it, the end of the sentence.

The anguish in his face showed exactly how much he'd hated every second of the conversation. Giving a terminal diagnosis to an eighteen-year-old and her distraught family is one seriously tough day at work.

I held myself together until Gracie took Laura off for a ride in the wheelchair. I watched them disappear down the corridor, still laughing at her joke. Then I doubled over with the physical pain of it. My legs had forgotten how to hold me upright. I was destroyed.

What on earth do you do when someone tells you that your daughter is going to die?

Well, here's what we did. We went to the Trafford Centre and ate burgers at Five Guys, bought wallpaper from John Lewis to decorate Laura's bedroom and went to the cinema to watch *A Star Is Born*, which, given the storyline, was a particularly bad idea but at least the dark cinema provided good cover. I cried for a good two hours, my mouth open like a mask of tragedy. Tissues would have given me away, so I kept my eyes forward in the darkness and let the tears roll down my face.

Once again, I called the family with bad news. They tried to be positive, just as I would have in their shoes, but this was the very darkest of days and I could see no hope at all. The triumphant recovery from surgery was forgotten: it had felt like a victory at the time, but I knew now that it was nothing more than a little skirmish prior to the real and devastating bombardment.

From that point on, I wore waterproof mascara every day because I knew I was guaranteed to cry. Mark was doing his best, and that manifested in keeping busy and maintaining a front of constant positivity, made easier by the fact that he'd refused to read any of the grim information I'd devoured online. Unlike me, he hadn't been prepared to waste time researching possibilities until there was a firm diagnosis. This meant that whereas I had a pretty good idea of what was barrelling towards us like a runaway train, Mark remained steadfastly confident that everything was fixable. As I was a 'glass half empty' kind of person, his natural optimism frustrated the hell out of me.

He did cry once, though, sitting at the kitchen table in the middle of eating a bowl of porridge. He suddenly threw his spoon down and sobbed, his head in his hands. I was momentarily horrified. It felt like I'd goaded him into some kind of emotional response and now I was witnessing exactly how much he was suffering too. It was unbearable to see him so distressed and, like a counterbalanced see-saw, his misery forced me to try to summon up some optimism and provide *him* with some degree of comfort or consolation.

Then just as quickly as it had started, it passed. He fastened up his tight-fitting 'Northern man' suit, picked up the spoon and went back to being his usual stoic self.

I knew now that his pain was as raw as mine, but he was just a great deal better at hiding it.

I was angry with everything and everyone. I couldn't countenance the unfairness of it all. Laura was just beginning what should have been the best time of her life. She'd worked so hard to pass her exams with the sole aim of studying in London. She was careful, risk-averse and sensible. Once, Gramps had written her initials in some wet concrete on the pavement, and Laura had only been one step away from phoning the police to hand herself in. She carefully assessed the potential hazards in every situation and avoided anything that she considered to be too risky. Laura's levels of vigilance were so extraordinary that she had a packed rucksack on the back of her bedroom door in preparation for the end of the world or a zombie apocalypse. In it she'd stuffed things that might prove useful in a civil emergency, including water purification tablets, first-aid kit, gaffer tape and fire-starting wool. She was an avid watcher of the news and followed current affairs closely, believing it vitally important that she and Gracie were up to date with world events in case there was a disaster looming on the horizon that they needed to prepare for.

Laura's nightmare actually became reality in 2013, when we found ourselves on holiday in Boston not far from the marathon finish line as two bombs were detonated in a terrorist attack. While it was a traumatic experience for all of us, the impact on Laura was monumental; her very worst fears had been realised – and she had survived. The experience gave her a new resilience which was going to prove vital in the years to come.

Being told that your child is going to die, completely out of the blue, is like falling through a trapdoor. The natural order of your life, the milestones you took for granted – the twenty-first, the graduation, their first home, perhaps one day a wedding and maybe even grandchildren – a whole life story on flickering Cinefilm, but the celluloid lingers too long in the projector, burns white hot and disintegrates.

That was the future you could have had. You can imagine it; you can almost taste the birthday cake … but it's not for you.

I had always thought Laura would do something extraordinary, but then I had always thought she would live. I would take ordinary now; I would thank you profusely and shake your hand, I'd be so grateful for normal and unexceptional.

How will I cope when Laura's friends grow up? How can I meet them in the street and ask about their jobs and their babies without the bitterness of bile in my mouth? How will I smile without it turning into a snarl? How can I be happy for them and not show the anger and envy that will be so obvious in my expression?

How will I live in the same village when, everywhere I turn, I'll be seeing her ghost?

'You know what you should do?' said Siobhan. 'Stop loving her a little bit every day. That way you can desensitise yourself. Do it by degrees, so by the time she dies you'll feel absolutely nothing.'

Back in September, when we had taken Laura down to university, I had cried for the entire journey, so sad that my little girl was leaving home and convinced she wouldn't come back. I wished that was all I had to worry about now.

'Don't borrow trouble from tomorrow,' they say around here.

Gracie and I had arranged a meeting at school; it was something neither of us had been looking forward to. As soon as we arrived in reception, it was evident from the unnatural hush that the whole school knew and they had collectively decided that loud noises might now be especially painful for us.

With the prognosis as bleak as it was, the last place Gracie wanted to be was school, but time with her friends and the normality of lessons would offer respite from the turmoil at home. She'd only just started her A Levels, so the timing wasn't great, but there was never going to be a good time to hear that her sister was going to die, and if Laura only had months left, then Gracie wanted to be there to share them.

I didn't want Gracie to look back on this time with regret. It was going to be hard enough to handle without any additional guilt; she just needed to take things one day at a time, so we agreed she could go into school if she felt like it, or stay home if she couldn't face it. We held each other's hand tightly and cried with Laura's teachers in the staffroom. Overnight, Gracie had become 'the one whose sister has terminal cancer'.

District nurses came to remove Laura's stitches. The scar was neat and tidy, but the stitches needed a firm tug with the tweezers. Laura was her usual stoic self and, although I was looking away at the time, she barely flinched. She could have her hair washed properly now, and Gracie did it for her with sisterly tenderness while she sat on a blue plastic stool in the shower.

That afternoon, we had our first visit to The Christie. We helped Laura out of the car, settled her in a wheelchair and pushed her through the automatic doors into the warmth of the foyer.

There were lots of people milling around, some having coffee in the M&S café or just waiting for their name to be called for an outpatient's appointment. Some were in wheelchairs, walking with sticks, pushing along drip stands or wearing bright scarves to cover patchy bald heads. My overwhelming impression was that everybody looked really sick and most of them were old. Goodness knows what unrealistic utopia I'd been expecting, but it wasn't this.

We met the oncologist in a spare office on the first floor, taking turns to shake his hand, which was dry and papery. He wore a suit jacket that was too big and hung from his shoulders, making him look like he'd shrunk in the wash. We'd been told that he was one of the longest-serving doctors in the hospital and we waited expectantly for him to hand down his wisdom.

His fingers made a steeple as he explained that Laura would have thirty sessions of radiotherapy, with a low-dose chemotherapy tablet called Temozolomide. Then she would have 'adjuvant' chemo: the same drug but in a higher dose, to kill any cancerous cells that lingered in the margins of the tumour site. I'd expected this, from what I'd read, it was how brain cancer had been treated for decades.

I turned to the long list of questions in my pink book. I wanted to know what else we could do, where we should look and how we could stop the inevitable progress of this disease. If I was a hare jumping up and down frantically, he was the world-weary tortoise who'd seen it all before.

I had no medical experience other than an Emergency First Aid at Work certificate, but I'd devoured everything I could find online about glioblastoma. I'd read extracts and abstracts thick with the names of contributing researchers, journals and papers, sensational news articles full of promises and hyperbole – anything I could get my hands on. Much of it was plain terrifying – seeing my daughter's cancer referred to as 'the Terminator' due to the dreadful survival rates was a particular low point, and much of the research seemed theoretical and speculative, decades away from becoming an effective or licensed treatment. All of it was difficult to understand and written to be read by medical professionals and scientists rather than naive and desperate parents.

I learned that Laura would probably only get a good response from the chemo if her tumour was methylated, as unmethylated tumours were statistically less likely to respond to Temozolomide. I had no idea what the word meant, but from what I'd read, it was important. The oncologist didn't seem to know either, and wasn't that interested, because, like Henry Ford's car, we could have any colour, just so long as it was black.

It was the only option on the table.

Attending doctors' appointments with an adult child is like walking a tightrope. I wanted to find out exactly what the side effects of this treatment would be and whether the benefits would outweigh them. I wanted to challenge the oncologist's perceived wisdom with the new things I'd learned and push him to think outside the box. But this wasn't my diagnosis and I still needed

Laura to trust her doctor, even if I had yet to make up my mind about him. Sometimes I wished she'd wait outside so that I could ask hard questions, but that was not an option so I fought to keep my face neutral, bit my tongue and did everything I could to maintain a positive front; I needed her to believe his treatment plan would work.

Whenever I walked through the kitchen, my eyes would snag on a creamy envelope propped up next to the fruit bowl. I knew it contained a gold-embossed invitation from HRH Prince Edward requesting Laura's attendance at St James's Palace for the presentation of her Gold Duke of Edinburgh's Award. The very sight of it made my heart sore.

I'd been so looking forward to a weekend in London, spending time with my girl at the end of her first term at King's. The rules allowed strictly only one accompanying guest, and I was smugly delighted to have been chosen as Laura's. I'd imagined us drinking cocktails in the hotel bar and laughing uproariously at some West End show like people in an advert. In my worst nightmares, I could never have imagined the situation we found ourselves in now. The invitation felt like a reminder of another life, where my biggest worry would have been what to wear and where to stay, and it squeezed my throat to think of all the things that were slipping away.

I hadn't torn it up and thrown it in the bin because a part of me still hoped for a miracle. When I first suggested to Mark that maybe we could still try to go, he had looked at me like I'd completely lost my grip on reality: Laura would be just twenty days post brain surgery, still undergoing radiotherapy and knee-deep in chemo. The sensible part of me agreed it was a ridiculous idea, but I kept the invitation, just in case.

As the date got closer and she seemed to be recovering well, I made tentative enquiries to see if they could accommodate a wheelchair and maybe even allow Mark and Gracie to attend too. When the reply came back as favourable, I casually floated the idea past Laura.

'Seriously, you think we could we still go?'

I nodded with more confidence than I felt.

'Yes! Absolutely, definitely, let's do it!'

Mark gave me a rueful look which clearly said *On your head be it*, but I knew the trip would give us all something to look forward to and, more than ever, this felt profoundly important.

Two days later, I took Laura to buy a dress. The shops were full of Christmas outfits; glitter and sequins designed for work dos and tipsy nights out in town-centre clubs. Gracie and I took turns pushing Laura's wheelchair from shop to shop, unfamiliar with the thoughtless challenges of steps, and racks of clothing too close together, searching for something appropriate to wear for a meeting with a prince. Laura didn't have anything in her wardrobe remotely suitable for royalty and even if she had, the steroids would have rendered it too tight. She wasn't keen on anything I suggested – all a bit frumpier than her standard uniform of jeans and T-shirt – but eventually we found a knee-length black-lace number that she grudgingly agreed to try on.

Siobhan was applying blood-red lipstick in the changing-room mirror, and she smiled as I caught her eye in the reflection. 'Nice dress,' she sneered. 'Bet I know what you're thinking, though.'

'Like hell you do,' I muttered under my breath, but she knew … the insidious thought that crept into my mind in the stuffy Debenhams fitting room was whether this would be the dress we would bury her in.

I had become fixated on Laura's funeral. I'd never organised one before, and I had no idea of the process. Who would we invite? Did you even invite people to a funeral? Where would we hold it? What songs would she like? Should I ask her for a list now? *Hey Laura, do you need anything? Oh, and while I think on, could you do me a Spotify playlist for your funeral?* We'd need a place big enough to include all her friends and family; definitely not a church but maybe a hall of some kind: it would need to be huge. She wouldn't want black-plumed horses, but I'd need some Taj Mahal-scale monument to her loss.

In the mean and miserable early hours, I planned for my daughter's death while she was still alive. What kind of sick-fuck mother was I?

Radiotherapy treatment is specific to the location of the cancer. When it's in the brain, a thick plastic mask is warmed up to make it flexible, then it's placed over the entire head and moulded to fit the contours of the face and skull. It's then mapped by a computer and target points are marked so radiation beams can be aimed at the tumours with pinpoint accuracy. During treatment, the mask is securely fastened to the table so that the patient's head can't move around. It looks like an instrument of medieval torture – a scold's bridle, or a head crusher from the Spanish Inquisition. Laura would have to go through this procedure thirty times: five days a week for six weeks.

The radiation made her skin red and raw, and it was horribly claustrophobic inside the machine, but she didn't complain, just got on with it in her own pragmatic way. The treatment itself was relatively quick but the daily commute was long and most of the day was spent in traffic on the M60.

Returning home after the first session, I wondered how on earth we were going to get through this, every day for six whole weeks. It seemed impossible, but like so many other things that followed, it was only impossible until it was done.

Over time, we built up a daily routine: breakfast was early or not at all, because Laura needed an empty stomach for treatment. Then she'd swallow down anti-sickness tablets, followed half an hour later by the chemo capsules, which she'd normally have to take in the car, balancing sachets of drugs and cartons of apple juice on her knees.

After the radiotherapy, we'd spend an hour or so in the M&S café, trying to tempt her to eat something. Having consumed the entire contents of the fridge when she was on steroids, Laura found that nothing tasted nice anymore and as a result her appetite dwindled away to nothing.

I was still half-heartedly flogging the dead-horse keto diet with my bizarre beetroot brownies, cookies made from coconut and sugar substitutes, and little breakfast egg muffins that she never had time to eat. I even locked horns with a senior radiographer who, to my horror, once tried to entice Laura with cake. She warned me that the best thing I could do would be to ditch the special diet and focus on building Laura up; this brutal treatment was about to launch a savage war on her body, and she was going to need all her strength to get through it. I was furious at the time, but she was probably right.

Throughout the winter, we travelled back and forth to The Christie under a heavy sky, which matched our collective mood. Nobody had anything to say; we just looked out of our respective car windows at the grey, rainy motorway. One evening, 'Happy Talk' by Captain Sensible came on the radio. The irony wasn't lost on me. We were not happy, nor were we talking.

The highlight of each dreadful day was the hour between tea and Laura's bedtime, when we'd snuggle on the sofa watching *I'm a Celebrity ... Get Me Out of Here!* – an hour of diverting escapism when every day felt exactly the same.

Mark and I had met when we both worked at Granada Television in Manchester. I was a management trainee, and he was a graphic designer who sauntered in late every morning wearing a leather jacket with the collar up. I thought he was a bit cocky, to be honest; his colleagues called him Sparky, and he always did have something twinkly about him. On the day we were introduced, he apparently went back to his office and and told his colleagues he'd just met the woman he was going to marry.

I still get a kick out of that, even after twenty-five years.

He asked me to marry him eighteen months later by drawing his proposal as a cartoon; he thought it might take me a while to work out the clues, but it took no more than ten seconds for me to say 'yes'. Once we had Laura, I went back to work part time, sharing a role in HR with my colleague Rachel.

Twenty years later she still worked for ITV – and she arranged a video message for the girls from Holly Willoughby and Dec Donnelly, all the way from where they were filming *I'm a Celebrity* in Australia. The girls were open-mouthed with surprise – it was a little moment of happiness that brought back smiles I'd almost forgotten; a small joy that cut through the misery of the day like an unexpected gap in the clouds.

Scan days were hideous, full of stress and the knowledge that everything could change in an instant. People in the cancer community talk about *scanxiety*; it's like Schrödinger's paradox, but instead of cats, you have two lives: one where the news is bad and one where it is less bad, perhaps even good. Two imaginary lives running in parallel.

Laura didn't have great veins; they did a decent job fulfilling their main purpose, but they ran for cover at the first sign of a needle. I watched as a nurse traced the faint roadmap of veins under Laura's baby-soft skin, pressing gently in her search for the most promising candidate, blue tourniquet wrapped around pale upper arm then removed with a sigh and an angry rasp of Velcro to be repositioned on the other arm.

I tried to supress the wince that clenched my stomach as the needle met the initial resistance of skin before breaching the surface.

'Sharp scratch, now.'

She drew back the plunger, but the barrel remained resolutely empty, so she angled the needle deeper and then tried again, closer to the surface. I could see the shaft wiggling obscenely beneath the skin as it failed to find its target. The nurse tried again, biting hard on her lower lip in concentration, then after a further failed attempt, went to seek help from a colleague. Protocol allowed each nurse just two attempts, and it was the fourth member of staff who was finally successful on the eighth try. I felt the collective sigh of relief in the room when the syringe barrel finally filled with bright-red blood.

Laura said very little, but I could see the tension in her jaw and the momentary flinch at each puncture of her skin. Her face was impassive; she had disappeared into some safe and pain-free space inside her head. I felt less than useless and wished for the thousandth time that this was happening to me and not her.

This was not a good day. Laura's head ached, she was vomiting repeatedly – leaving her dizzy from lack of food and sore from the needles – and she then had to lie perfectly still for an hour, to be assaulted by the deafening thrash metal of the MRI scanner as it took pictures of her brain.

Although the scan results were no worse than expected, Laura was so poorly that she ended up being admitted for IV anti-sickness meds and a drip to replace her depleted fluids. Exhausted and waxen, it was decided that she should stay overnight for monitoring.

With only four days to go before London, the trip was starting to look rashly optimistic at best, irresponsible and dangerous at worst.

Anyone who's had a brush with cancer will be familiar with the snake oil cures. Well-meaning people who share stories of the magical curative power of celery, alkaline water, sodium bicarbonate, lemon juice and a million other food stuffs and herbal products that may or may not have the slightest impact on cancer cells. It's utterly bewildering. A rational person knows that celery is unlikely to be the cure for cancer. If it was, surely, we'd all know about it by now – but what if we're wrong? What if arrogance means we'll miss the key ingredient that turns out to be effective? My stake in this game was the very life of my daughter, and while I wasn't prepared to gamble on it, if we didn't take *any* risks and did exactly as we were told, the most we could hope for was a year or so with her.

The long nights of research had thrown up a couple of treatments and supplementary drug protocols which *seemed* to be supported by a degree of evidence, albeit more anecdotal than scientific. I printed off journal summaries and highlighted news articles, then presented them to the oncologist at our next meeting – excited and optimistic that there might be something we could use to tip the balance in Laura's favour. He made no attempt to hide his exasperation and left the papers untouched on his desk, handing them back to me as we got up to leave.

In his defence, I was probably just the latest in a long line of parents and patients who thought they might have casually stumbled upon the cure for cancer in an internet chat room. But if we were facing a terminal diagnosis anyway, then surely it had to be worth trying? If it had been his daughter, would he really be content to treat her using the same protocol that hadn't changed in decades?

At the time, I felt crushed and frustrated by his dismissal, which seemed casual to the point of cruelty, and I couldn't accept that this was the very best we could do. If it was a matter of money, we would sell the house and sleep in a tent. Laura was too precious, and I never wanted to look back with regret, wishing we'd fought harder for her. I would exhaust every possibility before admitting defeat.

As we made our way out of the consultation room, a nurse patted me gently on the arm. 'I think that maybe now would be a good time to stop looking on the internet, Mrs Nuttall.'

I left the hospital feeling chastened and not a little bit foolish, but by the time we got home, disappointment had been replaced with a hot fury that made my hands shake.

How *dare* they write her off?

Naively, I'd believed the system would enfold us in a safe, warm blanket and present us with a gift-wrapped cure or at least a new drug trial, not just some ancient protocol that *might* give us a year. My confidence was diminishing by degrees, in the shrug of a doctor's shoulders and the patronising words of a nurse. We had two choices: do as we were told, or add a supplementary plan of our own and take a chance.

Initially, Mark had been deferential to the doctors and irritated by my belligerence but now even his faith was wavering. Laura was too exhausted to care, and her fierce independence had softened into a child-like trust that we would take care of her. Going out on a limb was risky, but it had to be worth a shot and so, despite the oncologist's reticence, we took a leap of faith.

The first thing we introduced was cannabis. From the moment Laura was diagnosed, complete strangers had begun to contact us, a veritable army of evangelical believers in the curative powers of cannabis, to the point where it felt like a cult. My email inbox swelled with articles championing the super-natural qualities of cannabidiol (CBD), tetrahydrocannabinol (THC) and full extract cannabis oil (FECO) – not that I really understood the difference. The idea of cannabis made me think of patchouli oil and musty joss sticks, hippies and students. I was deeply sceptical. It was still illegal in the UK, and I had absolutely no idea how we would even get hold of it, but Mark did his homework and convinced me that it was worth trying.

A friend of a friend, doing well with a similar diagnosis, offered to put us in touch with his source. We were sent a mobile number and a secret code word.

Mark did the talking, holding the phone out so I could listen.

'Hello? I'd like to ask about buying some *grease*, please.'

'Grease?'

'Yes, you see, our friend *Dan* thought you might be able to help us to get some—?'

'*Dan* gave you this number, did he?'

'It's for my daughter, she's got brain cancer, and he thought maybe you might be able to help us.'

The speaker's tone softened a little, and the conversation became significantly more cordial. Details were exchanged and a few days later we found ourselves driving around a housing estate looking for our 'man'.

The man actually turned out to be half of a middle-aged couple in a tidy bungalow with a neat garden. We sat on their chenille sofa and took in the china ornaments and framed photographs of various-sized grandchildren in matching school sweatshirts. It was not the seedy crack house of my imagining.

The woman made us cups of milky tea and told a story of breast cancer that had stubbornly refused to respond to chemo. Having exhausted all medical options, friends encouraged her to try cannabis, which appeared to offer some relief. Now she was in remission, and they had a little cottage industry supplying friends of friends. She asked about Laura, and I tried to tell her how little time we'd been given but all my mouth wanted to do was curl into a howl. I cried ugly snotty tears, twisting damp tissues through my fingers. She gave me a brisk hug, then took some of the £20 notes we'd handed over in payment and folded them back into Mark's hand with a shake of her head.

The *grease* was what is known as FECO, full extract cannabis oil – the whole plant boiled up with alcohol and condensed into a thick tar which is transported in plastic syringes. The FECO contains both CBD, which is legal and readily available in health food shops, and THC, the non-legal substance which creates the unpredictable psychoactive high. We'd been instructed to start with a tiny amount under Laura's tongue, increasing it gradually over days to the size of a grain of rice.

Feeling giddy with relief that we hadn't been arrested, or stabbed, in our first illegal drug deal, we drove our precious stash home, checking we weren't being followed.

Laura was understandably apprehensive as she took her first dose that night, Mark and I watching anxiously, ready for her to start bouncing off the walls.

'Can you feel anything yet, Laura?'

'No, nothing yet.'

Half an hour later.

'How about now – anything?'

Nothing happened, so she went to bed; it was a massive anti-climax. It would take us a while to get the hang of things, but in time cannabis would become a fundamental element of Laura's treatment protocol, and just part of her daily life. Even without the anti-tumour effects demonstrated by promising new research, cannabis lifted her mood and, perhaps more importantly, improved her tiny appetite.

The second thing we added was a combination of drugs used every day for conditions such as diabetes. These drugs are 'repurposed', which means that they are used to treat a condition other than the one they are licensed for. We found a clinical team to check Laura's blood results and prescribe a personalised protocol of metformin, statin, antibiotic and antiparasitic drugs, a cocktail designed to block a number of pathways, making it more difficult for the tumour cells to duplicate, and to encourage them to die.

We also contacted an integrative oncology nutritionist who interrogated Laura's blood results with a practised eye from her home in Texas and recommended a long list of supplements. Soon every parcel that arrived in the post rattled with the cheerful maraca sound of capsules and tablets in plastic bottles.

So, with two days' worth of tablets safely packed, we headed off to London.

Mornings are never good for Laura, but the day of the trip found her suffering a severe headache, and feeling sick and exhausted. We wavered at the door, unsure as to whether putting her through the stress of the journey was even remotely prudent.

'Laura, are you sure you want to go? It's a long journey and it's going to be a really long day. Honestly, it's no problem for any of us. If you're not well enough to go we're all fine with that.'

'We're going.'

'We're not bothered, honestly ... You go back to bed. Nobody minds, and it's not like we're even royalists, in fact—'

'Just get in the bloody car, will you?' Laura was insistent. We'd resolved to take our lead from her, so off we went.

My mum and dad came to the station to see us off on our travels, always keen to maximise any opportunity to spend time with Laura, even if it was just the fleeting minutes between the car and the station platform. They helped us negotiate the folding wheelchair and assist our poorly girl onto the train, their faces full of concern at how frail and generally unwell she looked. The magnificently resourceful Gracie then nipped down the train to negotiate with the guard in charge and got us upgraded to the quiet First-Class carriage. We made a pillow from a scarf and tried to get Laura as comfortable as possible so she could sleep for at least some of the journey down.

Before the ceremony, we pushed the wheelchair over to the temporary photography studio set up on the first floor of the Royal Over-Seas League. I wanted to remember every single minute of the day.

'Better buy them all,' whispered Siobhan. 'This might be the last chance you get.'

I ordered the full package: a family group and Laura holding a generic certificate, picking out ostentatious gold frames, the biggest and most expensive available.

Those photos are still in their plastic wrappers, stacked behind the sofa. I'm not sure they'll ever make it onto the wall because it's too painful to see the dazed flatness in Laura's eyes, the desperation in mine and those sharp, forced smiles with too many teeth.

The queue lining up to enter St James's Palace was a showcase of idealised young adults: strong, bright, adventurous and poised to succeed in whatever challenges life would throw at them. They were future leaders of industry, politicians, officers and academics, young people with a life to look forward to. I caught a few sideways glances from the other parents, drawing their own conclusions about the girl clasping her invitation in a borrowed wheelchair. I lifted my chin and fixed a smile into position. I knew I had to stop letting my fear of what was ahead of us spoil my enjoyment of the moment, but it was so much easier said than done.

Laura had been allocated a seat on the far side of the room, and her wheelchair was folded up and tucked away out of sight. She looked small and fragile among all that strapping youth, and I struggled to contain my trembling bottom lip. Royal palaces are no place for crying, but I did have a tissue concealed and ready just in case.

Prince Edward arrived, and Laura stood with the rest of her group to be asked charming questions about expeditions and future plans. Although she was still smiling, she looked pale, and I could see her sway slightly, as if trying to keep her balance on the deck of a ship. As the prince moved to another group, I used my best mime skills to ask if she needed to leave. She nodded in relief, and in a huge breach of royal protocol, we grabbed the wheelchair and bolted out of the state room just in front of Prince Edward.

The route out took us through a series of state rooms, each bursting with award winners and proud parents anticipating the guest of honour. Heads swivelled to the door in expectation, only to find a bunch of red-faced commoners pushing a squeaky wheelchair and apologising profusely. Our hysterical laughter echoed through the building as we made an unceremonious escape.

I stupidly misread the timetable and as a result we missed the last train home. I felt like the worst mum in the world, but thankfully Gramps came to the rescue, picking us up from Manchester then driving us to collect the car. My bad planning made it a ridiculously long day for Laura, but we'd pulled it off – just – and it had been glorious; nothing truly catastrophic had happened, and everyone was still alive.

Radiotherapy and Retail Therapy
December

The days that followed blurred together. We witnessed the arrival of the radiotherapy departmental Christmas tree with its tasteful baubles of silver and purple, and open tins of Quality Street chocolates appeared on the reception desk.

But we were struggling with Christmas.

The Brain Tumour Charity had been my first point of reference when Laura was diagnosed. They'd sent out useful literature and messaged from time to time to check how we were. Laura and Gracie had been invited to their Young Adults Christmas meet-up in Leeds, in a Mexican-themed bar at lunchtime, and as usual we were late. The bar smelled of stale beer and was virtually empty, but we spotted a few occupied tables towards the back and the bright-red charity T-shirts showed we were in the right place.

As we approached, it was clear that some of the young adults had sustained significant physical damage and paralysis as a result of their brain tumours and – to my absolute shame now – I had to fight the instinct to turn on my heel and run away. They were *not* the same as my daughter and this would *not* be our life. I couldn't process the unthinkable idea that Laura could also end up severely and permanently disabled.

Believe me, I have grown up a great deal since then.

I took deep breaths until the initial panic began to subside, then we introduced ourselves to a few friendly parents and enthusiastic charity staff, who encouraged us to leave the girls to make friends and enjoy the lunch.

Mark and I wandered around Leeds in a daze, numb to the frenzied Christmas shoppers rushing by at double speed as we moved in slow motion.

The first time I'd heard of glioblastoma (or GBM, as it is often called) was when Dame Tessa Jowell was diagnosed. I remember watching her address the House of Commons on her seventieth birthday. She spoke with such dignity and passion about the inadequate funding for brain tumour research, the poor survival rates and her hopes for the future; even then I had found it incredibly moving.

Following her death in 2018, the Tessa Jowell Brain Cancer Mission was launched, to improve treatment, research and survival. As part of the mission, a major new study was about to start recruiting participants. I read every detail available online, then fired out emails to all the doctors and professors whose names were associated with it. Laura was young and strong when she wasn't suffering from the side effects of treatment, and surely a perfect candidate for the study. My fingers were crossed.

Mark dragged the Christmas tree down from the attic and the girls helped me arrange the decorations while *Elf* played in the background. It was a Christmas tradition, not that anybody felt particularly festive this year. Each bauble felt loaded with significance: tatty paper ones made in primary school classrooms; a shiny pink *Baby's first Christmas*; snowmen with blue and red hats and *Laura* and *Gracie* written across their snow-globe tummies; decorations picked up abroad, like portkeys to happy holidays.

'This will quite probably be the last one you get with Laura, you know,' said Siobhan, as she watched me untangle the fairy lights. As if I didn't already know. As if I wasn't constantly filled with a paralysing dread that this could be our last Christmas together as a family of four.

The whole run-up to Christmas was frankly shit. I weighed it down by spending too much money, and loading it with unrealistic expectations, trying too hard to make everything perfect and memorable. I bought into the fake happy families, laughing and celebrating in TV adverts and Christmas specials.

I wanted us to be happy like them, but they only served to remind me how far from normal we'd become.

Laura and Gracie loved music and both girls played guitar; Laura had lessons on the bass, but Gracie preferred to just teach herself on an acoustic and would copy more proficient players on YouTube. When they were small and before streaming was a thing, I would compile CDs of songs that I thought they might like, a sort of *That's What I Call Mum*, and they'd be played on repeat on a small pink portable CD player in their shared bedroom.

One afternoon we were in the car and Avril Lavigne's song 'Girlfriend' came on the radio.

'We know this one, Mummy, it's on our CD – I love this song!' seven-year-old Laura piped from the back seat. Then there was a pause as she listened intently. 'The words aren't the same though – our one says *motherfuckingprincess*.'

I was a lot more careful about the versions I downloaded for them after that.

This musical brainwashing gave Laura a love of 90s indie music as well as a penchant for bad language. One of her favourite bands, The Cardigans, had a gig scheduled in Manchester. I had no experience of taking a wheelchair to a concert, but I called the venue, and they were happy to add her to the list so she could watch the show from a raised platform.

We were on our way there when I received a reply from the professor heading the trial: 'I am truly sorry to hear your terrible news & my thoughts are with Laura & your family. The trial will not be up & running until the middle of next year at the earliest & that will be too late, I am afraid. I am so sorry I cannot help.'

I was rooted to the spot. 'Too late.' Was I reading it right? I knew I was often guilty of overreaction, but it seemed that this professor was suggesting Laura would be dead by mid 2019.

I was flooded with the fight and fury of adrenaline, my hands shaking. I fired off a reply with trembling fingers: 'Thanks for your response, Professor. Obviously I am both devastated and clutching at straws but if she continues to be well and we see some effects from the repurposed drug protocol, would it be worth getting in touch with you next year? Kind regards, Nicola.'

To which he responded: 'Please do.'

Looking back, I'm sure that it was not his intention to crush our hopes, and he would probably be horrified to know how much it hurt, but my goodness it was painful.

The concert was fabulous, but although we really enjoyed the show, I couldn't get his words out of my head; they'd seeded in my mind, and they were now sending out choking tendrils of despair.

I decided not to share this exchange with Laura. Hope is a delicate and fragile thing, and my job was to preserve it for as long as possible.

The next morning, we went shopping before heading back to The Christie for another round of radiotherapy. Laura had always promised herself that in the event of that zombie apocalypse or the end of the world, she would treat herself to a ridiculously expensive leather jacket from All Saints. Zombies notwithstanding, she'd decided today was that day and after trying on what felt like dozens of identical black jackets, she made her final choice.

The enthusiastic sales assistant explained that the jacket would last decades and improve with every year of wear.

As Laura took it downstairs to pay, I blurted out: 'Thanks for all your help, that's good to know but she' – I jabbed furiously in the direction of stairs – 'has been given twelve months to live so she's not going to be around to see how good that jacket will look in ten years!' Then I promptly burst into tears.

I have no idea why I couldn't have just kept my mouth shut. I made myself cry and probably ruined that nice girl's day, too. I was a mean cow; furious with the world and everyone in it, but that's no excuse for my bad behaviour and I'm truly sorry I took it out on her.

Later that day I had a call from the Brain Tumour Charity asking if we'd be happy for them to include our story in a press release for the national media. I knew this would be a big ask. Laura valued her privacy deeply; she'd deleted all her social media accounts as part of her long-term plan for a career in the security services, so I wasn't optimistic that she'd agree to this level of exposure.

'Would you be OK with them writing an article about you? Not just you but the charity, too? They're hoping to get it into the *Daily Mail*. It could help raise awareness, you know, so people can get diagnosed quicker.'

She rolled her eyes. 'Yeah, that's fine, whatever.'

'Really … seriously?'

I had anticipated some debate at the very least, but it was becoming clear that Laura's priorities had changed. She wanted to help in whatever way she could, and if a news article might help another family recognise the symptoms of this horrific disease, it was worth doing.

After twelve days of radiotherapy, Laura's hair was starting to come out in handfuls. Until now, she'd still looked like herself and, although we knew this was an inevitable side effect, I still found it difficult to witness. I can only imagine how hideous it must have been to wake up to soft blonde clouds on the pillow every morning.

Laura's hair had always been thick and straight, and she'd worn it long for years, but now it was irritating and itchy. A combination of gravity and length meant it was pulling away at the roots, so she hacked it off, first with her penknife and then with scissors.

I picked up the skeins from the floor, twisted them into balls and saved them in a plastic freezer bag. Already they had faded from blonde to flat brown. I had no idea what I would do with the hair, but it was part of Laura, and I couldn't bear to toss it in the bin like rubbish.

The next day she asked Mark to shave off the remaining tufts.

The kitchen was flooded with bright winter sunlight, and she looked for all the world like a persecuted saint, sitting on a dining chair with the hand towel around her shoulders. We made jokes about her new look and how much it suited her, but her eyes were round and sad, and inside I was heartbroken for her. This visual transition into 'person with cancer' was both undeniable and inevitable. People would treat her differently from this point on.

Our alarm call the next morning was the sound of Laura padding unsteadily to the bathroom to throw up. The chemotherapy drugs accumulated in her system, leaving her exhausted and sick. Sometimes she was too weak to make it out of bed, so a pink bin was kept within reaching distance. Mark had also rigged up a doorbell system: the button was attached to the side of her bedside table, with one receiver in our room and one in Gracie's. On bad mornings, we would be woken by the electronic chiming of the bell and scramble, half asleep, into Laura's room, shaking with cold and adrenaline in preparation for whatever emergency was about to play out.

December was always a busy month in the Nuttall house, as both girls had birthdays in the fortnight before Christmas.

Gracie turned seventeen on the thirteenth, and we tried to make it special despite the cloud of sadness that was always with us. As usual, the day began with radiotherapy but then we met up with the grandparents and had a walk around the Christmas markets before taking Gracie to her favourite Thai restaurant.

For a parent, nothing can be worse than being told your child is terminally ill, but for a sibling, the loss is perhaps even more devastating. Not that there's a universal measurement scale for loss and grief – it's not like the heat of chillies or the clarity of diamonds – but siblings – and perhaps sisters – will always have a unique and unbreakable bond. In the natural order of life, you will lose your grandparents, then eventually your parents. Siblings, however, should be with you to the end; to witness all your trials and adventures, to stand by your side during the big red-letter days of life, to remind you where you came from and make sure you don't get too big for your boots. They're the only ones who share all your childhood memories – the in-jokes nobody else will ever understand, the stories, the dramas, the plans, the obscure references. What happens to all those memories when you are the only one left to remember them?

The Stars Will Still Be There

The girls were very different – in many ways, polar opposites. Laura was placid, cool, studious, self-contained and independent, almost to a fault, happy in her own company and always planning for the future. Gracie was an emotional roller-coaster, chaotic, warm, kind and sensitive; she lived in the moment and was much happier with other people than alone.

When Gracie was sad, she wept in the knowledge that she wouldn't have her sister by her side when she got married, and that her children would never know their Aunty Laura. All those things they had talked about doing together, she would be doing on her own. Gracie would sob her heart out and, despite my pathetic attempts, there was nothing I could do to make her feel better. It was all true, and it broke my heart to think that one day Gracie would be left alone in the world.

'It should be me with cancer, not Laura,' she told me one night, her eyes red with tears. 'She's the one with big plans who's going to change the world. I'll end up doing nothing with my life. Other people think it, too – I know they think the same: I can see it in their eyes. It should be me, not her.'

I held her tightly and tried my best to console her, convince her she was wrong and tell her how very loved she was. Over the years, there had been challenges, disputes and fallings-out – standard fare for any sisters – but the girls had never been closer than now, and there was nothing Gracie wouldn't do for her sister.

If I'm brutally honest – and I'm not proud of this at all – I often thought, as we drove down the motorway, that it would be better if we were wiped out by an articulated lorry jack-knifing across the carriageway, or some drug-addled joy rider driving the wrong way down the M60.

I knew it was unforgivably selfish and cowardly, but it would be so much less painful if the four of us could all die together.

*   *   *

I had been dreading Laura's A Level presentation evening back at her old school. It was the first time we'd been anywhere since she'd lost her hair and I hated the thought of all those concerned and sympathetic faces turning to look at us.

When we arrived, it was clear we stood out. Somewhere between a sore thumb and a C-list celebrity, everyone knew about Laura's diagnosis, but few came over to say hello. We lingered around the edges of the room, uncomfortable in the infamy. Lorraine and her daughter Iona provided emotional back-up; Iona had been Laura's best friend since nursery, and although high school found them in different friendship groups, they were still close. I knew that Iona would forever benchmark the life Laura would miss, and that every celebratory event would be a painful reminder of what we had lost.

Laura was awarded the subject prize for Politics and Government, and I almost burst with pride and delight. Not just because she was good at the subject but also because her teacher spoke at length about how she'd helped the other students in her class. She lined up with all the other winners for a group photograph under the Christmas tree, a row of smiley, long-haired girls and Laura, defiantly cool in black silk shirt, jeans and bald head.

'Look at all these lucky fuckers,' Siobhan said. 'How is it fair that they get to be normal? Not really surprising you're a bitter old cow, is it?'

It wasn't an easy night. We were surrounded by bright, beautiful girls who had just finished their first term at university and had a whole world of opportunity ahead: all that wonderful, glorious potential.

Laura enjoyed seeing her friends, but I'm sure the contrast was not lost on her and I tried not to be resentful on her behalf. My hopes for Laura had been fairly ordinary: have a good time at university, learn lots, get a degree, find a job she liked, fall in love, maybe have kids, and get her own home. Have adventures, lovers, friends and die an old, old lady. Just the normal everyday things that we all wish for our children: love, health, happiness, life.

We smiled and answered the same question a million times as we drank sour prosecco from plastic cups in the geography classroom.

'How are things?' (Head to one side, sympathetic voice.)

Sometimes it even went like this: 'My uncle had a brain tumour like Laura's.'

'Oh, did he? I'm so sorry to hear that. How's he doing now?'

'Well … he died, unfortunately.'

Awkward.

Bad news like ours isn't contagious, but I have seen people try to avoid us, taking a swift turn down a supermarket aisle, avoiding eye contact and then feigning surprise when we're in the queue for the same till. I absolutely understand this. I would have no idea what to say to me either.

Some of Laura's friends were wonderfully kind, organising fundraising events, dropping round with cake and flowers, or taking her out to the pub for a change of scenery. It can't have been easy; they were full of university life, new friends and the challenges of living away, while Laura's world had shrunk to the house, the hospital and the motorway that connected them.

There were also good friends who dropped out of Laura's life completely. Whether that was because they felt self-conscious or had nothing to say, I have no idea, but I do know that, as her mum, it's hard to forgive and I will certainly never forget.

Christmas feels mournful and off-key in a cancer hospital; perhaps it's the contrast between the piped festive music in the foyer, the sparkly trees in each department, and the stark fact that the building is full of people who are doing their best just to survive, hoping that this won't be the last one they see.

On our Christmas Eve visit, we brought chocolates and mince pies for the staff and the other patients. Laura was taken through for radiotherapy, leaving the waiting room empty except for a lady who was relaying details of her husband's treatment to a friend or family member on the other end of her phone call. I tried hard not to listen, but it was obvious that, despite the bright confidence in her voice, she was going through an extremely tough time and his prognosis was, at best, uncertain.

When the call ended, I took a deep breath and went over to where she was standing, and, after a moment's hesitation, I wrapped my arms around her and gave her the biggest hug I could manage. 'I know ... I know what you're going through,' I said into her hair as she cried. 'It's just so bloody hard, isn't it? And so bloody unfair.'

Then the door to the radiotherapy suite opened and her partner came out, followed closely by Laura. We both discreetly wiped away tears while gathering up bags and coats, then wished each other a happy Christmas. The smiles on our faces were shadowed by sadness; we both knew this might be the last Christmas, and the pressure to make memories just made it all feel that bit harder.

Christmas Day didn't start well. Laura rang her bell at 8:30 and we all rushed into her room, shivering around the bed like some alternative nativity while she threw up into the pink bin.

In the gaps between vomiting, we opened presents, ate lunch with the family and played games, but the day was punctuated by Laura's slow trips upstairs to be sick. We were like actors in some madcap farce, all heightened Christmas jollity and forced merriment until she left the room and we fell silent, smiles slipping from our faces. Despite her valiant attempts to be festive, Laura really couldn't stomach the food and eventually gave up. I helped her upstairs to bed.

Her absence was the biggest presence in the room.

I cleared the table and scraped the dishes furiously, screeching the knife down the plate as dry turkey and sprouts tipped into the bin, tears of anger and frustration running down my face. I was exhausted, not just from preparing the dinner but from all the emotional energy it took to maintain fake happiness.

Mum had followed me into the kitchen. She took the plates from me, then held me by my hands, looking directly into my eyes. 'Nic, I need to ask you something – are you sorry that you called her *Laura*?'

I took a deep breath. 'Yes. I'm sorry, Mum. I know this isn't what you want to hear, but absolutely – yes, I regret it with all my heart. Wouldn't you? Look what I've done! A hundred times – yes.' She held me in a tight hug but my body was rigid, filled with a rage that had nowhere to go.

I knew that my words were wounding and hurtful, but I *was* sorry. It felt like this was my fault and although my intentions had been good, I had cursed Laura with her name.

History was repeating itself.

I named my daughter Laura because once I had a sister called Laura. She died when I was five and she was just two and a half. If I'm honest I don't have many memories from that time, but the two I did have defined my childhood.

The first was of me and my baby brother Neil waiting in the back of a stationary car. My aunty and uncle were in the front seats, and this was unusual. Then Dad walked towards the car from a building, and the front window was wound down. His face was contorted into a shape I didn't recognise and then I realised that he was crying, tears streaming down his face.

I had never seen Dad cry before.

'We've lost her,' he sobbed.

In the second one, I am sitting on the toilet, swinging my legs and crossing my eyes to make the 1970s graphic wallpaper swim in and out of focus. Next to me, the bath is full to the brim with flowers. Wreaths and arrangements in a beautiful rainbow of colour, lots of pink. The smell was heavenly. I knew that I didn't want to go back downstairs because everyone there was sad.

Of course we had happy times, days out and holidays, but there was always a dark corner in our family. We didn't talk about it, but I always knew that we were different from other families, that we all carried a little piece of sadness with us, like seeds in a fold of paper.

Boxing Day continued in a similar pattern. Laura knew she needed to eat, but nothing tasted nice, and the tiny mouthfuls she did manage to swallow didn't stay down long. She was shaking from the lack of food but also with frustration. We did our best to distract her with trashy TV and board games, but a few more days of this meant we had to resort to steroids to resurrect her appetite and provide her with some desperately needed energy. She was brittle and painfully fragile, like the blown-glass decorations on the tree.

I was haunted by the ghosts of Christmas past: two little girls with fluffy, dandelion-clock hair and matching pyjamas, waking before dawn and rushing downstairs to discover a play kitchen or bunk beds for their dolls, a day full of magic and love. Then the ghosts of Christmas future – how could we ever find anything happy in a Christmas with just the three of us? It was too painful to even contemplate but it was always there, the spectre in the room.

I wished that we could go back to the beginning and start all over again. I wished that I remembered every single second of her life from the moment she was placed in my arms, so small and slippery. I wished that I had savoured and relished every day we spent together. If I could go back, I would do a better job at remembering everything. I would put my whole heart into each moment. I was often busy and distracted – maybe I was thinking

about work, what to make for tea, whether Gracie needed changing, the state of the world …

Why didn't I spend every possible moment staring into Laura's
eyes, trying to make her laugh, painting, playing games, splashing
in puddles? Why didn't I record more videos, take more photos,
record the sound of her voice?

I know why. Because, just like you, I thought I had all the time
in the world.

2019

It Takes a Village

January

A year ago, when our lives were normal and ordinary, I agreed to take Gracie to New York as a combined birthday and Christmas present. She'd spent years wearing me down until I'd finally relented and found myself booking flights and hotels. Laura had been obsessed with New York for as long as I could remember; her bedroom was decorated with a wallpaper of repeating black and white NY street signs. I thought it would be the trip of a lifetime for me and my girls, but Laura always had the power to surprise.

'That sounds brilliant, thanks, Mum ... but you go with Grace.'

'You don't want to come to New York?' I asked, incredulous.

'It's not that I don't want to come. I just have an image of my first trip there and I want it to be on my own – no offence to you or Grace.'

I tried not to feel too crushed by the rejection; it was probably for the best. There was little crossover between Laura and Gracie's interests, and keeping them both happy would have severely tested my skills as mediator and referee.

And now, the trip was upon us.

Since Laura's diagnosis, our family had a new shape. The structure, once supported by four, was now carried by three. It felt unstable and vulnerable. The idea of leaving the country and being thousands of miles away filled me with cold dread; it would be a desertion of my maternal duty. Laura would, of course, be in safe hands with Mark, and she was all for it; she knew Gracie badly needed respite from the cancer house, and we'd only be away for five days.

'She'll die,' whispered Siobhan. 'Something bad will happen and she'll die, and you'll be on the other side of the world, and you won't be able to get back and you will never EVER forgive yourself.'

It also meant that I wouldn't be there for the last day of radiotherapy, and my guts twisted at the thought of Laura ringing the bell to celebrate the end of treatment without me there to cheer her on.

It felt like having to choose which of my daughters needed me the most.

I avoided the decision for as long as possible and it wasn't until the day before the flight that I pulled a dusty suitcase out from the attic.

New York still sparkled with strings of fairy lights, but the giant Christmas trees had shed most of their needles and looked forlorn and hungover in the first days of January.

Gracie and I were equally subdued; we were struggling under the weight of this new life. It was a heavy rucksack that we couldn't put down.

Mark shared photos of Laura posing, bell ringer in hand, her smiling face moon-round with steroids and a rasp of new hair coming through. She had on the yellow Beatles T-shirt we'd bought on a trip to Liverpool, and I missed her with all my heart.

I'm sure that we had fun, visiting the Empire State and walking over the Brooklyn Bridge, but Gracie only remembers me as constantly anxious and distracted. I asked her not to share photos on social media as it just didn't feel appropriate, but she misinterpreted this and thought I was ashamed to be spending time with her.

Two days in, we had a spectacular argument. It began innocuously enough, with a disagreement about the location of the open-top bus stop on 49th Street, but it soon gained momentum and whipped up into an almighty row. We stood on the street corner, red-faced and sweating beneath layers of clothing, rotating our mobile phones to point the pulsing blue dot in the right direction.

'You do realise you still have two daughters, don't you? You might be a brilliant mother to one of us but I'm still here and I need you too!' she roared, loud enough for people to turn around and look.

'For fuck's sake! I'm doing my best here, Gracie!'

'You're doing your best for Laura, but what about me? *I'm* your daughter too and I need you, but you don't give a shit about me anymore.'

'I'm here, aren't I? With you, just like you wanted.'

'Yeah, but it's Laura you're thinking about, isn't it?'

'Tell me what you want me to do? Do you not want me to spend time with her – is that it? Are you actually *jealous* of her?'

'No, that's not what I'm—'

'—because if you're seriously telling me that I should be spending less time with Laura when I might only have months left with her, then I—'

'—I'm not saying that! I totally get it, but it's like you don't care about me now. I have so much going on in my life and you know fuck all about it. We used to be so close, you and me …'

She was right; we were distant and antagonistic these days, and I was hit with a wave of unbearable sadness. It felt like I was failing everyone.

Gracie stared at me angrily, her navy-blue eyes glittering with tears that she was too furious to let me see.

'I'm sorry, Gracie. I'm sorry if you don't think I've been there for you. Believe me, I am doing my best here but if I've made you feel this bad, I'm truly sorry. I love you so much, I love you both, and I promise I'll try to do better.'

'Fuck's sake, Mum – stop trying to make me feel guilty and sorry for you. You always do this, and it's not fair.'

We made up later over a shared red velvet cupcake.

It's obvious that a diagnosis like Laura's impacts the whole family and although it does at times bring you closer together, it can also set a wrecking ball in motion. We all end up damaged, whether it's a glancing blow or a direct hit.

Before the trip, I'd continually scoured the internet, searching for some revolutionary new treatment that could reverse the creeping invasion taking place in Laura's brain, or at least buy her time until some medical great leap forward. The most promising was a dendritic cell vaccination, which used tumour tissue to re-educate the immune system so it could recognise and fight cancer cells. The technology was still at clinical trial stage, it was shockingly expensive and contingent upon there being sufficient, properly frozen tissue removed during surgery. There was also a *very* long waiting list.

My research had suggested the treatment would cost £50,000, and despite having no idea where we might find that kind of money, I'd fired off a preliminary enquiry filled with hope and desperation.

Gracie and I were riding the subway out to The Bronx when the reply dropped into my inbox. It detailed the complex procedure for sending the frozen tissue to a laboratory, where it would be used to produce first a lysate and then a personalised vaccine. At the very bottom of the email, a guide price of £150,000.

My heart sank to the soles of my winter boots. It felt like the only lifeboat that could possibly save Laura was setting sail without us. That £150,000 was more than we'd paid for our house.

I didn't have a plan B.

I didn't want to spoil the last day of the trip, so I blew my nose, wiped away the tears that blurred my eyes, and packed this latest bombshell into the heavy rucksack. We dragged leaden feet around a rainy Little Italy and ate floppy triangles of pizza in a deli recommended on Trip Advisor for its 'authenticity', the windows opaque with condensation. Gracie rubbed my hand between hers and did her best to look on the bright side, suggesting increasingly ridiculous ideas for raising funds until I couldn't help but laugh. We ate the cannoli I'd promised her all trip, but its sharp edges stuck in my throat, tight and raw from crying.

The Brain Tumour Charity article hit the Mail Online almost as soon as we returned home. I'd added a link to a GoFundMe page, created at the last minute as we were never going to get a better opportunity to share Laura's story or raise funds.

Mark hated the idea. Charity was something we donated to, not something we needed. He couldn't even bring himself to ask for directions, so there was no way he'd ever be comfortable asking for financial help.

Pride is all very well, but it won't help you raise £150,000.

High-flying student, 19, who thought she had 'fresher's flu' was diagnosed with terminal brain cancer after a routine eye test – and now she's spending her last months making memories with her family.

Laura Nuttall, 19, from Lancashire, had unexplained swelling in her optic nerve …

She was later diagnosed with glioblastoma – an aggressive brain cancer …

Laura's family hope to raise awareness of brain tumours in young adults ...

It felt like we'd laid ourselves bare for the world to see, just when we were at our most vulnerable. I waited for the censure and blame in the comments. I waited for judgements about poor parenting and mobile phones. I imagined the readers looking for a reason for our bad luck: a house beneath an electricity pylon or built on a toxic dump, or a diet consisting solely of fast food – something we'd done wrong. We need cause and effect, because without it there's only the horrific conclusion that this is all just completely random.

My assumptions were wrong: the comments were nothing but kind and supportive, and by midnight we had already received donations of £5,000. By lunchtime the next day, my phone was hot with calls and messages from other media outlets asking for exclusive photographs and quotes, competing to cover Laura's story while it was newsworthy.

The local BBC News team sent a crew to interview the family for *North West Tonight*. They were kind and respectful of our broken hearts, sensitive to the fact that emotions were so raw and close to the surface. We were interviewed separately, in different rooms, although Ziggy did his best to feature in every shot.

At tea time we gathered on the sofa to watch the programme. Mark had picked up a chippy tea, and as we shared out polystyrene tubs of gravy and mushy peas, Laura's face filled the TV screen.

It was a tough watch. She sounded positive, brave and confident, although I knew she was more nervous than she appeared. 'I'm trying to get on with my life, trying to make it as normal as possible but it's quite difficult when you've got this ... got something inside you, trying to kill you.

'As soon as we found out, we were like, right, we need a bucket list. It's crazy thinking about these things – what you want to do before you die. When you're nineteen, you don't think about that sort of stuff.'

She still smiled when she talked, but, to me, she looked vulnerable and exposed without her long curtain of blonde hair.

The revelation, though, was Mark.

'This can happen to any human being in the world, and it happened to us, just like that, and it's devastating … I'm Dad. I fix things …' His voice cracked and he paused to compose himself, eyes filled with the tears he'd kept hidden from us. 'But I can't fix this.'

Mark was sharing emotions with strangers that he wouldn't or couldn't share with us; his honesty caught me by surprise. It hit a nerve with the audience, too – probably dads sitting on their own sofas, imagining it was their daughter, not ours.

By the end of that day, we'd raised £20,000.

'I feel really bad about this, Mum.'

'Why on earth do you feel bad? This is brilliant – people have been so kind, haven't they?'

'Yes, which is why I feel guilty. Why have they donated it to me? All this money could build an orphanage in Yemen or feed hungry children, or something else more worthwhile.'

I understood why Laura found this difficult to square: she had a straightforward, utilitarian approach to life and there were so many deserving causes desperate for funds. What was the life of one person worth? We could have used that money to vaccinate thousands of children against malaria or buy hundreds of food parcels, which would be objectively better for the world than trying to save this one girl. But in the end, when it's someone you love, all philosophical detachment is lost. She was my girl, and there was no price I wouldn't pay to keep her alive and well.

The mini media flurry continued into the next day, and despite being sick throughout the morning, Laura still managed to give two local radio interviews and another for *People Magazine* in

New York. It was impossible to fathom why an American audience would be interested in the story of a Lancashire teenager, but we were grateful they were. Any publicity was good if it helped to raise funds.

The kindness of complete strangers was astonishing, and I was awash with gratitude for the donations and messages of love sent from around the world. It felt like we had an entire army on our side. There were also emails from well-meaning people suggesting miracle treatments, conspiracy theories, and urging us to look to religion for a cure. I've no doubt having faith would have been really comforting, trusting everything was part of some great master plan rather than just the miserable random chaos of chance. When people promised their prayers, I was grateful; maybe the strength of their faith would compensate for my ambivalence.

I remember precisely when I stopped believing in God: I was nine and wearing my favourite yellow nylon jumpsuit – sleepwear of choice in the late 1970s. It crackled constantly with static electricity and was always saved for Thursday night so I could wear it to copy Legs & Co as they performed an interpretive dance to some chart hit on *Top of the Pops*.

I wandered downstairs late in the evening for a glass of water – probably thirsty from all that dancing – and swung through the 'cowboy' louvre swing doors into the kitchen diner to find my dad sitting on his own at the table. I think he'd probably been drinking, he seemed so sad. It was one of the rare occasions when he actually let his grief show, and I held his hand while he cried. He told me that he didn't believe in God anymore and although my mum had found a degree of comfort in Sunday church attendance, he couldn't resolve this compassionate God with the desperate sadness he felt at losing his baby girl.

Once he'd said it, it was so blindingly obvious to me that he was right, I didn't believe in God after that, either.

* * *

Sometimes when Laura was sick, she would describe feeling the tentacles of the tumours growing in her head. I could imagine it too, stretching out like a malevolent sea creature into the crevasses of her brain.

The first post-radiotherapy scan would show if the treatment was working but we had to be patient; too early, and it would only show trauma and inflammation and nothing useful. We needed a distraction and Laura needed something to look forward to; at that point, the calendar contained only the looming dates of her twelve cycles of chemo.

There was nothing I could do to improve the treatment process for her, or assuage the debilitating side effects Laura was experiencing; all control had been taken away. We just turned up at the hospital when the letters told us to and followed in the miserable steps of those who'd come before us.

But if I couldn't make the lows any better, I would try to bring the highs instead. 'You know what you were saying on TV about a bucket list, well have you made one yet?' I asked as I helped her into bed.

'Why, d'you think I'll be dying soon?'

'No, but you're going to have time on your hands without uni, so you might as well make the most of it and do some interesting stuff.'

The next day she dropped a handwritten list on the kitchen table.

Watch the filming of *Saturday Night Live* and meet Kate McKinnon
Visit the Heinz beans factory in Wigan
Drive a heavy goods vehicle
See *The Scream* by Edvard Munch
Visit the Churchill War Rooms
Go gold panning

Cross the equator
Have afternoon tea at the Ritz
Catch a big fish and have a photo taken holding it (ideally
   with Bob Mortimer & Paul Whitehouse)
Attend a rally/march for something I feel strongly about
Meet David Attenborough
Ask a question on *Question Time*

'Bloody hell, Laura, these are a bit random!'

'Yeah, well, you asked for a bucket list so there you go. I'd also like to visit a prison and go down a sewer.'

'Did you not fancy the standard stuff like swimming with dolphins?'

She rolled her eyes and walked out of the kitchen, biting down hard on a peeled carrot.

It was clear that I was going to need a great deal of help to make Laura's wishes come true, so later that day I posted the bucket list on Twitter. I also shared it with Sophie Raworth, who in turn generously shared it with her thousands of followers. Sophie and I had met in Tokyo where we were both running the marathon, and then again in the toilet queue at Blackheath Station the following April, when I was attempting a Guinness World Record by running the London marathon dressed as a Pendle Witch – complete with pointy hat and carrying a broom. When Sophie read about Laura's diagnosis, she had immediately called to offer her support and had already been instrumental in securing the extra seats for Laura's Duke of Edinburgh Award presentation.

I became a relentless sender of the brazen email. Gracie coined the phrase 'scrambled beg' to describe my efforts, and even I cringed at how overtly cheeky my requests were. But once Laura had been diagnosed, I lost all capacity for shame and became a firm subscriber to the principle that it was worth a try – they could always say no. My priority was to bring maximum joy to Laura's life; compensation for all the hours she was exhausted, sick and sad. I became the queen of the begging letter because, after all, 'Shy bairns get nowt.'

Most wish-granting charities were exclusively for sick children, but Rays of Sunshine just needed an application before Laura turned nineteen. On the day before her birthday, a billboard gave me a moment of blinding inspiration: Laura's all-time hero, Michelle Obama, was coming to London as part of her *Becoming* book tour. Meeting her was a wish way too ambitious to even make the bucket list but just maybe the gods were on our side?

Our designated Wish Granter, Holly, tried gently to manage my expectations: it was a *really* long shot. Tickets for the show had sold out in the blink of an eye and were now changing hands for hundreds on resale sites. But in the weeks that followed, the Rays of Sunshine team pulled in every favour they could to make Laura's wish a reality.

Holly was beside herself with excitement when she called to say they'd managed to acquire four tickets from an anonymous corporate sponsor. They were also working to get us on the meet and greet list but it was proving almost impossible. At least we'd see the show and be in her presence, and that was more than enough.

'Are we really, honestly, going to see Michelle Obama?' Laura asked, eyes wide, at least three times every day.

Without the Royal Navy eye test, it was unlikely Laura's diagnosis would have been so straightforward: she wouldn't have wanted to make a fuss about the headaches or persisted with the GP. I imagined her phone ringing unanswered on her bedside cabinet, and a late-night call to us from an unknown number, a solemn police officer explaining that my daughter had been found unresponsive in her student halls. We could so easily have lost her already.

So I phoned the Royal Navy to thank them for the vital role they'd inadvertently played in Laura's diagnosis. I was put through to the assistant regional commander and my wobbly start soon dissolved into incomprehensible sobs as I recounted Laura's story.

Rob was instantly kind and sympathetic, and after a consultation with his team, he invited Laura to pilot a Royal Navy warship from Liverpool down the Manchester Ship Canal, with the whole family welcome to join her on board. It was a chance for Laura to have the Navy experience she'd been denied, even if it was only for a day.

We arrived at the Liverpool docks under a bright blue winter sky. There was an unseasonal warmth in the January sun, but Laura needed every layer of her new Royal Navy uniform to keep her frail little body warm. She'd already been sick twice before we got there.

'Laura, are you feeling OK?' I asked repeatedly, until she got irritated and told me to stop.

'Just assume I'm OK until I tell you I'm not … OK?'

We sailed out from the docks and into the open waters of the Mersey, then down the ship canal with Laura at the helm of HMS *Charger*. We took turns at steering the boat – when we could prise my dad away from the tiller – and at regular intervals one of the cadets would be summoned to do 'wets', which meant rounds of tea and bacon rolls. I held my mug tightly, appreciative of any residual heat in the biting January wind.

We bid farewell to the crew at Warrington, where Laura was formally presented with the ship's crest and the HMS *Charger* rating – the band from the sailor's cap for the uninitiated. The crew stood in line and saluted Laura as if she was the most important of VIPs and my heart swelled to see the pride in her beaming smile.

'Anything you need … you let me know,' Rob said. 'She's one of our own now.'

* * *

We'd lived in Barrowford for twenty years, but I still considered myself a newcomer. I didn't have the history associated with going to school locally, or family connections to east Lancashire, so I could never have anticipated the way in which the local community united behind Laura. It took me completely by surprise, but if it takes a village to raise a child, maybe it takes a village to save one, too.

Our fundraising target was £150,000, to meet the cost of the dendritic vaccine. It was such a lot of money to raise on our own, so we were deeply grateful for the incredible support from our community. So many people raised money on our behalf in extraordinary ways: fell races, choir concerts, extreme sponsored walks, darts tournaments, pub quizzes, school talent shows and sleep-overs, an all-day sponsored run, bake sales, sponsored head shaves and raffles. A running friend even swam in a cross-Channel relay to raise funds. Complete strangers used their birthdays to request donations for Laura rather than presents for themselves. An old lady who'd never met Laura left £200 in out-of-circulation notes for her at the post office. Another sent Laura a voucher for afternoon tea at the Ritz that she'd been given by her husband for Christmas. We were able to return this with thanks when the Ritz (under an avalanche of persuasive emails and tweets), invited us down for complimentary tea.

Wish bracelets seemed a good way to raise funds; inexpensive and easy to post, hand-made threads with a dainty metal charm, mounted on square printed card. The theory was that when the thread snapped, the wish was granted. If only it was that simple.

We needed a motto that would capture the sentiment of the campaign and, after some time spent researching inspirational quotes, I presented Laura with a shortlist. I'd tried to avoid the most obvious clichés, but she still made retching noises as she read down the list.

We settled on two: 'We cannot direct the wind, but we can adjust the sails' and 'Storms make trees take deeper roots.' They seemed to strike the right balance of fatalism and optimism and we sold hundreds through local shops. We also sold hoodies and neck warmers emblazoned with 'Doing it for Laura'. Sometimes I'd pass a complete stranger wearing my daughter's name across their chest, which felt both touching and bizarre.

Laura was disappearing before us; cheekbones sharpening, eyes fading into purple hollows.

The district nurses came out to administer IV nausea meds to provide a brief respite from the chemo-induced sickness, but her appetite had disappeared entirely.

'We're trying everything to build her strength up,' Mark told the nurse, as she fed the used needle into the little yellow sharps bin. 'We've even given her gravy bones, not that she's happy about that, being a vegetarian.'

The nurse looked at me, eyebrows raised in surprise.

'Bone broth,' I corrected. 'We're giving her bone broth. We've not resorted to dog treats just yet.'

Changing Laura's bedding later, I noticed something sellotaped to the side of her bedside cabinet. She'd positioned it horizontally so she could read it lying in bed. It was from *Invictus* by William Ernest Henley copied out in her neat and careful handwriting.

I knew it wasn't for anyone else to see: it was a mantra, something to give her courage when things were bleak.

'In the fell clutch of circumstance,
I have not winced or cried aloud,
Under the bludgeoning of chance,
My head is bloody, but unbowed.'

Trains, Fast Cars and Superstars

February

If the terminal diagnosis had been mine, I would have taken to my bed like a consumptive Victorian, lying back on a mountain of pillows and having food brought to me on a silver tray. I would have succumbed. I didn't have the fight in me, unlike Laura.

There were times when she was exhausted and would sleep around the clock, but on the whole, she'd force herself to get up, get dressed and be productive. I'd try to pre-empt the worst of the sickness and plan events for the calm days between chemo cycles, ensuring that Laura always had something nice to look forward to.

February was full of good reasons to wear shoes and leave the house.

First, the Mission Motorsport charity offered to tick item three off the list, by inviting us to Silverstone where they held an annual event for wounded, injured or sick military veterans.

Laura loved to drive: she passed her test first time, then followed that up with an Advanced Driving qualification. She loved the freedom and independence driving gave her, which made returning her licence to the DVLA all the more painful: the seizure and craniotomy meant she was no longer legally allowed to drive, and this consequence of brain cancer was the one she found hardest to take.

Down at Silverstone, *Top Gear* presenter Chris Harris offered to take Laura for a spin around the racetrack. He wasn't quite a household name at this point and as she put her helmet on and climbed into the supercar, I heard her say: 'I hear you're kind of a big deal?'

She came back into the pit lane with the biggest smile, her eyes shining, almost breathless from the adrenaline rush of the laps. Then, out on the skid pan, she climbed into the cab of an articulated HGV, small and slight against the colossal truck. I watched in awe as she slalomed the eight-wheeler between cones, knowing how weak she was and how little she'd managed to keep down in the last few days. Laura never wanted to miss the chance to try something new, regardless of how bad she felt. She knew opportunities had to be grasped with both hands and threw herself wholeheartedly into every experience, knowing the inevitable exhaustion would be worth it.

Item twelve on the list was BBC *Question Time*. Rules on impartiality and political balance meant Laura wouldn't actually be able to ask a question, but she was invited to visit the set, meet the panel and watch the show being recorded at Chester Town Hall.

On the way, we stopped at the Trafford Centre, where I'd arranged a beauty counter make-over. I was hoping that some gentle pampering might boost Laura's self-confidence. Her face now told a story of chemo, radiation and steroids that was unmistakably cancer. I'd try my best to help by drawing on eyebrows, but my attempts were two ginger caterpillars that were never level.

The beautician did a much better job, making sympathetic small talk as she brandished her loaded blusher brush. Laura looked vulnerable and fragile under her laser focus, uncomfortable with the close scrutiny, but she emerged looking fabulous – if ever so slightly orange.

Fiona Bruce was intimidatingly elegant, but she was kind and generous with her time. She explained how the programme was recorded, showed Laura around and introduced her to the crew. The audience took their seats, raised their hands, and asked the pertinent questions of the day, which were skilfully avoided by the politicians. Later, when we watched it from our Premier Inn beds, tucked up with hot chocolate and individual packets of hotel biscuits, we spotted Laura's smiley orange face as the camera panned across the audience.

Item number twelve completed, or at least close enough for Laura's satisfaction.

The busier we were, the less time I had to think; thinking meant looking forward in time and the future felt like a gaping chasm to be avoided at all costs. I planned a girls' trip to London; we had so many activities arranged, I had to make a spreadsheet to keep track.

'You're going to wear her out,' Mark's mum, Beryl, told me sternly. 'She's got cancer and you've got her going all over the place. It'll do her no good, I'm telling you.'

In ordinary times, I would have searched for the cheapest hotel deal, but now it felt like every trip could be the last, so I scramble-begged a couple of lovely nights at the Waldorf Hotel.

As the taxi pulled up outside the granite facade with its liveried doorman, Laura was looking at the building opposite and the trickle of students filing out onto the pavement, talking, laughing, pushing folders into rucksacks and lighting cigarettes.

'That's where I had my lectures at King's,' she said quietly.

'Is it? Oh, Laura, I'm so sorry – I had absolutely no idea. Oh, God, how completely thoughtless of me. I'm so, so sorry.'

She needed no reminder of how much life had changed since last September when she was a shiny Fresher with the world at her feet, and I felt a crunch of guilt at cruelly dangling it in front of her. I tried to distract her, ramping up my levels of enthusiasm to manic, but the damage had been done.

Gracie and I left Laura in the hotel room to have a nap between fancy Egyptian-cotton sheets, arranging to meet an hour later at the noodle bar on the corner.

At the restaurant, we ordered our drinks and waited. I'd sent Laura the location and we knew she'd left the hotel, but the hour came and went, and still no sign.

'We shouldn't have left her on her own, Gracie. Something must have happened.'

'Like what? She's literally a hundred metres down the road. Do you want me to try her phone again?'

When eventually Laura did answer her phone, she was at another branch of the noodle chain on the other side of the city.

'How on earth have you managed that, Laura? We sent you a map with a pin! You can literally see this place from the hotel!'

I couldn't understand how she'd got so lost, but now it all makes perfect sense. This was nothing to do with map reading. She had just wanted to move through the anonymous streets of the city, like everybody else. A teenage girl with a beanie hat and a leather jacket going exactly where she wanted, on her own.

Afternoon tea at the Ritz was just as we'd imagined: a serene oasis of palm trees and golden chandeliers, where silver teaspoons tinkled on fine china to the gentle accompaniment of the resident pianist on his baby grand. We'd dressed conservatively to blend in with the middle-aged ladies from the home counties, but we fooled no one: the bald head and caterpillar eyebrows were a neon sign flashing CANCER. Laura was treated like royalty, though, and the tea, cakes and scones were replenished until we couldn't manage another mouthful. She was even invited to choose songs for the pianist to play, but we decided Radiohead didn't really match the ambience.

The girls were momentarily star-struck when Sophie Raworth breezed in and pulled up a chair. She happened to be on a BBC training course nearby and popped in to join us for tea and a scone, despite the fact that her jeans didn't quite meet the dress code.

Item eight on the bucket list completed – and with a sprinkle of celebrity stardust.

I'd bought tickets for the stage production of *All About Eve* not long after Laura was diagnosed – a Christmas present and a defiant act of hope. She was a devoted Gillian Anderson fan and so excited at the prospect of seeing her live on stage. A few pleading emails to the production company got us moved from our cheap seats in the stalls to a private box, where Gracie and I had a childish argument as to who was sitting next to Laura. As the safety curtain rose and I pulled out my phone to turn it off, a message flashed up on my screen suggesting we might like to remain in our seats when the show finished.

After a fabulous performance and rapturous standing ovation, we lingered uncertainly with coats and bags until the theatre had emptied.

Then Gillian Anderson appeared from a side door, crossed the auditorium and took the stairs up to our box.

I was instantly nervous; she had the unmistakable, slightly intimidating aura of an old-school film star. Delicate, much smaller than her huge stage presence had suggested, and ethereally beautiful with her face scrubbed clean of stage makeup, she chatted with the girls, signed Laura's programme, and generously posed for photographs until her PA signalled that our time was up.

We blundered out into the street, giddy and incredulous that we'd *actually* met Gillian Anderson in real life, then wandered back to the hotel for a late-night feast of leftover Ritz scones.

Visiting a prison was never going to be especially straightforward – they're hardly a tourist attraction, but a new Twitter friend suggested lunch at The Clink restaurant, located within, and staffed by the inmates of, HM Prison Brixton.

As we made our way out onto the street the next day, the doorman raised his arm to hail a taxi for us. He knew Laura's story and we'd kept him up to date with our daily adventures in the city.

'Where you off to today, ladies?'

'Brixton prison,' replied Gracie with a straight face.

'Come again?'

The Clink has a mission to reduce reoffending by giving inmates in the last eighteen months of their sentence the opportunity to train for qualifications in catering or horticulture. Practical experience and transferable skills make it easier to find employment on release and help stop the cycle of reoffending.

On arrival, we were thoroughly searched: personal belongings, phones, wallets and bags were securely stored in lockers before we were given a (slightly terrifying) briefing and taken through the looming gates into the prison itself. We ate with plastic knives and forks, for obvious reasons, and there was no alcohol available, but our lunch was beautifully presented, and delicious. We would have taken so many photos if our phones hadn't been locked away. Our waiter, Mohammed, was a polite young man with six months of his sentence left to serve. It was hard not to be curious about the nature of his crime, but we'd been firmly instructed not to ask. It didn't stop us speculating in the taxi on the way back to the hotel, though. I hope that Brixton is just a memory for him now.

The great thing about the bucket list was that new items were added all the time. It was Laura's policy to say *yes* to every experience she was offered. If life was going to be short, she was going to squeeze maximum joy from it. We only really regret the things we don't do, after all.

On our last morning in London, we took the tube to Edgware Station, where we'd been invited to visit the Northern Line training facility. Tube-driver Clive showed Laura and Gracie the basics and they took turns on the simulator, opening and closing virtual doors and maintaining the safety of their computer-generated passengers. Then in our orange, high-vis jackets, we joined Clive in the cab as his train filled with real people.

Gracie had the honour of announcing to the passengers, 'This train is for Kennington via Charing Cross. Mind the doors, please.'

When our passengers had disembarked and the train was empty, Clive let Laura drive the short loop which turned the train around before it headed back north. She was thrilled, her face a picture of concentration as she went through the security checks, closed the doors, and put the morning's training into practice.

We left with a carrier bag full of TFL merchandise, including a knitted hat – which Laura was particularly grateful for as her head was always cold. I was equally grateful when I lost my ticket on the way back and the guard, spotting Laura's hat with its distinctive logo, waved us through with a complicit grin.

Initially, the loss of Laura's hair was visceral and shocking, but soon, and to my surprise, we just stopped noticing it. Humans are very adaptable, I suppose, but when I look back at photos from this period, I'm astonished to see that she really did have absolutely *no* hair, *no* eyebrows and *no* eyelashes.

If we walked down a street, it was obvious from the double takes that Laura's bald head identified her unequivocally as a poorly girl. And as the gaze shifted from her to me, it would be met with narrowed eyes and a hard stare that Paddington would have been proud of.

I wanted to protect Laura and defend her from the casual judgement in those lingering looks but, to be truthful, there were times when I would use this to our advantage, and I was not afraid of pulling the cancer card if it would make Laura's life a bit easier. The queue to enter the Sky Garden bar was very long and it was a cold night so I had no qualms in marching to the front and asking the door staff, very politely, if they would make an exception for the sick girl with no hair.

Mark, Gracie and I were facing the prospect of a family without Laura, and we each handled this in very different ways.

I worked to fill Laura's days with adventures, things to look forward to and reasons to get out of bed, but I wonder if this was as much for me as it was for her. Too much free time for thinking and I would be sucked down into a miserable vortex of fear, grim facts and statistics. So instead, I made myself busy, researching treatments and sending emails late into the night until I finally fell into a sickly, dreamless sleep.

Mark maintained his mantra that 'everything was going to be okay', despite all evidence to the contrary. At the time, I thought the only explanation could be that he'd somehow failed to grasp the seriousness of the diagnosis, but actually I think he physically couldn't bear the thought of losing his girl and it was only denial that allowed him to remain functional.

Gracie sometimes joined me on the bench with the realists, but other times she could be swept up in Mark's unsinkable positivity.

Chemo accumulated into and depleted every cell in Laura's body. Each month she became progressively weaker, desperately sick and drained of energy. Despite another visit from the district nurses and one from our GP, Laura just wasn't improving, so with all home-based options exhausted, we drove her back to The Christie, where she was admitted.

The magic Ondansetron drip helped to get the sickness under control and she was rehydrated with fluids, but inevitably the oncologist wanted her back on steroids. There was an uneasy stand-off.

'Could it be that maybe the chemo is too strong for her? Would it be possible to reduce the dose?' I asked tentatively, not wanting to irritate the oncologist.

'No, the dose is correct. The problem is with the additional treatments you are giving her – this is what's causing her sickness. I have many other patients who have no sickness at all …'

'… you are making her unwell; you are causing the sickness with the supplements and the cannabis; you are a terrible, unfit mother who is poisoning her own daughter. This is all your fault …'

That's not actually what he said, but that's what I heard.

I felt crushed, and horrifically guilty. I'd checked for any potential counter-indications and sought advice on what Laura should be taking. But maybe I'd crossed the line and we were doing more harm than good? Reluctantly we agreed to take her off any supplements until she improved.

'What have you done?' Siobhan whispered on a loop, as I failed to find sleep that night.

Laura was fragile and so pale she was almost blue; a diet consisting of apples and the odd packet of Skips had dragged a stone from her already thin frame. The days she wasn't sick were a cause for celebration, but a dark cloud hung over us all as we tried to work out where to look next for help. The bucket list became even more important, not just as something to look forward to but also as a reason to get out, to draw on those eyebrows and interact with the cancer muggles.

I guessed that item seven on the list would be the most difficult to achieve: crossing the equator would probably be ridiculously expensive, the travel insurance alone would be thousands and where would we go and what would we do if she became ill while we were away, hundreds of miles from home?

Then, completely out of the blue, I received an extraordinary phone call.

'Hello, this is Captain Dave from British Airways. Am I speaking to Nicola Nuttall?'

'Um … yes?'

'How would you like to fly business class to South Africa so Laura can cross the equator? And then you can both spend some time on safari?'

It was the kind of call that only happened in Disney films. I fumbled to find words of sufficient gratitude; we were being offered the trip of a lifetime and I frantically waved Laura over so she could listen to the rest of the call.

Good timing meant that Captain Dave had read about Laura during the year of British Airways' centenary and to celebrate, they were giving 'money can't buy' experiences to one hundred lucky people.

A small part of me worried that it might be too much for her; we had some really busy months coming up and I didn't want her to end up exhausted.

She just laughed at me. 'As if there's any way on earth we're not going! Don't worry, Mum, there'll be plenty of time to sleep when I'm dead.'

Snakes and Ladders
March

Our lives would, for the foreseeable future, be punctuated by the three-month scan. Four times a year, a letter arrived in the post printed on recycled paper, then a date was circled on the family calendar like a final exam.

The relative relief of a 'stable' MRI only lasted until the apex of the arc between scans – then the anxiety escalated as the date raced closer. Sometimes I convinced myself that the news would be bad, only to be surprised and relieved. I knew equally that when I let my guard down and worried less, the chances of bad news would have multiplied exponentially.

This scan was stable, so we could finally take a breath and start organising our April trips. In addition to South Africa, we also had a visit to New York arranged and an elaborate plan to tick item one off the bucket list simmering on the back burner.

I knew we couldn't travel without insurance, and so began the soul-destroying experience of calling policy providers for a quote. Each required a long and painful explanation of Laura's diagnosis while the sales agent evaluated the risks and I crossed my fingers.

'… and have they told her it's terminal?'

Every call left me feeling bruised and most companies (even those who promised cover for travellers with medical conditions) refused point blank to cover us. I did find a policy eventually at a cost of £1,500 for five days in South Africa and £2,500 for the same period in the US. Just as well the flights were free.

Life settled down to a level of equilibrium: we were getting better at anticipating the bad days, and good days were almost normal. Laura had never wavered in her determination to go back to university, but had grudgingly conceded that staying closer to home would be more practical. She'd submitted her application to UCAS in January and now had a place to study Philosophy, Politics and Economics at the University of Manchester. I found her poring over their website, trying to decide which accommodation package to choose. Although I made encouraging noises, I still couldn't imagine how this could possibly work when she was debilitated for a full week every month and struggled to get herself out of bed. But I knew how important it was for her to have something to aim towards, to imagine a future undefined by cancer, so I helped her draw up a shortlist and hoped for a dramatic improvement in the coming months.

Days later, we received a phone call that the pessimist in me had been half-expecting, and which sent us right back to square one of the Snakes and Ladders board. Despite numerous reassurances from the oncologist to the contrary, there wasn't nearly enough frozen tumour available to produce the dendritic cell vaccine. We had sent Laura's preserved tissue from Salford to the London laboratory for analysis, a complex and costly procedure as it needed to remain frozen at -70 degrees, only to discover that instead of the $1cm^3$ of tissue required to produce an effective vaccine we only had a sliver.

All our eggs had been in this basket and the disappointment was crushing. I tried my best to remain positive for Laura and Gracie, but I couldn't see where to turn next. We were tantalisingly close to meeting our fundraising target and had been assured by the clinic that Laura's name was nearing the top of the waiting list, but without the requisite tumour tissue it was all futile.

It was hard not to feel despondent, but after a few days of wallowing in frustration, I was back on the laptop trying to fashion a plan B. But for every innovative clinic working to improve life for people with cancer, there was another, perfectly poised to empty the bank accounts of the desperate. We were easy prey in a lawless jungle.

Laura didn't seem to be eligible for any trials, and although we sought second and third opinions there was nothing available beyond the 'standard of care' protocol that hadn't changed in decades. It was becoming apparent that any additional treatments would be outside the UK, but having spent the best part of fifty years trusting the expertise of the NHS it felt like a huge leap of faith to look elsewhere.

Some of Laura's favourite days were the most unexpected. One of Neil's oldest friends, Michael, a DC in Greater Manchester Police, asked if Laura would be interested in spending the day with the force, and she jumped at the chance.

Michael had arranged a schedule full of surprises, starting with the firearms unit. As Laura was shaking hands and meeting the team, I could sense she wasn't feeling well, so I surreptitiously took her off to the bathroom where she proceeded to throw up.

'Please don't tell anyone, I'll be absolutely fine in a minute,' she said, wiping her mouth with a paper towel. 'If you tell them, they won't let me do anything and I might never get this chance again.'

She rinsed her mouth with water and walked back into the room, wearing a smile so bright that nobody noticed she was grey and slightly clammy.

Laura watched with wide eyes as the armed response officers went through their daily target practice and talked her through their safety protocols and procedures.

'Do you want to have a go now?'

'What, with an actual gun?'

This sickly girl who'd been vomiting in a toilet just thirty minutes ago was now in position at the firing range, wearing ear protectors and shooting real bullets from a gun. I did my best to hold back the tears, but her expression of fierce tenacity filled me with pride. I tried to film her on my phone, but every bullet made me jump, so the footage was a bit wobbly. Even the armed response officers were impressed with her accuracy and rolled up the target sheet for her to take home, where it was given pride of place on the bedroom wall.

Laura left the firearms unit fizzing with adrenaline and excitement, the morning's sickness just a memory.

We then ate breakfast with the chief constable in his glass-walled office, balancing cups of tea and bacon rolls, nodding furiously as he talked us through the challenges of twenty-first-century policing. We dropped in to see the police helicopters at Barton airfield, enjoyed a demonstration from the exuberant drug-detection spaniels and visited the public order unit, where Laura was kitted out in full Robocop riot gear. It was a whistle-stop tour of police careers and Laura loved every minute of it.

As we left, she told Michael it was one of her 'top three days of all time'.

The public order training team invited us back to take part in a major riot simulation – not necessarily the most appropriate activity for a girl with terminal brain cancer but, a few days later, we were running around in the dark wearing hard hats and hurling wooden bricks at the police. The scenario saw firefighters and ambulance crews called to an orchestrated traffic accident before the police were ambushed by rioters (mostly local college students), who threw impressively replicated petrol bombs and bricks. It was all very realistic and a little bit thrilling.

The Stars Will Still Be There

The memory of Mark and Laura shouting pretend abuse at the police from inside a darkened tram carriage, like bit-part actors on a police drama, will stay with me for a very long time.

I often thought about the young doctor who first identified Laura's symptoms at Homerton hospital back in October. I was convinced that, if she hadn't acted so quickly and arranged for Laura to be scanned that night, we might have already lost her.

I have no idea whether individual patients stick in the mind, whether they merge into a faceless crowd or whether for reasons of self-protection and bandwidth, the memory is shaken clean like an Etch A Sketch on a nightly basis, but I felt compelled to thank her and tell her about Laura's progress since that fateful night.

I searched for her profile on Twitter and sent a message of thanks to the person I hoped was Amber and promptly received this response: 'I am the doctor who saw you and your daughter that night at Homerton. I still remember it often. I can't tell you how much your message means to me, so thank you for taking the time out of what I'm sure has been a hectic few months to thank me.

'One horrible part of being a doc is finding that terrible things happen to wonderful people and, though impossible, you can only try your best to make the whole experience a bit less awful. It looks like Laura's been doing some amazing things since her diagnosis and I can only send you all my love, support and best wishes to you. Thanks for making my day.'

On Mother's Day, we had all the family round for afternoon tea. As usual I'd prepared industrial quantities of cake. Neil's partner Georgina arrived wearing a T-shirt which read *Ice Ice*, with an arrow pointing downwards. It took us a minute or two to work it out, but we couldn't have been more excited with the news that they were expecting a baby in October. We finally had something good to celebrate and I saw smiles shining on faces that had been drawn with sadness for months.

Laura and Gracie were thrilled at the prospect of a new baby cousin and were already suggesting names and planning adventures.

I was delighted and clinked my glass to toast the wonderful news, but my joy was tinged with something like sadness.

'Ahh,' Siobhan whispered, 'such a shame Laura won't get to meet her cousin, but "them's the breaks". I don't make the rules.'

International Ambassador
April

Laura's bucket list was a great starting point, but many of the nicest days we experienced were suggested by complete strangers. Like Donna and Phil, who kindly invited us to spend the day on their farm, where we fed calves and lambs, helped with milking and Laura got to drive what looked to me like the world's biggest and fastest tractor.

Her next trip was down to Litchfield for the first meeting of the Brain Tumour Charity young ambassadors. It felt like I was waving Laura off on a primary school residential, only this time she was sick, bald and knew nobody.

All of the ambassadors had been affected by brain tumours in some way, but Laura was the only one in the middle of her treatment. They shared rooms and stories, scars and scan pictures. Then they built rafts, made towers from crates, and sat around the campfire at night. Some had lost strength on one side of the body, some had memory loss or slowed cognition, but they shared an understanding – Laura didn't have to explain why she was taking thirty tablets a day or might need to rest between challenges. She came home happy, exhausted, and covered in bruises, and with a bag of washing that we had to turn around quickly as the next day we were off again.

The very idea of a trip to South Africa seemed so unlikely that I'm not sure I truly believed it would happen until the car came to collect us. But they were definitely expecting us at the BA check-in desk, as Laura had one all to herself, with her name on the screen instead of the flight number. We were escorted to the executive lounge, where I tried not to overdose on free Danish pastries before the short flight to London.

Eddie, who had managed first-class guest services at Heathrow for years, met us on the tarmac and escorted us up to the Concorde Lounge, which was a whole other level of fancy. He had met pretty much everyone through his job, and we would have happily listened to his stories for the rest of the day.

'Are you interested in football, Laura?' he asked, and when Laura confirmed that yes, she was, he disappeared and returned holding out his mobile phone. 'I have a friend here who'd like to have a chat with you.'

Sir Alex Ferguson was on the other end of the line. I'm not sure Laura caught every word, but apparently they discussed the ideal clothing for a safari, which was brilliantly surreal.

Captain Dave invited us to take a look around the cockpit and introduced us to his first officers, Ryan and Holly, who would be joining us on the trip.

My own bucket list had contained two things: one was tea at the Ritz, and the other was, just once, to fly anything other than economy class. I ticked this off my list as we settled into our seats, which were private little pods, with Laura and I facing each other, top to toe. Once we'd perused the menu, dinner was served on china plates with real cutlery. We watched a couple of movies, then I changed into my first-class pyjamas.

Laura raised her eyebrows. 'I cannot believe how ridiculously excited you are by plates and pyjamas, Mum.'

It was such a treat to be able to sleep horizontally in a bed on the plane rather than smeared against a window with my mouth open.

The cabin crew woke us just before we crossed the equator for champagne and photos on the deck. I think Laura would have preferred more sleep, but that was number seven ticked off the bucket list.

As we touched down in Johannesburg, Laura began to experience severe head pains, so we waited on board until they'd eased and asked for a wheelchair to take her through the terminal. Having been so excited about the trip and the flight I was now starting to panic that I'd made the most dreadful mistake in bringing her this far from home.

I hoped that it was just tiredness from the journey. Sure enough, as soon as we arrived at Leopardsong, she slept, awaking to feel much brighter.

We were staying in a small, rustic lodge with a thatched roof, a slow ceiling fan moving the warm air around. I pulled back the curtains to see actual wild animals, and we rushed outside to take a million pictures of the kudus that grazed in front of the lodge. Within days they'd become part of the scenery, but that first sighting was breathtaking.

Refreshed by sleep and a toasted cheese sandwich, Laura was ready for anything.

Colin, who owned Leopardsong, came over to introduce himself. As a friend of Captain Dave, he'd been fully briefed on how tough the last few months had been for Laura and wanted to make sure she had the best possible time. She was explaining how much she missed the freedom of driving, to which he replied,

'Fancy driving this?' pointing to a massive ten-seater safari jeep.

'Are you serious? Yes, absolutely!' She grinned.

'You know, she doesn't actually have a valid driving licence …!' I squawked anxiously.

I could think of a hundred reasons why this might not be a good idea, but Colin was already teaching Laura the rudiments of handling this huge beast of a vehicle.

Dave, Holly and Ryan came along for the ride and soon we were bumping along the tracks and trails of the reserve, through the gates and out into Dinokeng. We saw zebra, impala, warthogs, wildebeest and buffalo, but the best thing I saw was the enormous smile on my girl's face as she navigated the tricky terrain. I couldn't remember when she'd last looked so alive, and it was magical.

Then, as if we hadn't already had enough excitement for one day, Colin asked, 'Would you like to go up in a microlight? It's a brilliant way to see wildlife, from the sky, but if you do, it would have to be right now, as the weather's about to break.'

A sensible mum would be thinking about the things that might go wrong, or the risk of invalidating the ludicrously expensive insurance policy, or the fact that this was still our first day and Laura must be exhausted, but one look at her face and I knew that 'Sensible Mum' was not going to be involved in this decision.

We drove out to the dirt runway and met our pilot. He was wearing flip flops, and the microlight looked like a scooter with wings taped on. Laura snapped some goggles over her eyes, and they shot off down the runway. Seconds later, she was waving down at me and pointing out giraffe – later, she told me that just at that moment the pilot was asking her if she believed in God.

Looking back, I wonder what on earth I was thinking, but opportunities like that were precious and rare and it was only right to grab them with both hands. The day ended with an evening game drive, watching an orange sun melt like an ice lolly into the lake while listening to the sounds of hippos at play before dinner and bed.

We soon discovered that a safari holiday is not ideal for people who like to sleep in, as the best time to see animals is sunrise and sunset.

'Listen, Laura, we don't have to get up for the early game drive, we can just do the evening ones. I know you need your sleep.'

'I'll sleep when I'm home, Mum. I'm going to do absolutely everything.'

Every morning, 5:30 would find us wrapped in blankets in the back of the jeep. We never missed an opportunity, and were rewarded with sightings of black rhino, cheetahs, crocodiles and spectacular lions against the backdrop of a glorious African sunrise.

After the early morning drives, Laura would go straight back to bed. She was struggling with the nausea that stopped her eating, so I was sustaining her with the snacks we'd brought with us, and some high-calorie meal-replacement drinks we used as a last resort.

The second time she drove the safari jeep, ominous black clouds began rolling over the horizon, followed by neon flashes of lightning, then thunder and an absolute deluge of rain. We were soaked to the skin and Laura was struggling to see as the rain poured over her hat and ran down her face, the Jeep having no windscreen or roof for shelter. The tracks we were bumping along soon became slippery and waterlogged.

'Right, Laura, you've got one chance of getting us up this hill,' Colin said calmly, as parts of the red clay road disappeared in front of us.

Extreme weather and wild animals made for an exhilarating ride, but Laura held her nerve, and got us all safely back. She couldn't stop laughing: she was drenched and dripping, but justifiably proud of how she'd handled the jeep, I was in awe.

* * *

For a sick girl, Laura was ridiculously busy in April. No sooner had we returned home than we were back in London to watch Michelle Obama on her *Becoming* book tour at the O2. Securing tickets had been a colossal challenge, and the final breakthrough came after Jane, the CEO, made friends with a US senator on holiday. Luckily for us, he'd made the schoolboy error of saying, 'You holler if there's anything I can do to help y'all!' Strings were pulled, and our names were added to the meet and greet list alongside those who had personal links to the lady herself, or who had paid an eye-watering amount for the opportunity to meet her.

Our bags and phones were stored for safekeeping and we were invited to join a post-office-sized queue, the front of which disappeared behind a white curtain. It felt like waiting to see Father Christmas in his grotto when you're a child, with a dash of *The Wizard of Oz*.

When it was our turn to pass through the curtain, there was Michelle Obama, looking just as gorgeous as you'd imagine – smiley, elegant and very tall. I'm sure she'd met an endless line of people before we made it to the front, but she looked genuinely happy to see us and we were enveloped, one by one, in a deliciously fragrant hug. She asked Laura lots of questions about how she was doing, her downy bald head providing a handy clue as to the challenges she was facing.

Because we couldn't take our own photos, a professional photographer was on hand to record the event for posterity.

As we lined up for our picture, Gracie said, 'I'm going to look really small next to you.'

To which Michelle Obama replied, 'Oh, honey, you just tell your friends I was stood on a box.'

When the group shots were emailed through to me, Michelle was holding tightly onto Laura's hand.

* * *

We were spending a lot of time travelling back and forth to London, so it was just as well I was able to pass Laura off as under sixteen, using Gracie's railcard. We were banking on the assumption that it would take a brave ticket collector to challenge the age of the poorly girl with no hair.

Our next trip down was for a visit to 10 Downing Street. I'd expected security to be tight but didn't anticipate that we'd have to knock on the door.

We stood on the doorstep, giggling. 'Go on, knock on the door then, Laura.'

'No, you do it.'

'No, you do it!'

Michael, our guide, gave us a fascinating tour of the building, during which Laura made herself comfortable in the prime minister's Cabinet Office seat, and might even have filched Theresa May's pencil! She also had the rarely granted honour of perching on Churchill's reading chair, when she was momentarily rocked by a sudden head pain.

We took tea in a reception room full of portraits, gold-plated treasures and Chippendale chairs worth tens of thousands. Then we dashed over to the Houses of Parliament to catch the end of Prime Minister's Questions from the Visitors' Gallery. Later we had lunch in the Strangers' Dining Room with then-Home Secretary Sajid Javid. It was peculiar to eat lunch in a room containing so many instantly recognisable faces, but we played it cool, until Sajid asked Laura, 'Would you like to spend a day at MI5?'

MI5 was Laura's dream job, and she could hardly contain her excitement at the thought. 'Yes! Absolutely! I would love to if it's possible, and not too much trouble – thank you so, so much.'

'Leave it with me and I'll see what I can do.'

That's the last you'll hear about that, I thought cynically, as we said our goodbyes.

April's final trip to London was much harder work, for me at least. Between hospital visits and bucket list trips I'd been 'training' for the London Marathon. Not proper training – just the odd run when time and circumstances allowed. I'd taken part a number of times before, but this one was especially important because I was running to raise awareness and sponsorship for The Brain Tumour Charity, something we were doing alongside fundraising for Laura's treatment.

The BBC Events team had asked if we would like to be interviewed before the race; it wouldn't take very long, they promised, but it would be early, and they'd send a car to the hotel for us at 6 a.m. Laura agreed, in her role as young ambassador, she knew it would be good publicity for the charity, but as soon as she got into the taxi, she began to feel ill, and as the cab pulled up in Greenwich, she opened the door and immediately threw up on the grass, to the horror of early runners and security staff. She looked so pale and fragile, and I berated myself for putting her through all this unnecessary fuss.

Thirty minutes later she was live on the BBC wearing her Brain Tumour hoodie and a great big smile. Laura's ability to put mind over matter never ceased to amaze me, but as soon as the interview was over, she headed back to the hotel for more sleep.

Laura had arranged to meet me at Tower Bridge, a highly emotional point in the race, not just because it's such an iconic landmark but because it's roughly halfway and always packed with the loudest supporters. I slowed my pace to look for her, hoping she'd be with the rest of the Brain Tumour support crew, but there was no sign of her. A runner covered in purple body paint collided with me as I searched the crowd. He yelled angrily at me for getting in his way, then sprinted off, leaving me with a violet stripe down my arm.

If Laura wasn't there, did that mean she'd been taken ill? I spent the next ten miles imagining various dreadful scenarios. Siobhan joined in, of course: 'She's on her own, in all these crowds. She might pass out and get trampled or be lost and confused on the street somewhere – oh, this was a verrrry bad idea.'

Then, at mile twenty-three, I heard a voice above the crowds. 'Mum! Mum! Over here!'

I'd almost gone past when I saw her, shouting and waving her arms to get my attention. I crossed the stream of runners and made my way to the barrier, sobbing with the relief of finally seeing her.

'I've been so worried about you, Laura! Is everything all right? Are you feeling OK?'

'Yes, yes, I'm having a great day – everything's fine.'

'I love you so much, I've imagined all sorts!' I cried.

'I love you too, Mum, but go on, get it finished now,' she replied, as I crushed her into a hug.

The last three miles went so much faster with a light heart.

Gracie
May

We had always been so close, Gracie and I, but these days I was constantly busy, leaving her feeling isolated and trapped by a situation none of us would have chosen. One night I found her punching her bedroom wall in frustration, tears making vertical stripes down the face mask she'd just applied, making her look like a heartbroken ghost or the world's saddest clown.

'You know what, Mum, the first thing anyone says to me is, "How's Laura?" or "How's your mum and dad?" I don't even count any more, they ask me because they don't want to bother you, but how do you think that makes me feel?'

I was so preoccupied with trying to fix Laura that I'd barely given Gracie a thought, and now she was really struggling. She'd told me as much during our fight in New York, but despite initially making more of an effort, I'd let things drift.

She was angry with me because who else could she be angry with? Her beloved big sister was sick and, at some point, Laura was going to die and leave her and it didn't help our relationship that Laura and I were constantly disappearing to exciting places she wasn't invited to.

I knew that I was handling this badly, but I had no idea how to make things better.

I suggested we both went for counselling, but she refused.

'What's the point in talking to some stranger? They're not gonna be able to make Laura well again, are they, so how can they fix anything?'

She had a point. I was avoiding anything that might poke at the bricks of the wall I'd created around my heart; I needed it to be strong, otherwise I wouldn't be able to function. I tried to make amends by taking Gracie out shopping – the very definition of a guilt trip.

There were still some good times: beautiful, ordinary days in half term when the girls would lie in bed till lunchtime, Laura watching *Saturday Night Live* on her phone, Gracie Snapchatting her friends, then between mouthfuls of cereal they'd play Mario Kart like they were eight again, screaming and laughing as Toad and Koopa Troopa battled for first place. I'd watch them from the doorway, wishing I could save them just like that: forever in pyjamas and gradually emptying the fridge.

When the girls were little, they played imaginary games, employing an assorted cast of weary half-dressed dolls and tatty teddies. Laura was like a trainee story-liner for *Casualty*, always planning some natural disaster, heinous crime or dramatic plot twist. Gracie was fond of a Disney princess and preferred a happy ending, but if Laura had conceded to play with her, she'd have to go along with her dark and tragic plot lines.

'Pretend your baby has pneumonia ...' Laura would say to Gracie, and her little face would fall at the disaster and turmoil her sister was injecting into the perfect imaginary world.

Maybe Laura just loved the drama, or perhaps she had already known that life could be cruel and random and nothing should be taken for granted.

The first item on Laura's original bucket list had been to watch *Saturday Night Live* being filmed; a topical sketch show with an all-star cast, a musical act and a different guest presenter every week. It's huge in the US and has been since the 1970s. A friend of a friend helped us get tickets for the penultimate show of the season. Virgin Atlantic agreed to fly us out and I'd messaged all the most famous hotels to see if we could stay somewhere lovely rather than just somewhere we could afford. With the extortionate cost of travel insurance everything else really needed to be as close to free as possible.

The Plaza Hotel offered us a room for $199 a night, good value for any New York hotel, but especially one on the corner of Fifth Avenue and Central Park. I'd seen the lobby featured in *Home Alone 2*, so I knew it would be lovely. As I wrestled suitcases out of the taxi and tried to work out how much I should tip, a smiling doorman appeared in navy coat and white gloves and whisked our cases onto a tall, golden luggage trolley. I held Laura's arm to steady her, and we walked up the steps into the foyer, to be dazzled by the car-sized chandelier, enormous architectural floral displays, and the heady scent of hundreds of lilies.

Omar, the concierge, checked us in and escorted us up to the 14th floor. He opened the door and stood back with a flourish to let us enter.

I hovered awkwardly in the corridor. 'Sorry, but are you quite sure this one is ours?'

'Oh. My. God!' said Laura, stepping around me.

The room was filled with extravagant bouquets of fragrant white roses, and on a small table there was a chocolate sculpture of New York, complete with yellow taxi, Empire State Building and candy-green big apple. It was in fact a suite of rooms: an airy living room with writing desk, fireplace and sofas, a powder room, closets the size of bedrooms and gold taps in an enormous bathroom. On the nightstand, next to a vast expanse of bed, there was even a photograph of our family – a selfie taken that day in Lytham – and now displayed in a gold frame. Laura's eyes were wide, her mouth open in shock. Omar explained that the room also came with a butler, who would be happy to run baths or press clothes for us. I assured him that we would just about be able to manage those things for ourselves.

I think we would have both happily spent the entire trip in that beautiful room, but I'd made plans to do as much as possible during our short stay; after all, who knew if we would ever get the opportunity again.

Laura was a big fan of Sandra Bullock and her heist movie *Ocean's 8*, so I'd arranged for us to visit Veselka, the 24-hour Ukrainian diner featured in the film. We had lunch with the owner, Tom, with Laura sitting in Sandra's very seat. We ate potato pancakes and pierogi while he shared the history of the restaurant, before taking us down to the basement to watch a small army of Polish ladies rolling out dumplings.

From there we headed to MoMA – the Museum of Modern Art – where I'd arranged for us to have a guided tour. Conscious that Laura couldn't stand for too long, I carried a handy folding stool so she could just sit and appreciate the serenity of Monet's waterlilies and the chaos of a Jackson Pollock.

Laura had watched *SNL* for years, uploaded from YouTube to the tiny screen of her phone, and she was ridiculously excited at the thought of being there in person. She'd asked to watch the dress rehearsal rather than the live performance, in the hope that it would last that bit longer. Omar arranged for the house car – a Tesla with gull-wing doors and blacked-out windows – to take us down to the Rockefeller Center, and we emerged from our limo like rock stars. It was a brilliant night, Emma Thompson hosted, the Jonas Brothers performed, and Laura laughed as loud as anyone in the enthusiastic audience, hyped to a frenzy by a floor manager wearing headphones and waving a clipboard to encourage applause.

After the show, we were given a backstage tour and introduced to the cast, which by a stroke of luck that week also included Tina Fey and Amy Poehler. Everyone we met was lovely and really interested in what we'd thought of the show. Laura looked fabulous, her hair a little peach fuzz mohawk, her eyebrows pencilled in and relatively symmetrical, and with the biggest smile on her face. She was thrilled when Pete Davidson told her he liked her All Saints leather jacket, but the highlight of the night was a big bear hug from her idol, Kate McKinnon, who was so generous with her time despite the fact that the live show was only an hour away.

Number one on the list was most comprehensively ticked.

It was a wrench to leave The Plaza, but good to be home and together again. I loved travelling with Laura: she was great company, and we didn't so much as bicker. But I was always conscious of the weight of responsibility. If something did go wrong, so far from home, it would go wrong really badly, there was always a small exhalation of relief when we made it home safely and without drama.

But the positive energy generated by all these fabulous experiences was fragile and so easily shattered. I jogged past Barrowford Cemetery on one of my sanity runs, and noticed a team of workmen constructing three new blocks for memorials and the interment of ashes. Siobhan helped me work out the maths as I ran: twenty-eight spaces on each side times three, makes one hundred and sixty-eight. Will a hundred and sixty-eight people die in this village before Laura, or will I bring flowers up here to talk to a square of slate with her name on? I carried on running and although the thought was too painful to contemplate, I still worried it like a wobbly tooth.

When we had lived in the world of the well, charity had meant donating to good causes that tugged at our heartstrings, reminding us how lucky we were to be healthy and live in a safe country. Now we were on the receiving end of charity, and filled with gratitude for hands that reached out to catch us.

The Willow Foundation offered a week of family time in a cabin on the banks of Loch Lubnaig, where we played board games and swam in the loch (for about ten seconds). Laura found a survival skills course in the visitors' guide and spent the day in her element: foraging for food, building shelters and starting fires. In the evenings we'd listen for bats with the sonar detector and star-gaze from the warmth of the hot tub.

As we were already in Scotland, I made a plan for number six on the bucket list, and on our way home, we headed to Wanlockhead to meet world champion gold panner, Vincent Thirkettle.

Laura's fixation on discovering gold first became apparent in a school diary. Aged about six, she'd written in neat, joined-up handwriting that her ambition was to become a 'gold digger' when she grew up … ah, the innocence of youth.

We spent a glorious afternoon standing in the river as Laura, in pink wellies, learned the fine art of gold panning. Vince got her started and soon she was swirling the silt in the pan, tipping out the river debris until only the smallest and heaviest material remained. Gold has a very high density, so it's always at the bottom of the pan when it looks like there's almost nothing left. How very apposite. It might have been beginner's luck, but to Laura's surprise she managed to pan a decent number of gold flakes and an actual real-life nugget too – not enough for us to retire on, but she was delighted, and took her treasure home in a tiny bottle filled with water like a precious metal snow globe.

When this is all over. If this is ever over. What will be left of us?

We would never be the same people we once were.

I was fundamentally different as a wife, daughter, mother, friend.

Would I be able to function normally again? What would normal even look like?

I understood now why so many couples split up after a death, a murder, a great trauma. If the shape of your grief doesn't match with your partner's, how can anything else?

But if you do drift apart, like continents on a fault line, you do so in the knowledge that no one else will ever truly understand what you've been through; those battle wounds like matching tattoos, and the secret of just how dark life can be.

To live through something like this, alone, would have been utterly bleak, and yet it was still possible to feel lonely, when communication had been distilled to just the practical and perfunctory.

I worried that I used up all my love on Laura and I didn't have enough left to sustain Gracie or Mark. The future was desolate and too bleak to contemplate; the past was full of happy memories too painful to bear – so we could only live in the present: meals, dog walking, medication, and remembering on which day to put the bins out.

Two Lauras

June

Hospice. The word chilled me to my core, it signified the very end of things. It meant there was no longer any chance of recovery: it was a hushed and wholesome place for painful goodbyes.

Our local hospice was famous for its annual fundraising pub walk: hundreds of participants in bright T-shirts staggering across fields, their blisters hurting less and less with every half pint. They stood in crowds with red faces and rucksacks outside pubs, like flocks of some exotic and thirsty migrating bird. The hospice offered a range of therapeutic services and Laura was invited to come and enjoy some relaxing reflexology but I had to fight back a panic attack every time we drew up in the car park – just the act of walking through the door felt like an admission that Laura was going to die, and soon we'd be turning left to the in-patient rooms rather than right to the therapy suites. I knew that it was also a warm and welcoming place, nowhere near as grim as you might imagine, but still no place for my nineteen-year-old daughter.

Outside, back in the real world, we did all we could to carry on living. The winter before, on a dark and poorly evening, Laura and Mark had watched an episode of *Inside The Factory*, which had featured the Heinz plant in Wigan. I think they might even have been eating beans on toast at the time, but, either way, it had made it onto the bucket list.

We'd driven passed the site on the M6 hundreds of times: the huge '57' illuminated in red was a signpost that meant we were nearly home. It wasn't easy to arrange a visit – they tended to be restricted to royalty and film crews – but following an onslaught of emails (and not all of those from me), we were invited to spend the day there.

Food production is a serious business, so we were kitted out in white tunics and trousers, with hair nets, hats, protective footwear and high-vis jackets with our names printed on.

The Wigan factory is a massive fifty-five acres and the biggest food-processing site in Europe, producing up to three million cans of beans a day. The dried beans arrive from North America, to be rehydrated and mixed with the secret sauce, before being steamed inside the tin. It was very impressive. Laura did some taste-testing, tiny in her oversized white uniform and smiling broadly as we took photos of her raising a spoon of chicken soup to her mouth. We left with boxes of Heinz products printed with Laura's name, and for each member of the family a personalised bottle of their iconic ketchup.

Bucket list item number two was complete.

The next day, I was lying on my back on a mat in the Pilates studio when a memory so powerful left me winded. For years we had come down to the leisure centre on a Sunday morning. I'd go to my class at 9:30, the girls would wait in the lounge until 10 a.m. when they would run down the corridor for their taekwondo lesson in the studio next door. While they waited for the teacher to arrive, they'd pull faces through the glass panel in the door and try to make me laugh.

The memory of such ordinary happiness and the overpowering feeling of loss hit me like a train. Tears ran down my face and into my ears. I had thought those days would last forever.

Bucket list item number four was to see *The Scream* by Edvard Munch, and by happy coincidence it was on temporary display at the British Museum. I'd studied Munch in sixth form and knew what to expect, but instead of *The Scream* I found myself drawn to *The Sick Child* – a painting of Munch's sister Sophie, who died of tuberculosis aged just fifteen. He painted this scene often as it was such a traumatic moment in his life, but I don't think I'd really appreciated its emotional power before. It was an image of a pale girl looking out towards an open window while a grief-stricken woman clasped her hand, head bowed in sadness and grief.

Too close, too familiar.

I'd timed our trip to London to coincide with the premiere of the new Richard Curtis film, *Yesterday*, a romantic comedy that was also a love letter to The Beatles. After a military-grade email campaign, we had managed to get Laura and I on the guest list for the event at the Odeon Leicester Square. Laura had bought a beautiful new dress: black with a long net skirt and a bodice covered in tiny, embroidered flowers. Accessorising it with big boots and her leather jacket, she was stunning, her (not quite) bald head starting to look more of a fashion statement and less of a side effect.

We headed up the yellow carpet, past the bank of paparazzi photographers, and asked a fellow guest to take our picture in front of the *Yesterday* backdrop. As we were about to enter the theatre, Kate McKinnon arrived in a flurry of camera flashes. She looked across and called out to Laura, opening her arms wide for a hug. Laura's face was a picture of astonishment – she just couldn't believe Kate had remembered her. The photograph I took of them together will always be a favourite: they both look beautiful, and Laura's smile could power a whole city.

It was an amazing night, spoiled only by the chemo kicking in earlier than expected and 3 a.m. sickness – Laura's life was becoming a ridiculous roller-coaster of extreme highs and dreadful lows.

Back home and still chemo-sick, we took Laura to an open day at the University of Manchester. She'd already accepted her place but wanted to get more information on the course and meet the head of department. She was so frail I still couldn't begin to imagine how she would ever be strong enough to look after herself and walk between halls and lectures, but we had to remain positive: she still had another three months of recovery before term started.

When Laura was really sick it was hard to imagine her ever being well again. Then when she was well, it was easy to forget just how sick she was.

She also had a level of pragmatism and insight that would constantly catch me off guard. It was almost as if she could see the world from above now, while we were all still scrabbling around on the ground. Her perspective had changed completely.

We were talking about the diagnosis one day – something we didn't actually do very often – 'You know, Mum, I'm really grateful to be here right now. Sometimes we don't realise how important things are, until they're almost taken away, like going to university, and I know it sounds weird, but in some ways, I feel more alive now than ever.'

I think I understood: we spend so much of our lives sleepwalking, and hoping for better days ahead, that we don't appreciate the blessing of every single day, the people in our lives and the small pleasures of just existing.

Since the dead-end disappointment of finding out we didn't have enough tumour tissue to make the vaccine, I'd been scouring the internet for other options, broadening the search to include clinics overseas.

We scheduled a telephone appointment with a professor based in Germany, whose clinic offered treatments designed to stimulate the immune system into recognising cancer cells so they attack and destroy them with T-cells: immunotherapy in its simplest form. He offered a customised vaccine that could be created using white blood cells rather than the frozen tumour tissue we didn't have. It was the best option we'd found, so we arranged to take Laura over to Cologne the following month.

We knew this was unlikely to go down well with our oncologist, and that he would argue that the evidence was insufficient to prove efficacy, but we didn't have time to wait for the results of a five- or ten-year peer-reviewed study. There was a ticking time bomb in Laura's brain, and we were prepared to do whatever it took to keep her alive. The fundraising had given us the luxury of options, but even without it we would have sold the house and slept on the street if it kept Laura alive.

I'd always believed that we were making huge leaps forward in cancer treatment; after all, deaths from breast cancer have almost halved since the 1980s. But I had no idea that there was a big black hole when it came to brain cancer. In fairness, there were some good reasons why research was difficult: the number of people with the disease is relatively small, it's difficult to get drugs through the blood-brain barrier, and it's not easy to access the site of the cancer – you can't just cut chunks out of the brain, after all. It's also significant that within each tumour there's a variety of cell types (known as heterogeneity) and as there aren't drugs to kill all the different cells, some will remain, and eventually regrow.

None of this detracts from the grim reality that brain tumours kill more children and adults under forty than any other cancer.

If you compare the upward survival trends for more common cancers it's pretty stark: 78 per cent of people diagnosed with prostate cancer will still be alive after ten years,* for breast cancer it's 76 per cent,† but for those diagnosed with glioblastoma, just 5 per cent are still alive after five years.‡ And there was probably a good reason why I couldn't find a ten-year survival figure.

---

* https://www.cancerresearchuk.org/health-professional/cancer-statistics/statistics-by-cancer-type/prostate-cancer

† https://www.cancerresearchuk.org/health-professional/cancer-statistics/statistics-by-cancer-type/breast-cancer

‡ https://www.thebraintumourcharity.org/brain-tumour-diagnosis-treatment/types-of-brain-tumour-adult/glioblastoma/glioblastoma-prognosis/

With these depressing statistics you might imagine brain tumours would be a priority for research, but the fact is historically, less than 2 per cent of the national spend on cancer research has been on the brain. There have been no new brain tumour treatments available in the UK in Laura's lifetime, compared with fifteen for breast cancer and sixty-four for blood cancer.* Obviously, all cancers are bad and need a cure but it's hard not to feel aggrieved by the lack of funding and the reluctance to invest in brain cancer treatments.

Glioblastoma is horrific – it's undoubtedly a bin-fire cancer – but there is worse: a brain cancer that affects children, mostly between four and eleven, it's inoperable, displays symptoms for a matter of weeks and has a median survival of nine months. There is still no cure for diffuse intrinsic pontine glioma (DIPG), just as there was no cure for Neil Armstrong's daughter, Karen, when she died from it – in 1962.

I was five when my sister Laura died, and for a long time I didn't understand why we lost her. As a child, I hadn't been brave enough to ask, conscious of the pain in my parents' eyes when her name was mentioned, but when my Laura was diagnosed, I looked for a connection, needing to find some way of joining the dots and making rational sense of this apparently random bad luck.

In family photographs – tinged with brown and orange like everything in the 1970s – I could see that my sister had a slight turn in her eye. I'd seen the same in children with DIPG: could she have had a brain tumour too?

Mum had always told me that Laura had gone into convulsions, which might well have meant a tonic-clonic seizure, but other than that, she was told very little, and what she was told,

* https://www.braintumourresearch.org/media/our-blog/blog-item/
our-blog/2020/03/27/the-high-price-of-brain-tumours#

she struggled to understand. I understood: I knew how it felt to be overwhelmed in a tsunami of shock.

I wish I had more memories of that time, but I just don't. I remember fragments, the sound of the radio in the ambulance that took us to Laura's physio appointments and the smell of the Women's Royal Voluntary Service tea stall in the hospital. I remember sitting in the car and being told she had died.

I remember the flowers in the bath, but I'm pretty sure I didn't go to the funeral.

I remember that her favourite colour was yellow, and she had a beanie doll that she loved and that went in the coffin with her.

I don't remember how I felt, or even if I cried at all.

Was I a heartless child who felt nothing, or did I wander the house wondering why there were suddenly two children and not three?

When somebody asked me that most casual of questions: 'Do you have any brothers or sisters?' I wasn't sure what the right answer was. Nobody had told me what I should say, and I was frightened of getting it wrong. I was on safe ground with the brother thing, but did I have a sister? It felt like a trick question.

A few years ago, Neil had been engrossed in a copy of *Autotrader* magazine while his then-wife Leo had a reading with a medium.

'You're one of three but everyone thinks you're one of two.' She had told him. Maybe we wear old grief on our faces; maybe she could smell it.

More vivid than the memories are the two recurring nightmares I had throughout my childhood. In the first, Neil was a toddler and I'd lost him somewhere in Liverpool Museum just as it was about to close. I ran frantically from room to room trying to find him before we were locked in forever.

In the second, I came home from primary school as normal, but when the front door was opened it wasn't by my mum, but a complete stranger. My parents had moved to a new house and hadn't left a forwarding address.

I can't remember all that much about my childhood, but I remember exactly how blind panic felt.

I hadn't expected to find out I was pregnant in the middle of studying for a masters, moving house and six months before the wedding, but it was a wonderful surprise regardless. The first thing I did was phone the dressmaker and ask her to forget those alterations she was about to make to my wedding dress as we were going to need every inch of material now. Then I called the venue, and fortunately we were able to move the wedding forward from October to July 1999.

Once he'd got over the initial shock, Mark asked, 'If it's a girl, would you like to call her Laura? Because I'd be absolutely fine with that.'

It was as if he'd read my mind. 'I'd love that, Mark – it would mean the world to me.' I hugged him tightly as hormonal tears leaked from my eyes.

The timing wasn't ideal, but I was delighted. I'd always wanted to be a mum and enjoyed a good pregnancy followed by a scary emergency caesarean in the final gasps of the twentieth century.

My mum and dad both cried when I told them my baby's name. I wanted them to be able to say it without feeling sad anymore. In naming my daughter I also wanted to remember my sister.

We'll never really know why my sister Laura died or if there was a connection. Mum requested a copy of the coroner's report, but forty-four years after her death, there were no records available. Added to this, my sister lived and died in a time before MRI and CT scans and even if records had been available, they probably wouldn't have helped, or prevented this from happening.

I called my daughter Laura to make my parents happy, but instead I broke their hearts all over again.

Pushing Our Luck

July

Laura loved live music, so I took her to as many gigs as I could. I'm sure she'd rather have been out with friends than her mum, but she'd tolerate me and my big bag of emergency medication and snacks if it meant a few hours in the company of Dido or Janelle Monáe.

Back in 2016, Laura persuaded me to take her to her first music festival to celebrate the end of GCSEs. It was an ambitious plan as it was in Lisbon, but she'd worked out all the costs and logistics and presented her case. Laura could be very convincing, especially when she was well prepared: we were once given a twelve-page PowerPoint presentation on why she should be allowed to have her ears pierced.

There had been talk of going again, but our lives were so different now. I wavered for weeks as to whether it was ridiculously stupid or a brilliant idea to take both girls away. I knew there were risks involved, but there was also a good chance it would be wonderful, and we'd make unforgettable memories together, so in a moment of optimism I bought them tickets for Christmas, convincing myself that we could always sell them on if Laura wasn't up to it.

The girls were really excited at the prospect of music and sunshine and Laura seemed relatively stable, so I booked flights, an Airbnb, and a hefty travel insurance policy. I tried to convince Mark to come along, telling him what a good time he'd have with us; there was also a part of me that wanted to share the responsibility, as travelling would be easier as a team of four. But he couldn't be persuaded.

We spent the first day on the beach, reading books and enjoying the glorious sunshine. In the evening we went into the city for food. It was busy and still quite hot; soon Laura started feeling light-headed and sickly. She needed to lie down before she fainted, so we cut the evening short and got her home. I was starting to regret that we hadn't brought the cannabis with us – we hadn't wanted to risk getting arrested, obviously, or jeopardising the trip, but already Laura's appetite had petered away to nothing, and she was looking fragile.

On the first day of the festival, after some top-level negotiations, I managed to get us access to the elevated viewing area with its folding seats. There was no chance Laura could stand to watch the bands, the walk from the train station had been enough of a challenge. Halfway through Weezer's set Laura started to feel hot and dizzy, she told me that she didn't feel great, and that her fingers and lips felt tingly. Trying not to panic, we lay her down behind the seats and a friendly bystander ran off to find her something to eat in case the episode was just down to a drop in blood sugar – but it was becoming apparent that she really wasn't well.

Someone must have alerted security because very quickly a team of medics arrived with a wheelchair. They strapped Laura in and took her down to ground level in the world's slowest platform lift just as the helpful bystander arrived back with a tray of hot chips, a plastic fork stabbed into the middle, asking Gracie for his 5€ back.

Fortunately, it was still relatively early in the evening and the medical tent had yet to fill with the casualties of drink and drugs, so Laura had the full attention of a team of enthusiastic young medics. I tried to explain her cancer diagnosis, but the language barrier made it tricky and those who did understand were clearly wondering what had possessed me to bring a sick girl to a music festival.

It was a question I was asking myself.

Laura's blood pressure and pulse were found to be extremely low, so she was quickly wrapped up in a foil blanket and attached to a drip. I believe it contained electrolytes and glucose but with my knowledge of Portuguese it could have been anything at all. I'd completely lost control of the situation – this had been a bad idea, I had been reckless and thoughtless and put Laura at serious risk.

Laura closed her eyes and slept, despite the pulsing bass from the stage that made the ground and everything on it vibrate. Meanwhile Gracie was pacing outside the tent and crying down the phone to Mark, who, with his usual level of sensitivity, essentially told her to get a grip. It was hard not to panic: all we could do was hope that the slow drip of fluids into Laura's bloodstream would work some kind of magic.

The medics were preparing to send us to hospital in an ambulance when Laura started to come back round. Her colour was more human and less waxwork, and she was adamant that she felt absolutely fine. They removed the canula and disconnected the drip and we thanked them profusely for their kindness.

As we walked slowly back to the station, I had the feeling that we'd got through the night by the skin of our teeth.

'I can't tell whether you're irresponsible or selfish or just stupidly optimistic,' Siobhan whispered.

'I'm a fucking idiot,' I replied.

After a good night's sleep, Laura wanted to give the festival another try. 'We haven't come all this way to stay in the apartment, have we?'

'Yes, but what if you get ill again? If you end up in the medical tent two days running, they're going to be calling Portuguese social services. I already look like the world's most irresponsible mother.'

Most importantly, I didn't want Laura feeling unwell and unsafe in a field with 50,000 other people. She did look much better, though, and so I agreed we'd have a second attempt. Luckily, things all worked our perfectly: we watched Johnny Marr and Vampire Weekend, had a great night and nobody ended up attached to a drip.

The trip to Lisbon Oceanarium was less successful. As soon as the taxi dropped us at the entrance, Laura began to feel wobbly, so we borrowed a wheelchair, then a headache descended and almost inevitably she began to throw up. We pushed the chair between the bathrooms, the gaps between bouts of sickness getting shorter and shorter until we were forced to find a first aid room so she could lie down with a sick bowl.

There was a particular look Gracie would give me when things were going wrong, especially when Laura was ill. She looked to me for reassurance, checking to see that I was handling things and that everything would be OK. More often than not, I was able to say something appropriately comforting, which gave the impression I was in control, but this time I felt she was starting to see through me with those wide, navy blue eyes. She was beginning to discover that I didn't have all the answers and that I was making it all up as I went along.

We made it home without further incident. It was a huge relief to be back in the UK, but I was left feeling cross with Mark for not coming with us when we really did need there to be two adults, and furious with myself for putting Laura's health at unnecessary risk.

There was a fine line between seizing every opportunity and looking for trouble, and I needed to learn the difference.

The clinic was in an office block, above a gym, on a wide, tree-lined Cologne avenue, studded with high-end furniture shops. The staff wore white trousers and lime-green tunics; the doctors, white coats over jeans and T-shirts. Our professor was Belgian, buoyant and enthusiastic.

'And how is the family Noottall?' he asked with a broad smile, then listened intently to Laura's story and pored over her scans, before scribbling a complicated flow chart to explain exactly how he would treat her.

He recommended electro-hyperthermia with an injection of Newcastle disease virus (NDV) for five days every month. NDV is a pathogen for chickens but is harmless to humans: it has no side effects, but gives the immune system a nudge by migrating to the tumour cells and sending out alert signals. It acts like a highlighter pen, drawing attention to the cells that are dangerous. Cancer cells are masters of disguise, but if they're recognised as alien, killer T-cells can be activated to destroy them, which is the whole point of immunotherapy – I think. Then, once Laura had finished her twelve cycles of chemo, he'd introduce the dendritic cell vaccinations. To get the ball rolling, he drew half a pint of Laura's blood into thirty individual vials with multi-coloured lids, ready for analysis.

Later we sat with coffees in the café next door. 'Every month?' Laura said, eyebrows raised.

'I know, it feels like a lot, doesn't it? But he seems good, don't you think?'

'Really good,' Mark agreed. 'I liked him.'

'Yeah, but what about uni? How am I going to get a degree if I'm here for a week EVERY month?'

It was a fair question.

'Maybe you can do lectures online or remotely – some universities do podcasts, I think,' I said, with more confidence than I felt. For me, there was no point worrying too hard about the degree: keeping Laura alive and well enough to study was our biggest priority, and this seemed like our best option.

The summer meant Laura was finally able to spend time with friends who were home from uni for the holidays. It was good to see them dropping round to take her out for a drink or even a short walk round the park.

Olivia took her out to an escape room in Manchester – she came home flushed with happiness and told me that it was the first time in forever she'd actually felt like a normal person and not just like someone with cancer.

Laura received an unexpected video call from another student who was home for the holidays: Nobel Prize winner, Malala Yousafzai. It had taken many emails and a few surreptitious phone calls with her assistant, but it was worth it a hundred times over to see Laura's face when she realised just who was on her phone. They talked mostly about university – Malala was at Oxford studying the same PPE course Laura would be soon be starting in Manchester. She asked Laura what it had been like to have her life derailed so dramatically – something else they had in common – and offered a tour of the city if we were ever in Oxford.

Sometime later, Malala's book arrived in the post. Inside she had written,

'Dear Laura, thank you for your support.

I am inspired by your strength and resilience.

Never give up.

Best wishes, Malala.'

When Malala calls you resilient, you're definitely on the right track.

Mark and I planned to take alternate trips out to Germany with Laura, as we needed to at least keep some semblance of normality for Gracie. But at that point, the whole endeavour still felt like a massive leap of faith. We couldn't get a travel insurance company to cover the trip because Laura was having treatment abroad, so we had to hope that the EHIC card would provide us with the basics if anything went badly wrong.

After the disaster in Portugal, I decided that, on balance, it was worth taking the cannabis to Germany: if Laura had an appetite and ate well, she'd be stronger and less susceptible to inconvenient fainting.

Mark was horrified: 'What happens if you get arrested or something? They don't mess around, the German police – they'll have sniffer dogs and guns in the airport, you know.'

We made up just enough tiny capsules to last the week and hid them in a medication bottle nestled next to some strongly perfumed washing capsules in my suitcase.

My heart was thumping ridiculously hard as I grabbed the case off the conveyer belt. It was still locked, so that was a good sign. I tried to look as casual as possible, chatting animatedly to Laura while wheeling the suitcase passed the three heavily armed security guards and out onto the concourse, where I finally took a breath. Forty-eight is definitely too late in life to start a new career as a drug smuggler.

I'd prepared for the possibility of arrest by translating into German details of Laura's diagnosis, as my German vocabulary was otherwise limited to telling someone I was thirteen and asking where the youth hostel was. The Germany word for cancer is *Krebs*, which makes sense when you think about it. So, I carried a card with '*Meine Tochter hat Krebs in Kopf*' printed on it, just in case.

Laura found the ten-minute walk to the clinic challenging; when we finally arrived, she was breathless and weak and needed to lie down on the floor of the lobby to avoid passing out. For the umpteenth time that day I questioned the sense in dragging her all the way to Germany when she was so poorly.

'Wow, great work trying to save her,' Siobhan whispered sarcastically, as I tried to help Laura up off the floor and into the lift. 'Anyone would think you're trying to do me out of a job.'

Thankfully, she did improve as the week progressed, with plenty of naps, freshly baked *Laugenbrezel*, Pringles and carrots.

Every day Laura had a small amount of blood taken, then she was attached to a drip and given an injection of the Newcastle disease virus. She would then lie on a waterbed, with a water-filled 'bag' clamped firmly onto the side of her head, the electrohyperthermia, in the form of radio waves, was directed through it to the tumour site. The session lasted about fifty minutes and it didn't hurt – at worst it could be slightly uncomfortable – but Laura often slept through it or listened to podcasts. Sometimes she would use it as an opportunity to learn something new, practising Morse code as her head was gently heated.

We knew there were no guarantees, but it felt good to be doing something proactive to give Laura the best possible chance of survival. As long as it wasn't making matters worse or causing any side effects, it had to be worth a shot.

People travelled to the clinic from all around the world. On the third day we heard English voices down the corridor and introduced ourselves to Toni and her son Charlie, who was being treated for medulloblastoma. We went for coffee and cake once treatment was finished for the day and Toni explained how Charlie had initially been treated in Turkey but now the tumour had grown back, and it was this recurrence that had brought them to the clinic.

'I don't think I'd really considered that it might come back,' Laura said in a quiet voice, as we walked slowly back to the apartment.

My heart ached for her.

On bad days, it felt like Siobhan was stalking us, hot breath in our ears, tapping impatiently at her watch with a long fingernail to indicate that time was running out. But on good days, why the hell couldn't Laura be the one who survived to live a long and happy life? After all, she was probably the only person in the entire world with that precise combination of treatments. Why couldn't it be her? Someone would have to be first, and we were heading into new and uncharted territory.

'It's All the Fashion Now'

August

With the summer coming to an end and the new university term approaching, we ploughed on with the bucket list, adding new things all the time to keep Laura busy. She'd long been obsessed with Uncle Joe's Mint Balls and loved to see how things were made, so a trip to the Santus sweet factory in Wigan was almost inevitable.

This little factory, with it's heavenly minty scent, was the polar opposite of the huge Heinz plant down the road. The sweets had been made the same way since 1898, using just sugar, peppermint oil and cream of tartar, cooked in copper pans on open fires and traditionally hand-rolled. They'd been on the same site next to Wigan train station since 1919, when only committed Methodists could apply for a job, and wages were paid directly to their mums.

Laura, wearing white coat and blue hair net, was encouraged to help stretch out a batch of warm sugary toffee. It looked like sweet dark lava, and although she didn't have the strength to lift it, she did help with the kneading – and naturally left with a hamper of sweets.

When Laura was really sick and sofa-bound, she and Mark had enjoyed nothing more than sitting in front of the fire watching *Mortimer and Whitehouse: Gone Fishing*. She loved the good-natured teasing, the panoramas of lush British countryside, and the occasional big fish.

'I'd love to do that – just spend the day somewhere lovely, fishing with them.'

And that had become item number nine on the bucket list.

It took months of communication before we finally arranged a date, which happened to be Mark's birthday, so the trip was a treat for him too.

We had the best day. It rained non-stop so we sheltered under umbrellas for much of it, but we laughed till our faces hurt, ate birthday cake and tried to catch fish. At one point we nipped to Waitrose across the river to warm up with a hot drink, watching the customers do a double take as they walked past the coffee shop into the store. It's not every day you see legends of comedy behind the newspaper stand of your local supermarket.

Always keen to learn new skills, Laura took the fishing very seriously and, to her delight, she caught the biggest fish of the day: a pretty 2lb pike. Maybe it was just beginner's luck but Paul caught nothing at all, and Bob only caught tiddlers, although as far as I can remember he did manage to stay on his feet, so that was a bonus.

Gracie and I could whip up an argument out of nowhere, probably because our personalities were so similar; Laura would always act as the peacemaker, and Mark would put his 'tin hat' on and retreat until peace had been declared. She and I once drove back together from a family party and by the time we got home, sparks were flying.

Once again, we were stuck in a circular argument that left us both wounded and tearful. The debate continued for hours, with Mark attempting to mediate. There wasn't a right or a wrong party here, just two people who were in a great deal of pain at the idea of losing someone they loved. Punch drunk and cried out at 1:30 a.m. we finally went to bed without really resolving anything.

An hour later we were back up and on high alert. Laura was violently sick, again and again, without respite. This wasn't the normal chemo sickness, so we bundled her into the car and headed to Burnley General.

It was one of those bad vein nights and twice we had to find a doctor as the tissue of Laura's arm swelled alarmingly with the fluid that should have been flowing through her veins.

Around 6 a.m. we took her home. She was back on an even keel but exhausted and for the first time really very low.

She asked me:

'What if this is just my life?'
'Am I just waiting for it to come back now?'
'What if I get really sick when I'm away?'
'How am I going to cope at uni?'

And then, worst of all …

'What's the point?'

She was so small and sad, and it broke my heart all over again.

I did my best to cheer her up with *Bend it Like Beckham* and pizza, but it was as if she'd opened up to show me how she really felt, just for a moment – and I wondered if it was me being strong for her, or the other way around.

The argument with Gracie had been overshadowed by Laura's sickness but she still guilt-tripped me into taking her shopping and employing me as her changing room gopher, swapping sizes and carrying bags.

Patching up our relationship with regular retail therapy was becoming expensive, but Gracie was my absolute rock. She was full of kindness and compassion and would always be there to comfort me when I was at my lowest ebb. She could read my mood better than anyone, and in moments of weakness she was my strength. It was such a lot for any seventeen-year-old to cope with, and although we sometimes clashed, I was so very proud of her kind heart and her new maturity.

* * *

Sajid Javid was true to his word and Laura spent a fascinating day behind the scenes at MI5. She told the Director General her plan was to work there after graduation, and asked if she could take a picture of his bookshelf to get ahead with some background reading. Then she spent a day at BAE systems, with the new Typhoon jets rolling out to join the RAF and the prototype Tempest fighter jet – so space age, it will be controlled by eye movements. Laura also had the chance to land a virtual fighter jet onto the deck of an aircraft carrier, which was surprisingly stressful. She was brilliant, and took the task very seriously, her face stern with concentration.

Shortly after, Laura and Mark also had the opportunity to visit the Ron Haslam Race School at Donington Park, where she was taught to ride a motorbike and master her gear-changing technique, before five laps around the track riding pillion with world champion 'Rocket' Ron himself.

Laura was pale and speechless when she got off, her arms still locked in position, legs trembling. As Mark sat her down and bought her a warm drink from the café, the man beside him in the queue said, 'Was that your lass on the back with Ron?'

'Yes, I think she's still in shock,' said Mark, looking over at a stunned Laura.

'Bloody hell, I'm an instructor here and there's no way you'd get me on the back with him.'

Probably just as well that I wasn't there, as I'm not sure that I could have coped seeing Laura holding on for dear life as they flew around the track, overtaking the other riders at 158 miles an hour … while doing a wheelie.

You might have thought, looking at Laura's bucket list and the things she's done, that none of them are especially 'girly'. You would definitely have a point. From being small and playing dress-up with her friend Iona, Laura only ever wanted to be the prince or, at a push, the witch. Unlike her sister, she was not interested in being any kind of princess. The posters on her wall were of Jessica Ennis rather than Justin Bieber, and the only dressing-up outfit she had truly loved was Captain Scarlet, and she wore that until the trousers finished halfway up her legs.

Over the years Laura had introduced us to a couple of boyfriends, but none had lasted very long, and she didn't seem particularly involved, so it wasn't a huge shock in 2017 when she came home drunk one night and told me in no uncertain terms that she was gay. She was then horribly sick, and Gracie and I had to get her in the bath before putting her to bed with a bucket within grabbing distance.

She didn't mention it again for a while and I certainly wasn't going to force the issue. As long as she was happy, I had no problem with who she might one day fall in love with. Three months later, she told Mark, who was equally unruffled by the news.

Soon after the diagnosis, Laura decided that she wanted to tell the rest of the family. If she only had a short time left to live, then she wasn't prepared to waste it pretending to be something she wasn't. My mum was very enthusiastic and completely supportive, my dad was a bit quiet but only because it took a little longer for him to process the information. He didn't really know any gay people (apparently) but obviously he was happy for Laura to be whoever she was. 'Anyway,' he said. 'You all know that *Pride* is one of my favourite films. I cried more than anyone when the coaches full of miners arrive at the end.'

Nanna Beryl was the one we were dreading telling – a lovely lady who doted on her granddaughters, she was traditional in her beliefs and did not have a reputation for tact, so anything could happen.

Laura took her into another room to tell her and we crowded behind the door to listen.

'Honest?' was her first response. Swiftly followed by, 'Well, it's all the fashion now.' And then, 'And you've got the hair for it I suppose.'

'It's not the life I'd have chosen for you, Laura, but that doesn't mean I won't support you,' was Beryl's final world on the matter.

Laura was loved by all of us, and nothing could change that.

As a young ambassador, Laura was always looking for ways to promote the work of The Brain Tumour Charity. She had distributed hundreds of Head Smart cards to schools and surgeries, and shared her experiences in the media, but it was while we were away in South Africa that she had had her big lightbulb moment.

'Why don't we see if we can get a group together to represent The Brain Tumour Charity at Manchester Pride?'

Before we'd returned home, she'd got the OK from the charity, applied, paid, and was rallying friends and fellow ambassadors to take part. It was a perfect opportunity to cross number ten off the bucket list, definitely fulfilling the criteria of 'a rally or march for something I believe in'.

Pride weekend was gloriously sunny. We were all kitted out in our red Brain Tumour Charity T-shirts, accessorised with wings, flowers, flags, rainbow skirts, bucket loads of glitter and anything else we could think of.

All except Mark – he came down the stairs wearing a blue T-shirt with the words *Proud Dad* printed in rainbow letters. He was a man of few words, but sometimes his tenderhearted gestures spoke volumes.

Each group had a designated place in the parade, so we sat on the kerb in front of the chip shop cheering and clapping as we waited for our turn to join the stream of walkers. My dad had seen many things in his seventy-two years on earth, but he learned a great deal more that day, his mind forever opened by Pups, Bears and The Sisters of Perpetual Indulgence. Every day's a school day, after all.

When our time came, we walked the route between the decorated floats and the marching bands, shaking the charity collection buckets and handing out Head Smart cards. There was so much support out on the streets, we sang along and danced to the music played on loudspeakers. I was so proud to be walking alongside Laura as she just smiled from ear to ear – I wanted everyone to know that she was my girl.

There's a wonderful photograph from that day. Laura is beaming, her arms raised in triumph and her head tilted back, eyes to the sky. She looks so perfectly happy. My dad is standing to the side of her looking for all the world like a CIA bodyguard ready to jump in front of a bullet for her, which he would have done without a moment's hesitation.

Laura had made it her mantra to say *yes* to as many things as she could, even if she was tired or things were difficult. She knew that opportunities needed to be taken whenever possible and shouldn't be squandered. A family wedding in France clashed with the end of treatment in Germany but instead of travelling home, Mark and Laura took a series of trains across Europe and joined us there.

It was a glorious weekend. The little gites I'd booked in the Périgord Vert were basic but surrounded by a beautiful meadow of wildflowers with a lake and a little swimming pool. We went on walks, played boules, and watched Gracie wrestling with an inflatable crocodile in the pool. Evenings were spent playing cards and drinking cheap French cider while insects buzzed around the light fittings.

On the last night Laura was struggling to keep her eyes open as we played Sevens.

'I'm so tired and I know I need to go to bed, but I don't want this night to end.'

It brought a lump to my throat. *Me too, kid, me too.*

'This One's on Us'
September

Earlier in the summer, Laura had been invited to join a local band on stage with her bass guitar for a rendition of 'Seven Nation Army'. She hadn't played in years and there'd been no time to rehearse, but you would never have guessed that she was nervous. It would have been so much easier and a lot less scary to politely decline, but what if the chance never arose again? We were so proud, watching her perform in front of the crowds at Blackstock Music Festival, effortlessly cool in her skinny jeans like Kim Deal from Pixies.

Another of Laura's guitar heroes was Johnny Marr, and on the afternoon we returned from France, I had a call to ask if we'd like to go and watch his show in Manchester that night.

A couple of hours later Laura, Mark and I were introduced to Aly and Ory who ran the fan club, and had helped arrange the tickets.

'Would you like to meet Johnny before the show?'

We waited nervously outside the dressing room for the sound check to finish, then Johnny bounded up the stairs and invited us in, he found us drinks and spent the best part of an hour chatting about Manchester, music, marathons and playing bass guitar. He was really interested in Laura's story and asked lots of questions about her life and plans for the future. It was a privilege to spend time in the company of such an extraordinarily lovely man.

Playing in front of an adoring, capacity audience must be one phenomenal high – it was spine-tingling just to watch. Then, before Johnny played the final song of the night and after he'd thanked the audience he said, 'This song is dedicated to my new mate, Laura. God bless you – this is for you … take care.' He went on to play, 'There Is a Light That Never Goes Out' for her. She was thrilled to bits; I sobbed all the way through.

Next day we headed down to London. Following some top-draw badgering, we'd been given tickets to watch Phoebe Waller-Bridge's incredible one-woman show *Fleabag*. Laura was a huge fan and loved the TV show based on that original play. Sixty-five minutes later, we emerged blinking in the bright daylight after an astonishingly brilliant matinee show.

As we ambled back through Covent Garden, we passed Trevor Sorbie's flagship hair salon and I had the bright idea of getting Laura a fabulous new haircut. She didn't have a great deal of hair as yet, and what she did have was wiry and grew straight up like a Play-Doh barber shop customer, so it definitely didn't have anything you could describe as a style.

I checked the price list from the doorway. I would never have dreamed of paying those prices at home but if, by chance, they had availability with a junior stylist then it was fate, and I'd happily treat Laura to a really good cut. They did have an appointment available if we were able to pop back in thirty minutes, so we filled the time with ice cream and a quick bookshop browse, soon we were back at the reception desk.

'I'm really sorry, but the junior stylist who was cutting your hair isn't here now, so it's going to have to be one of our directors instead. Is that OK?'

I gulped, trying to remember by what factor that would increase the cost of the cut.

'Umm, yes, of course. That's fine.'

Laura was taken through into the dazzling salon, which seemed to be populated entirely by the beautiful people of London, while I enjoyed a pot of loose-leaf tea, having turned down the glass of fizz.

I watched as Laura's hair was cut by a real artist, delicately snipping away while giving tips on how to care for chemo hair and encourage it to grow. There wasn't a great deal to work with but when she was finished Laura emerged looking like Mia Farrow in *Rosemary's Baby*: her hair had been cut in an elfin style which emphasised her expressive eyes and slender neck.

I no longer cared what it cost – this woman had waved a magic wand and it was worth every penny. My eyes filled up just to look at Laura and the huge smile she was wearing.

We were escorted to the reception desk to pay, but the fabulous stylist shook her head.

'This one's on us.'

There were hugs all round and we all ended up in tears, the stylist, receptionist and me. It was the most wonderful and unexpected kindness and Laura was delighted with her new look.

I don't remember exactly how I persuaded Gracie to take part in the Great North Run; I think my dad might have been responsible, or maybe we both caught her in a moment of weakness, but this was where we found ourselves, in our Brain Tumour Charity vests on the start line with 57,000 others and absolutely no training.

We ate cider ice lollies, Jelly Babies and stroked every dog we passed. Gracie entertained the other runners by describing in great detail what she planned to eat when the torture was over: 'Thick, white toast with lashings of salted butter,' she said, as the other runners groaned with ecstasy at the thought.

At one point she disappeared into a platoon of marching Roman centurions but the three of us crossed the finish line together, with Laura there to cheer us in, making the whole experience even more emotional. She'd been helping at the recovery tent with my mum and the other Brain Tumour Charity volunteers. We had made a point of talking to everyone running in the turquoise and red of the charity, so many of them taking part in memory of someone they'd loved and lost to this horrific disease.

Gracie fell asleep on the bus journey back to Newcastle. I looked across the aisle to see Laura holding her hand above Gracie's face, to shield her sleeping sister from the sun blasting through the window, and a lump formed in my throat. We both knew it was tough for Gracie, and to see Laura's love for her in this simple act of kindness made my heart brim with pride for them both.

After an exhausting day and a long journey back to Lancashire, Laura had another early start the next morning. She was taking a train from Preston to Glasgow and then on to the Firth of Clyde, where she'd be sailing with the Ellen MacArthur Cancer Trust.

Cancer is a lonely place for a young person whose friends are at school or college; the chasm between the world of the sick and the world of the well is huge, and regardless of how close you might have been before, that bridge is a tricky one to cross. The shared experiences have become so difficult, and even the language has changed. The world of the sick is littered with initials, acronyms and procedures that have no place in the world of the well.

It's tough for both parties, and if something is difficult or uncomfortable, we avoid it, which leaves the sick person even more isolated. The Ellen MacArthur Cancer Trust tries to address this by bringing together small groups of young people who are 'in the same boat' and giving them a sailing trip of a lifetime, creating new friendships and unforgettable memories.

One of the things Laura enjoyed most about her bucket list was having new stories to share with her friends. It meant there was more to talk about than just treatment and how she was feeling. It gave her a library of interesting and exciting experiences that friends genuinely wanted to hear about.

Laura had a brilliant time in Scotland: she made friends, learned new skills, took part in a baking competition, and played lots of Uno. She told me about a time when the crew were caught out in stormy conditions, and she had to lean right back over the side of the boat to provide ballast while being soaked by the waves and the rain. I imagined her as Lieutenant Dan in *Forrest Gump*, lashed to the mast in a storm and making his peace with God, but I hope it wasn't quite as dramatic.

When Laura had been really sick, I'd asked the oncologist if perhaps her chemo dose was too high. He had assured me it most definitely was not and that all responsibility for her sickness lay with us and the additional supplements we were using. But then I noticed that the dosage had been significantly reduced and, as if by magic, the sickness stopped; she was functional for the full five days that she was on the tablets, rather than a wraith shuffling between bathroom and bed.

Curious, I phoned the hospital pharmacy to be told that the change had been made to reflect her weight loss, but the weight loss had happened months ago, when she'd first been weaned off steroids after surgery. Laura was 18 kilos lighter now, but her chemo dose hadn't changed. No wonder she'd been so sick.

I was furious with myself for not picking up on this sooner: I knew of people who'd claimed to sail through oral chemo, so we'd just assumed Laura was unlucky. She'd lost so many unnecessary days to sickness, precious days that we wouldn't get back. I was disappointed in myself and now it felt like trust in our oncologist had hit a new low. Apologies were made when the error was discovered. A few months later, he retired, and we were assigned a new oncologist, Dr C.

The one positive we could take from this discovery was that the next five months of chemo would be easier because the dose would finally be proportionate to weight. It was just in time, as we were now getting ready to take Laura back to university.

When she had first been diagnosed, we'd been told that going back to uni would be impossible, but a year on, Laura and I were opening up those IKEA boxes and getting ready to take them to Manchester. She was a fledgling that we'd nursed back to something close to health and here she was, getting ready to fly all by herself.

Letting go a second time was never going to be easy, not after the year we'd had. Laura was still on chemo and needed to be reminded to eat on a regular basis, but it was no surprise to us that she had decided to live in halls. If she was doing this, she wanted to do it properly, and be a real student.

I cried less this time, maybe because she was only an hour away or because I knew how hard she'd had to work to get there. I was happy she was well enough to go, but all my instincts were to keep her safe and warm till all her feathers had grown back.

She was often sick, and nosebleeds were an issue, so I would offer to come and collect her, but she wanted to manage the symptoms herself as best she could. 'Laura do it' had been the refrain of her early childhood, and she was no different now.

She had always been brave and independent, but bravery isn't always about needles and motorbikes – it's also walking into a lecture theatre when you have no hair and your eyebrows have been drawn on in a hurry because you were throwing up an hour before.

We missed Laura dreadfully when she was away at uni. I'd been involved with every single aspect of her life for the past year, but now I just had to trust that she was taking care of herself properly. One silver lining was that it meant I had more time to spend with

Gracie before she too left for uni. She was going to have the opportunity to reinvent herself in a brand-new environment; a fresh start where what she revealed, or didn't, was entirely up to her.

That month it was my turn to take Laura to Cologne. We were growing to love our adopted city, dodging the bikes and scooters, finding nice places to eat, and developing our own little routines. Other than the long travelling days it wasn't difficult: treatment was relatively painless and only lasted an hour, leaving the majority of the day free for Laura to catch up with lectures, most of which were available as podcasts.

I'd walk around the city so as not to distract her, and after tea we'd binge a Netflix series or watch a subtitled film at the Kino. I loved spending time with her, just talking – sometimes about the future, or the incredible things we'd experienced in the last year; sometimes just absolute rubbish. It didn't matter, I just loved to hear her talk.

When Laura was first diagnosed, I became obsessed with holding on to everything she'd written; her handwriting became a talisman to me, and I needed to save every single piece as if the very essence of her was contained in the loops and formations of her letters. Maybe one day I would piece all the words together, and, in that patchwork, find some kind of answer.

Not long after our trip, we had a phone call in the early hours with the news that Georgina had given birth to a beautiful baby girl: Alice Elizabeth. She'd arrived a little earlier than expected but both mother and baby were doing well.

Laura came back from uni on the train, and met us at the hospital. It was pouring with rain, and we splashed through huge puddles in the car park with coats held over our heads. We'd been so thirsty for good news and Alice was loved at first sight. I was just so happy that Laura had managed to meet her baby cousin; it had seemed almost impossible back in March, but here she was in her Johnny Marr T-shirt, relatively healthy, smiling like a Cheshire cat, and holding our brand-new baby in her arms.

Kintsugi
October–November

Sometimes we find great truths in works of philosophy, history or maybe religious texts. And then sometimes they are placed in front of us, printed on a table mat in the Bolton branch of Wagamama. 'Kintsugi is the Japanese art of mending broken pottery. Instead of concealing the cracks, gold is used to emphasise the beauty of what was once broken. The moment we accept and share our struggles is the moment we begin to paint our own cracks with gold. Wear them with pride as they are a map of a life lived, leaving us stronger and more beautiful than before.'

Laura had arranged to see her surgeon, Mr L. I think she wanted to show him how well she was doing. There was definitely an element of 'look at me now' and he was suitably impressed by how well she'd responded to treatment. I think in some irrational corner of my mind I hoped he'd be so amazed that he'd exclaim the initial diagnosis must be wrong.

'Bless! The depth of your delusion is quite astonishing,' Siobhan said, instead.

The likelihood was that Laura would have another tumour, and although there were few prospects on the horizon, our strategy was to keep her alive as long as possible in the hope that a breakthrough cure might be found in her lifetime.

With Laura settling into university life, I went back to work.

Our family business was an indoor play centre called Giddy Kippers, the usual set-up of soft play sessions, café and birthday parties. We had re-mortgaged the house to open it when the girls were small, they'd basically grown up there and both worked weekend shifts as soon as they were old enough – they even featured on the company logo. We were very lucky to have Michael, our manager, who'd been part of the family for years and kept the place running, leaving us free to concentrate on Laura.

Taking care of someone with a diagnosis like Laura's, certainly at the beginning, is a full-time job. I've no idea how we would have coped if we'd been working full-time or didn't have the means to research treatments or take her to appointments. The trips to Germany were only possible because we'd been incredibly lucky with our fundraising. Once you step beyond the treatments approved by NICE and the parameters of the NHS, things get very expensive very quickly indeed.

I found going back to work tricky: it was lovely to see everyone, but my fuse was considerably shorter now. My whole perspective on life had changed and it had reduced my patience. Where once I would cheerfully handle a disgruntled customer, now I couldn't be trusted not to tell them to get a grip.

It must have been difficult for Laura too, as she had so much more to worry about than Freshers' Week or submitting assignments. She had a night out planned with her best friend Olivia.

'I feel really nervous about going out.'

'Why? You'll have a brilliant time with Liv.'

'I don't know how to just be normal anymore.'

'Oh, Laura, you are normal.'

'People look at me and see "cancer girl". I don't want to be that person, I don't want cancer or a bald head to be the things that people remember about me. I don't want it to define me.'

There was so much more to Laura. She would change the world if she was given time. I had every confidence she still would.

* * *

When we travelled to Cologne, Laura was able to relax in the knowledge that I'd tried to anticipate every eventuality, printing off an itinerary and micro-managing each element of the trip. Travelling with Mark meant she needed to stay alert, as he employed what he called a 'rally driver mentality', which meant that he dealt with situations as they arose. He wasn't big on planning and had a bit of a reputation for being late.

October was his turn to take Laura to Cologne, and on Monday morning he called me from the airport.

'Everything OK?'

'All good here … hang on, why aren't you in the air? Have you been delayed?'

'Not exactly.'

'Go on.'

'We were a bit late and …'

'Please tell me you didn't miss the flight.'

'Not exactly, but we were too late to check any luggage in.'

'So what's happened?'

'Well, Laura's on the plane, with her small case, and I'm getting a flight later this afternoon. I couldn't take the cannabis on as hand luggage, couldn't risk it.'

'So … she's on her own?'

'She said she'd be fine.'

'And does she know where she's going?'

'Yes. I wrote it down for her, she's stayed there before, hasn't she?' Mark sounded unconvinced.

Early mornings were always tough for Laura, and I hated to think of her navigating the train from Dusseldorf to Cologne alone and having to find the apartment, before going to treatment. She phoned me later that morning, laughing because she'd spent hours wandering up and down the street looking for building 106 when Mark had actually written 10b. I saw the funny side eventually, and these things happen, but it was always going to be hard for me to relinquish control.

Back in Barrowford, Gracie had a lot on her mind. She was planning to study film production, choosing universities relatively close to home so she could spend as much time as possible with her sister. There were so many things for her to worry about: Laura – obviously – but also A Level grades, assembling her portfolio and quite understandably, qualms about living away. Unlike her fiercely independent sibling, Gracie liked to be home; family was important to her and the idea of being self-sufficient was as terrifying as it was thrilling.

Twice a year the sixth-form kids arranged a mid-week night out at a local club. Gracie left early to get changed at her friend's house. She was a bit anxious about going, as these events had become loaded with unsustainable levels of significance – their equivalent of the Met Ball.

I'd agreed to collect her at the end of the night, but the call came hours earlier than expected.

It was one of Gracie's friends: 'Hi, would you be OK to come and get Gracie now? I think she's ready to come home.'

'Already? It's not even nine yet. No problem, just give me a sec and I'll set off.'

Ten minutes later I had another call, from a member of the club staff, asking how long I was going to be as Gracie was now unconscious. I drove as fast as I possibly could, ran up the steps and into the club to find her passed out in a side room under the watchful eyes of security staff. Two of them helped me to carry her out to the car, then laid her across the back seats. I had no idea whether it was just alcohol, but she was incoherent, barely conscious.

'Do you think I should take her to hospital?' I asked the bouncer.

'Nah, she'll be right. Just keep an eye on her tonight. She'll have one hell of a hangover tomorrow.'

I drove home, alternately berating her for being so irresponsible and begging her to stay awake and not be sick in the car.

There was no way to get her upstairs, so I laid her on the kitchen floor and covered her with a blanket. I needed to make sure she didn't choke, so I sat beside her and monitored her breathing.

In my heart I knew this was a cry for help. I stroked her hair and told her how much I loved her, thankful that she was home and safe.

She was very sick and subdued the next morning, sorry for herself and deeply apologetic.

It was no coincidence that her night from hell had landed on the first anniversary of Laura's initial diagnosis.

When Laura was home, I found it really hard to let her go back to Manchester. She let slip that her university diet had been mostly Pringles and Haribo sweets, so I portioned up curries and home-made soups to freeze and bought ready meals she could eat at her desk: anything to make her life a bit easier. I worried that without someone to coax her, she wouldn't bother to cook, her iron levels would get low, making her liable to dizziness and passing out. I worried that she wouldn't tell me if she felt ill, and I worried that she might suffer another seizure.

Laura wasn't finding the transition easy either. She was trying to enter wholeheartedly into university life, but was often exhausted and struggled with late nights; she needed to avoid the strobes and flashing lights of nightclubs and couldn't really drink alcohol. She was also disappearing off to Germany every month, so it wasn't easy to to make friends.

She phoned sometimes when she was feeling stressed or anxious, but before she'd discuss the matter, I had to promise that I wouldn't say either, 'You can always defer to next year' or, 'Shall I just come and get you?'

I'm sure there were times when she wanted to do exactly that, but she was bravely resolute in her determination to stick it out. Until a night when she was really sick, and we got one of those awful, dead-of-night phone calls from her – the kind that slap you from asleep to wide awake in seconds.

Shaking with nervous adrenaline and the sick feeling of early morning shock, we raced over to Manchester. Laura was curled up in a ball on her bathroom floor, her skin grey and icy cold. We scooped her into the car and headed to the nearest hospital. After a quick triage she was hooked up to a fluids drip with a cocktail of anti-sickness meds and antibiotics. She was freezing, so we covered her with our coats, and she slept a little while Mark and I exchanged worried glances across the bed.

A city centre A&E in the middle of the night is a scary place. There were twenty patients on the corridor waiting for beds, and a number of shady individuals trying to sneak past the security guards and into the restricted areas. I can't imagine how hard it must be to take care of sick people while being verbally abused and keeping one eye on the drugs cabinet – it really must take superhuman courage as well as unconditional kindness.

While Laura slept, a woman in her twenties wearing a bomber jacket and a high ponytail sauntered into the room. 'Hiya love, have you got credit on your phone? I need to call me mum, to tell her I'm in hospital.'

She bounced down on the bed and with furious fingers, fired off a number of texts, all of which seemed to be telling 'Nate' that she 'didn't have his money'.

A nurse came in and shooed her away, then for the rest of the day I got messages asking, 'Who dis?'

* * *

We'd built a good relationship with the team at The Brain Tumour Charity. Laura had recently organised a local Twilight Walk, which had been well supported with over a hundred walkers taking part, and lots of delicious contributions to the homemade cake stall. She presented each finisher with their medal and thanked them for taking part, standing patiently in the cold and dark to greet the final walkers.

Then I was invited to speak at their annual conference at the head office in Farnborough. I was more than happy to talk about Laura but everyone in the room would know more about brain tumours than me, and I wasn't sure I'd have anything especially new or interesting to say. I was, however, really grateful for all the support we'd received and thought it would be a good opportunity to thank them on behalf of the thousands of families like ours.

In the end, I didn't so much speak as ramble on incoherently for ten minutes, cry a couple of times and then kick over my glass of water.

I think the conference loosened my tongue a little too much. On the train back up to Preston, a poor man had the misfortune of sitting next to me and making polite conversation; he got the whole epic story. I'm sure he got off a stop early and walked the last twenty miles just to give his ears a rest. Sorry about that, Clive.

It's a Wonderful Life
December

Christmas and birthdays are weighted with an unwieldy significance when you're dealing with a terminal diagnosis. Will she see another one? Can she make it to the end of the year?

Laura had never been especially interested in Christmas – unlike Gracie, who loved every aspect and refused point blank to deviate from a single family tradition. But Laura's diagnosis had changed her perspective on the value of time, and now her priority was to spend it with the people she loved. Although we didn't dwell on how much she might have left, she knew it wasn't infinite, and she wanted to spend it wisely. Having said that, she would still happily waste a day in her bed watching back-to-back episodes of *Criminal Minds* on her phone.

As Laura was doing her best to live a relatively normal university life in between monthly chemo and weeks in Cologne, we'd slowed right down with the bucket list adventures, but we did manage one 'grand day out' before the year ended.

Wallace and Gromit always held a special place in Laura's heart. She'd adored the films since she was really tiny, and when things were stressful, we'd often find her on the sofa, with a warm blanket and *The Wrong Trousers*. It was definitely the on-screen equivalent of comfort food for Laura.

When I contacted Aardman and told them her story, they were only too happy to invite us down for a tour of their studios in sunny Bristol.

Nick Park is a gentle, unassuming Lancastrian with the most incredible talent for telling stories with modelling clay. Laura was fascinated by the sketches of her favourite characters that decorated his office walls, and we were careful not to pay too much attention to the top-secret development ideas on the notice board behind us. Very few people have won four Academy Awards, five Baftas and a gold Blue Peter badge; it would be fair to say that he had one very full and shiny trophy cabinet.

We were shown around the workshop, an Aladdin's cave of Plasticine, fabrics, googly eyes and tiny props, then watched the animators working with Morph and his mischievous friend, Chas. Laura even filmed a few stop-motion frames herself. The whole building was full of the most extraordinary talent; every desk we walked past had some amazing creation either on paper or in 3D. It was quite magical.

Laura was presented with her very own Morph in a cardboard box, and a Wallace and Gromit sketch drawn for her by the man himself. I took a photo of her, beaming as she held an Oscar statuette. She might have been almost twenty but there were still times when I'd catch sight of that wide-eyed little girl.

Although December was Mark's month for Cologne, the dates coincided with the end of term, so Gracie and I went out too.

The whole city had become a giant Christmas market and in between treatment sessions we were able to spend time together as a family, just wandering around the stalls and stopping for hot chocolate and *gluhwein*.

When I asked Laura what presents she might like for her birthday and Christmas, I was quite prepared for something usual. In previous years the girls had sponsored rescue greyhounds and paid for goats to be distributed to families in Africa.

Laura already had a plan.

'Right, so what I want to do, instead of getting presents, is for us to open up Giddy Kippers on Boxing Day, invite lots of families who are struggling … like carers, and families that are vulnerable, or refugees, and have a massive party with food and presents and everything.'

'You want to do that instead of getting presents?' Mark asked.

'I've got everything I need already, and how good would it be to use what we have at our disposal to make other people happy.'

My first instinct was to say that it was a mad idea, but the more I thought about it, the more it made sense. So, while Laura got on with her university work, we set about making it happen.

I contacted local primary schools, charities and social workers to invite the families who'd benefit most, rounded up an army of volunteers and contacted all the local supermarkets and suppliers to see if they could help with food. Once word got out, we were inundated with people who wanted to help or buy presents for Father Christmas to distribute.

It was a revelation: focusing on making other people's Christmas happier changed our own for the better. On Christmas Eve, we even made it out to the cinema for our annual pilgrimage to watch *It's a Wonderful Life*. It meant the world to have Laura sitting next to me, eating mince pies, and giggling with her sister. She'd come through so much this year, and we were all different people now, older by way more than twelve months, battle-scarred but united.

When Laura was first diagnosed, I would have seen her twentieth birthday as a major achievement but now we were here, there was no way this was anything close to enough. We wanted another twenty, thirty years at the very least.

I would never, ever be ready to let her go.

In contrast to the previous year, Christmas was lovely. Ziggy tried to open everyone's presents and Mark and I prepared dinner for the whole family as the girls watched *Flushed Away* just like they did every Christmas morning. Last year had been horrific but now Laura was managing to eat, her hair was growing back and although she was still fragile there was a new strength and a resilience to her.

The Boxing Day Bonanza was a big success. Our initial plan to serve a cold buffet had snowballed into a full Christmas dinner for 250 guests. Michael and a team of enthusiastic volunteers managed the kitchen, and we offered face painting, games and the best Father Christmas south of the North Pole in a grotto bursting with presents.

One little boy told us it was the best Christmas he'd ever had, and a dad told me it was the first time he'd seen his daughter smile since her gran had died earlier in the year. A small girl asked

Laura's friend, Iona, if it would be OK if she took a little box of rice home for her tea, so we made sure that she, and every single family, left with a huge pile of leftovers, chocolates, biscuits and presents.

I was so grateful to the volunteers who'd given up their Boxing Day to help, all of whom insisted they would love to do it again next year, and I was so proud of Laura for being the driving force and the very heart behind the event.

Even though she was dealing with the worst life could throw at her, Laura was completely focused on trying to bring happiness to other people.

Caitlin Moran captured this brilliantly in *More Than a Woman*: 'So often in people who have been through great illness, or torment, and come out the other side, there is something extra to them. Although it is never the method you would wish for them, there is a kindness, a steadiness, a strength, an ability to find everyday life absolutely joyous.'

In the days between Christmas and New Year, when the lights go on at three and you're never more than half a metre from a chocolate orange, we stayed in our pyjamas all day and watched films. We squashed into Laura's bed and pointed to the places we'd like to visit on the huge map on her wall, and we shared the stories of where we'd been and the people we'd met.

I took the girls to the cinema to watch *Little Women*. It had been decades since I'd read the book and I'd completely forgotten that one of the sisters, Beth, becomes very ill. As the film progressed, I hoped that I'd got it wrong, but the story was moving inevitably towards her death.

In one of her final scenes Beth sits on the beach with her sister Jo and gently tries to prepare her for the fact she's going to die. 'It's like the tide going out. It goes out slowly, but it can't be stopped.'

To which Jo replies, 'I'll stop it.'

My throat squeezed tight in the fight against more tears.

As we left the screening Laura said what we were all thinking: 'That's pretty much like us, isn't it?' and it broke me just that little bit more.

2020

Kopfkino

January

We spent new year in Wales. It was lovely to be squashed up tight in the little cottage. The girls shared a bedroom, and we snuggled together in the tiny lounge. Laura watched *The Sound of Music* for the first time and was quite literally on the edge of her seat as the Von Trapps raced to cross the border. We wandered around bookshops, visited abandoned churches, and celebrated the end of 2019 with fish and chips.

Mark drove the car in circles on the deserted beach, whizzing round on two wheels while we all squealed with excitement, Ziggy, in the boot, tried in vain to grip with his claws as he slid from one side to the other. Gracie leaned as far as she could out of the window whooping loudly with her arms in the air.

'Hold onto her legs, Mum, she's going to fall out!' Laura shrieked from the front seat.

Gracie and Zig even went paddling in the ice-cold sea while we looked on in abject horror.

January was scan month.

It was the last thing I thought of before sleep finally arrived, and my first thought when I woke gasping in the middle of the night, blood pulsing in my ears, heart racing. The Germans have the perfect word for it – *Kopfkino* – which literally translates as 'head cinema': the worst-case scenarios that keep you awake, hard to switch off and impossible to walk out of.

How many clear scans could we hope for before our luck ran out?

Ironically, Laura's first uni assignment was a reflection on Nagel's essay 'Death'. It felt like crappy timing to me.

'Actually, Mum, it's quite good, this. Nagel says that death's only bad because it deprives us of life's experiences, but because harm can only be felt when you're alive, and nothing can be felt after death, the harm is felt only by those left behind, who mourn the person they have been deprived of.'

I didn't need some old philosopher to tell me that it was those left behind who'd suffer.

On the morning of the scan, Gracie received an unconditional offer from the University of Salford, which meant no pressure to achieve predicted grades. Laura and I danced around the kitchen, absolutely thrilled for her.

Our buoyant optimism lasted all the way to the hospital, when we were caught unawares by bad news.

There was a spot on the scan.

It was small, roughly 4 mm across, but Dr C didn't think it was visible in the previous scan, which meant it was growing. It could still be a number of things and would be tabled for discussion at the weekly multi-disciplinary team meeting. It was definitely too small to operate on, so it would most likely be a 'watch and wait' scenario.

We assumed our usual positions: Laura was pragmatic, Gracie and I devastated, and Mark pretty much in denial. When we took the scans out to Germany with us, Professor VG didn't seem overly concerned; he had no plans to change the treatment protocol. We just needed to hold our collective nerve and crack on.

When the ground was cold and hard, I put the dull balls of Laura's hair on to the bird table, in the hope that it could be used to warm nests and at least do some small good in the world.

Three of the cemetery plots were now taken.

When Laura was invited to a Brain Tumour Charity social in Manchester, I suggested that maybe the parents could meet up at the same time – somewhere else of course, so as not to cramp their style.

It felt a little awkward to start with, as after all the only thing we had in common was a child with a brain tumour, but very quickly we were sharing heartbreaking stories and comparing the good and the utterly dreadful experiences we'd had trying to navigate treatment. We were strangers and yet we understood each other completely, probably better than close friends or even family.

One of the parents said the saddest thing I think I'd ever heard: 'He's my only child. If he dies, am I even a mum anymore?'

The thought had never crossed my mind before and it made me realise just how lucky I was to have Gracie.

Laura had spent the afternoon at a board game café, and it was good to see her laughing and among friends. I wrote at the time: 'There is so much more to her than a cancer diagnosis, she is beautiful and kind, she has ideas, opinions and plans for the future, but when people first meet her, they only see the bald head and the scar. Cancer is the elephant in the room, so big it squeezes everything else into a tiny corner.'

She'd recently taken the bold step of joining Tinder. In typical Laura style, her bio was a list of pros and cons about herself – no one could accuse her of overselling – although she did at least mention her skills with a Rubik's Cube.

Dating with cancer is a tricky business, with two options: either full disclosure, running the risk of scaring the date away; or hold back and wait, but till when, exactly?

There would never be a good time, and it would obviously be unfair to mislead, but cancer was such a tiny fraction of all the things she was.

I really wanted Laura to fall in love. If her life was going to be short, I didn't want her to die before she'd been swept off her feet by someone who adored her. I wanted her to have at least one wonderful, epic, love affair, and the possibility that this might not happen crushed me. I'd always hoped she would have the chance to have a baby too. But now saving her life was the priority, and there'd been no mention of egg freezing before radiotherapy or chemo.

Should I have asked about it? I had the dreadful feeling that I had missed something hugely important. 'Not exactly on the ball with that, were you? Shame really, but that boat has well and truly sailed now,' Siobhan reminded me.

Children definitely featured in Laura's seven-year plan: she wanted four. I imagined a little ninja army – they'd be schooled in flags of the world, the NATO phonetic alphabet, American state capitals and have their taekwondo black belts long before they started primary school. She would be strict rather than indulgent, scheduling trips to museums and maxing out their library book entitlements.

I wanted a part of Laura we could keep, like a cutting from a plant.

Was that normal, or had I become some twisted Frankenstein, trying anything I could to keep my daughter with me?

Meet Hilary

February

When Laura was in Year 8, her engineering class won a school's design competition and was invited down to the House of Commons to receive a certificate. It was all very exciting, and all very busy – as they set off from Euston, she somehow found herself still on the platform as the tube train doors swished shut and the train departed, with the rest of her group, and the teachers, inside.

'What did you do?' I asked in horror, when she arrived home that night.

'Well, I stayed calm and didn't panic and just got the next train. I felt a bit sorry for the teachers – you should have seen the look on their faces as the train set off and they saw me standing there on the platform. Anyway, did you know that Hilary Benn isn't actually a woman?'

Now she was off to spend a weekend in Amsterdam, with the other students on her politics, philosophy and economics course, a cancer diagnosis, and no teachers. It felt like the outward-bound residential at primary school – would she make friends? Would her roommates be nice? – but now I was also worrying about medication, head pains and low blood pressure too.

But this was an opportunity for Laura to be *normal* and she grasped it with both hands, sampling vast quantities of cheese and visiting both the Anne Frank and the sex museum. A photo popped up on my phone of Laura and her friend, Lisa, sitting on a giant swing, high above the city, legs dangling perilously; another of her smiling on a bridge over the canal. They'd hired bikes, but Laura told me sheepishly that she'd actually fallen off – her balance still wasn't great.

She'd decided not to take the cannabis with her to Amsterdam (coals to Newcastle, I suppose), but did try some of the local brownies.

Lisa asked, 'How do you know if you're high?'

'Look at your pupils and see if they're dilated.'

'Laura! Your pupils are huge!'

'You're joking, this is barely four out of ten!'

My daughter had seemingly become an expert on psychoactives.

This seems an appropriate time to introduce Laura's alter ego: Hilary.

Hilary (a portmanteau of 'high Laura') is who Laura became when she'd taken slightly more cannabis oil than needed, or it was just a particularly potent batch. We normally tried to keep her levels down at a steady six but on occasions she found herself riding an eight or a nine. Hilary was very entertaining: she said yes to everything and enjoyed loud singing, giggling and energetic dancing round the house. Sometimes she'd agree to things that Laura would have no recollection of the next day. And sometimes she arrived at the very worst moment, just before a tutorial or an interview, unpredictable but great fun.

Although she was now juggling the demands of assignments and lectures, Laura still had a policy of saying 'yes' to every new opportunity. The Royal Navy invited us to a Trafalgar Day dinner in London, and when the brand-new aircraft carrier, HMS *Prince of Wales* was docked in Liverpool, we received an invite to the VIP reception, to be attended by lots of sparkling local dignitaries. It felt like a great honour just to be asked.

The commanding officer welcomed us all on board and members of the crew circulated with celebrities, balancing their glasses of champagne with napkins of finger food. I was making small talk with the Speaker of the House of Commons, Lindsay Hoyle, and his wife, when I noticed that Laura was looking really pale.

'You OK, chick?'

'Not really, I need to lie down … now.'

Laura was alarmingly grey, and I knew if I didn't get her down soon, she would fall of her own accord. I was trying to avoid causing a massive fuss, but we needed urgent help. One of the crew ran off to find a chair; another to find a receptacle for her to throw up in.

It was horribly awkward. Everyone was so kind and helpful, but hundreds of people were looking across to see who was creating all this drama. Eventually, when her head stopped spinning, we were taken down to the officers' mess.

There are no lifts or staircases to take you between the nine floors of an aircraft carrier, just ladders and bulky hatches to climb through. It's definitely no place for cocktail dresses or high heels.

In the space of an hour Laura had faded from fabulous and relatively healthy to a frail little girl having her forehead stroked by the ship's medic. The pains in her head were quite severe and she complained that the sides of her skull felt like jelly. My stomach was clenched in a knot of worry. This sounded really bad: was it caused by the spot on the scan – had it grown already?

Touch Wood

Lockdown

Laura would often talk about how lucky we were, and she was absolutely right. If something like this was going to happen, then it was good that it happened when it did. She had completed her A Levels and got the grades she needed, she'd spent the most fantastic summer in Chicago, and had only just started at university so hadn't really got stuck into the course at that point or made any particularly close friends, so it had been no great wrench for her to leave London.

We had met people who'd endured months and even years of traipsing back and forth to their GP with worrying symptoms before even being referred for an initial scan. Whereas for Laura, the space between the headaches and the diagnosis was just a matter of weeks.

Maybe lucky wasn't exactly the right word, but it could certainly have been worse.

And now we found ourselves in a global pandemic.

Well, who could have anticipated that?

We were definitely lucky that Laura wasn't having her radiotherapy and chemo during the Covid months, lucky that I could be with her at every appointment and lucky that her treatment wasn't delayed as a result of the monstrous challenges facing the NHS.

We were also incredibly fortunate to have been able to travel and do so many exciting things that would simply have been impossible during the pandemic – casually jumping on planes, attending concerts and visiting factories without a second thought.

As it was, during lockdown we had time with Laura that she would ordinarily have spent living in Manchester. Gracie no longer had exams to revise for, and the sun was shining. In our small corner, where we had lost no one we loved, Covid gave us space and time to be together. We had no work to do, nowhere else we needed to be, no deadlines and no social obligations.

Instead we created a vegetable garden out of an unloved terrace and watched it flourish with giant courgettes, feeble cauliflowers and long-legged spinach. We sorted out drawers, cupboards, wardrobes and bedrooms and revelled in the short-lived serenity of organisation. We clapped, we baked, we read books in the sun, held family quizzes over Zoom and played Sock Sumo and Mario Kart. We walked the fields and the lanes of the village, spotting herons and kingfishers while Ziggy splashed furiously in the water, telling each other on a daily basis how very lucky we were to live just there, with countryside all around us. Sometimes we'd walk at midnight to look at the stars or watch lightning flash across the sky, running back home when the rain came.

The only cloud on the horizon, other than the spot on the scan and the pandemic itself, was how on earth we were going to get Laura out to Germany for the first of her two vital dendritic cell vaccinations. Flights and ferries had been cancelled worldwide, and with borders closed, we were going to need to get creative.

In desperation, I made enquiries as to how much it would cost to charter a small plane to Cologne, in the optimistic hope that it might be less expensive than I feared. It wasn't. I tried not to yell 'How much?' and instead just made a gasping noise, then told them there was someone at the door.

We really did need a plan, so I posted a plea on social media to see if anyone had a suggestion. The wonderful people of Twitter came up with all kinds of ideas, including military planes into Stuttgart and cross-border routes via France and Belgium. They offered rooms for stopovers if we chose to drive and found options from London and into Hamburg. But Laura found the standard journey to Cologne a stretch even on a good day, and we were loath to add extra days of travelling.

I also began negotiations with the British Consulate in Dusseldorf: even if we did get across to Germany, we needed to make sure we'd be allowed to enter the country. There were a great number of forms to complete, and letters of authority would be required from the clinic to explain why Laura needed the treatment so urgently and why she couldn't have it in the UK.

Then my friend Steph called. 'I think I might have actually solved your problem, and you're not going to believe this!'

She'd shared my tweet and it had spread its wings and fluttered around until it landed on the laptop of a lovely man called Jonathan. He worked for a private bank which had a fleet of jets currently idling on a runway, so he offered us a plane and a couple of pilots to take us to Cologne and back.

It was the most amazingly generous offer, and I must have thanked him a hundred times during the conversation we had later that night. Might even have cried a bit too.

The next day I had a call from Jonathan's PA, who asked, 'Which airport would you like to fly from?'

Imagine the luxury of being able to choose!

We had a tentative agreement with the consulate; they had cleared our entry with the Federal Police, but the final decision would lie with Border Force when we arrived in Cologne.

Days later we arrived at Blackpool airport and stood with our bags on the runway. It was almost like we were hailing a taxi: right on schedule, a beautiful silver and blue plane arrived to collect us. No queuing, no security, no waiting around – our bags were popped in the hold and off we flew.

We'd decided it would be a good idea for Gracie to come too, in case one of us did get sick or ended up in hospital with Covid; but if I'm truly honest, I just didn't want her to miss out on the opportunity to fly in a private jet.

We fastened our seatbelts across huge white leather seats that could be turned to face the centre aisle (ideal for when you're negotiating an in-flight trade deal or peace agreement), and slid away the table for take-off. The pilots had provided us with sandwiches, drinks and snacks and we felt like A-list film stars munching our Jammie Dodgers and M&Ms.

I would have been more than happy just to stay in the air for the whole day, but little more than an hour later we touched down in Cologne.

The German lockdown was slightly less strict than the one we were experiencing in the UK: small shops were open, but restaurants and cafés only offered food to take out. Roughly half the people were wearing masks but there was plenty of outdoor socialising.

We watched all the Harry Potter films (again), ate a large number of halloumi wraps and the girls enjoyed a round or two of chopping-board tennis. Gracie hired a scooter in the Volksgarten, and we took turns speeding up and down the closed road. They played on the swings, and we ate ice cream nearly every day.

Sometimes it felt like they were just eight and ten and the last decade had never happened.

When did I stop crying every single day? I can't remember the actual date: maybe I cried all day to start with, then weaned myself down to the luxury of just once a day. In the beginning we were like swimmers, fighting against the waves and the tides, regularly going under, and choking on mouthfuls of salt water, unable to see the horizon or even know which way up we were. This time felt like a temporary lull, the winds had dropped and we could lie on the surface, floating and letting the water carry us rather than having to fight against every wave.

It was eighteen months since the surgeon had given his grim prognosis and, although it was only an estimate Laura was very conscious of the date. It was almost like an extra birthday. Anything beyond this was a bonus.

The glorious lockdown summer continued. We did have the anxiety of a closed business and no real income, but there wasn't a great deal to spend money on anyway, and at least we were together.

Laura continued to complete assignments and worked on our family tree (no aristocratic lineage but one or two convicts). Gracie cut Mark's hair with clippers and we left our handprints in primary coloured paint on the bottom shelf of the newly cleared out cupboard, for another family to find one day and wonder who we were.

A greenhouse arrived. We'd ordered it months ago, when the whole country took up gardening and seeds became black-market currency. Laura laid out all the components on the grass, thoroughly checking every item off the list to ensure it was complete before methodically assembling it, with only the tiniest assistance from Mark. She was never happier than when she had a project and a booklet of instructions in thirteen languages.

We sat round the fire pit till late at night and watched the International Space Station pass overhead while Ziggy tried his best to chase the bats that would tease him by flying low, before swooping skyward.

Laura had her final vaccine scheduled for May in Cologne, but before we began worrying about how to get there, Jonathan called and offered to take care of it again. How privileged we were to experience this once-in-a-lifetime opportunity twice.

As the German restrictions became tighter, I was no longer allowed in the treatment room with Laura, so I read my book until she was finished. So many different languages were spoken in the airy waiting room, but each family shared the same desperate need for a miracle.

We were incredibly lucky: without the kindness of friends, family and strangers we could never have afforded this treatment, and if Laura had been diagnosed during Covid, raising the funds would have been almost impossible – no concerts, no races, no events, and countless worthy causes competing for funds. We had so much to be grateful for, and most of all, the fact that Laura was currently well.

The idea that she might die soon filled me with dread, but it wasn't what scared me most. The thing that terrified me was the likelihood that I would watch this brilliant, brave, intelligent girl disappear before my eyes. That she would be taken away from me slowly, and in agonising stages. That she would be pumped up with steroids, which would swallow her face until it was only her eyes that I recognised. I was afraid that Laura, the smartest person I knew, would start to experience cognitive decline, lose her memory, fill with rage and confusion and not know who we were or how much we loved her. I was scared she'd lose her mobility and be restricted to a wheelchair, that this proud, independent girl would eventually have to rely on us for all her personal care.

I wasn't sure I would be able to bear it. What if I wasn't mentally strong enough?

The eminent brain surgeon Henry Marsh wrote in his brutally honest memoir *Do No Harm*: 'Death is not always a bad outcome, you know; a quick death can be better than a slow one.' This man, who spent so much of his working life operating on brains, wrote that if he had a malignant brain tumour: 'I hope that I would commit suicide, but you never know for certain what you will decide until it happens.'

I knew it was weak to let these thoughts into my head, especially when Laura was doing so well. I needed to be more like Mark and focus on living in the moment.

These were the months of courgettini for tea, jigsaws and long summer evenings spent watering the garden.

Laura grappled with Descartes and even sat some exams from home, sticking a note on her door with Blu-Tack so we didn't interrupt her. Studying wasn't easy when the sun was shining and we were all home, only too happy to provide a distraction.

Once, sitting at the kitchen table eating lunch – which almost certainly included Pringles and a carrot – Laura looked up from her phone and said to me: 'I'm so glad I'm still here.'

It just made my heart burst. We knew nothing was promised now – there was another scan looming on the horizon, a dark cloud in an otherwise bright blue sky. When anyone asked how she was, we'd say, 'She's doing great, thanks …' – before lurching dramatically to lay our hands on the closest approximation of wood or laminate we could find – '… touch wood!'

Most of the time Laura was really well, taking herself out for short runs and walking the dog; she was less tired too, and definitely not as sick.

Until suddenly she wasn't.

Just before the scan Laura had a crushing headache. She also became horribly sensitive to light and stayed in her darkened bedroom all day, wearing sunglasses to go to the bathroom because the daylight hurt her head so much. Before the diagnosis we would have called it a migraine, but now every headache was a portent of doom.

Gracie looked at me with those eyes, begging for reassurance that everything would be OK, and it made me think of my mum.

When my sister Laura died, I'd just turned five and Neil was sixteen months. I wondered if I had bombarded my parents with questions like:

'Where has Laura gone?'
'Why can't she come back?'
'Did we do something wrong?'
'Am I going to die too?'
'Are you going to die?'

Maybe I didn't, though; maybe I thought it safest not to ask.

I wish I knew what had gone on in that five-year-old head, but I can't reach that girl. I have no idea where she went or what happened to her.

A few years later she brought home a bunch of wildflowers, drooping bluebells and sticky cow parsley. 'I brought you these, Mum.'

'Oh … that white one's called Mother Die. We don't want that in the house.'

I remembered how my insides clenched into a tight fist. I had given my mum a posy of flowers that could kill her – what kind of monster was I?

If my sister had died in this century, my parents would have been given counselling rather than tranquillisers, a doctor would have explained why she'd died in ways they could understand, and if it made no sense, they could have searched for the words on the internet.

Someone would have given me a picture book that told me it was OK to feel sad and maybe I would have had some counselling too, or at least someone to keep an eye on me at primary school when I was lost and scared.

Maybe if we'd talked about her, I would have been able to handle the long-term effects better, rather than allowing the knot of anxiety in my childish tummy to calcify into a big hard ball of teenage guilt. The human brain doesn't like gaps in a story, so without being told why it happened, I assumed that it must have been my fault, and everybody would have been happier if it had been me that died rather than my sister. All that culminated in a pathetic attempt at a paracetamol overdose, a short hospital stay and some talking therapy, only eleven years too late.

So, when I saw Gracie having those same feelings and I could see how badly she was being affected, I felt horribly guilty. I had no excuse. My mum was only twenty-six and she'd had to balance her grief with the demands of a precocious five-year-old and a baby. Sometimes I think the only way she survived was by cracking on and hoping that the ship righted itself eventually, without too many souls lost overboard. She didn't have the luxury of wallowing in grief, sleeping for days or even talking about it. Maybe that's Northerners, or maybe it was just the 1970s. I should have been doing better – not only was I fifty but I had experienced it from her side too.

When the results came back, the scan remained stable. We celebrated with cheese pie, Heinz beans and *The Usual Suspects*.

Having a Moment

July–August

Once Laura had set her mind on something, she was difficult to dissuade.

On a family holiday to Wales in her early teens, Mark had bet £5 that she wouldn't jump in the river and swim under a waterfall. Naturally, she did it – there was money involved, after all. I'll never forget her trying to pull skinny jeans up over wet legs, blue with cold. Gracie did it too, but without the cash incentive; partly due to her fear of missing out and partly because wherever Laura went, Gracie was always close behind.

Laura, having watched Mark do a tandem jump the year before, was determined to throw herself out of a plane. Obviously she needed written permission from her consultant and had to wait until it was safe for the parachute centre to operate, under new Covid rules, but on the first day they reopened for business both Laura and Gracie were booked in to jump.

They bubbled with excitement, and I tried really hard to be cool about it. People jumped out of planes strapped to complete strangers every day, what could possibly go wrong?

They were last to jump from the plane and we strained our eyes to work out which splash of brightly coloured parachute was which as they floated from 15,000 feet, and through a cloud of spiky rain, before bumping back down to earth. Gracie had been convinced she was flying over France, confusing Blackpool with the Eiffel Tower, and was especially delighted at how tiny the cows had looked from up above.

It wasn't one of the original bucket list items, but it was something Laura had always wanted to do. We all believed the list should never be completed, only added to, and as she would say in an interview later that year, 'It's not done till I'm done.'

A day spent with the girls was never wasted. On days when Laura was sad, we'd choose uplifting films to cheer her up, and when she was happy, we'd walk in the fields and inhale the green of the meadows behind the houses.

We took a trip to see Antony Gormley's haunting sculptures on Crosby Beach and, after a picnic, ran around with the dog, chasing the waves until they chased us back. Then to Formby, where we ate ice cream and looked for red squirrels before yomping through the sand dunes.

Formby has a huge, flat expanse of sand, with the biggest sky I think I'd ever seen. The sun was setting into the sea, and it felt like we'd stepped into a watercolour painting. Zig raced up and down chasing seagulls and the girls and I traced the patterns made by waves and looked for shells – until we noticed we'd actually been cut off by the tide and Gracie had to give first Laura and then me a piggy-back to dry land. We couldn't stop laughing at how ridiculous we must have looked.

Laura told us we were having a *moment*. On the Brain Tumour Charity young ambassadors' course, they'd talked about how life is made up of moments, and she wanted us all to remember this one.

'Looking back,' she said, 'we had the best childhood, playing out all day with the kids next door and having adventures. I wouldn't change a single thing about it.'

'Remember that time when the four of you got up really early and went out for a long walk with breakfast in your little backpacks? No sign of you when we got up, no note or anything.'

'Oh, yeah, and when we got back you pretended to be on the phone to the police, reporting us as missing.'

'I had a pretty good idea where you were but the look of horror on your faces …! It was probably a bit mean.'

'Always left a note after that, though, didn't we?' She laughed.

With wind-burned cheeks, hair made huge by the salty air and one exhausted, sandy dog, we stopped in a pub for tea on the way home.

If that is not your idea of a perfect day, then you have no business here.

I vacuumed the car. It wasn't something I did very often. Now, though, long strands of golden hair previously glued to the seats or attached like Velcro to the floor mats worked themselves loose and disappeared into the vortex of the Hoover. My heart felt sore and sad: I missed my little girls.

One drove her own car now and the other had new hair: darker and wiry, not like these long blonde threads. In her dreams, however, Laura still had long hair. She would wake up happy that it was back and then have to remember it wasn't.

I missed the frantic drive to school: each new term would start with good intentions, but the girls would take it in turns to get progressively later, which meant the car journey had to get faster and faster in order to still meet the school bus. I missed them fighting over who would sit in the front seat and thereby control the radio. I missed us singing and playing music really loudly with the windows down like gangsters.

Sometimes Gracie took Laura out for a drive or to wave at grandparents from the garden, and I would be momentarily paralysed by the thought that they could be in a car crash, hurt or even killed. If I heard a siren when they were out, I imagined a car rolled on its roof or a head-on collision. I'd lost confidence in the safety of the world, I knew now that anything could happen.

I didn't want to become a helicopter parent or wrap the girls up in cotton wool – or maybe I did. When they were younger and I hadn't seen horror quite so close up, they'd had all the freedom they could want, but once you've met the big bad wolf on a dark night you never really feel safe again.

Despite not actually sitting any exams due to the pandemic, Gracie passed her A Levels and, after that notorious logarithm had been moderated, she was awarded an A, B and C. She'd missed months of school when Laura was first diagnosed and had worked really hard to catch up, so her grades were well deserved, and we were all immensely proud of her.

A trip to Cyprus was going to be Laura's 'Well done, Gracie!' present, and although I had filed it under 'Might never happen' for the sake of my sanity – the trip for the pair of them was definitely on, subject to negative Covid tests on arrival.

Gracie, with memories of Portugal still fresh, was adamant they should take Laura's cannabis along, but I worried that without a middle-aged mum to serve as decoy, they were more likely to be stopped by the police.

Ten days of sunshine and halloumi was just what the girls needed. They sat in the sun, snorkelled and read books. Gracie sent me a video of Laura launching herself off a cliff and into the sea, to which I replied, 'Cliff jumping … seriously, Gracie!?!'

They returned home just as the travel corridor to Cyprus closed, narrowly avoiding two weeks of quarantine. It was good to have them back – with only a few weeks before they would both be leaving for university I wanted to spend as much time as I could with them.

We were still finding interesting new vehicles for Laura to drive, so when I'd suggested monster trucks, she had laughed and said, 'Hell, yeah!'

She loved every moment, reliving her safari days in an off-road Land Rover through rough, muddy woodland, then in a series of trucks like reverse Russian dolls, each one bigger and more ridiculous than the one before it. Eventually, she needed a ladder just to climb into the cab. But nothing fazed her – she'd just clamber in, pull the seat forward so she could reach the pedals and then she was away, driving up ramps and down steep hills, squashing cars beneath gigantic wheels and slaloming between tiny plastic cones.

The car park was fringed by majestic oak trees and the ground was littered with fat, juicy acorns. I packed my pockets with them and when they were full, I filled a carrier bag I'd found in the car. I would grow them into saplings, I decided, and give them to people at Laura's funeral.

Even in life I am in death.

We arrived home to a letter for Laura with the salutation, 'Dead Laura'. It was just an obvious typo, of course and we did laugh about it, but was there ever such a difference between an 'r' and a 'd'? Good job we weren't sensitive types.

The Life Is Good?

September–October

I collected Laura's tablets from Boots.

'Does she pay for her prescriptions?'

'No.'

'What's the exemption?'

'She has cancer.'

The pharmacist looked at Laura's date of birth on the script and did a double take. Even after twenty-two months it still felt surreal that this was actually our life.

Sorting tablets was a serious responsibility. Laura took roughly thirty each day, some three times every day, most daily or on alternate days. I prepped four of the weekly boxes at a time: twenty-eight days of tablets, each brightly coloured daily box divided into quarters. After consulting the big wipe-clean board, I would pop capsules from plastic packs – a cackle of silver foil as they were released from the pod – and tip tiny white tablets into the palm of my hand. Some were round, or lozenge-shaped, and shiny, chalky, peach or bright blue. Some were dusty and bitter, and others redolent with the golden smell of turmeric. I would be left with a mountain of discarded packaging, like the empty egg sacs of some strange sea creature or the silvered exoskeleton of an alien insect.

On scan days Laura was always subdued, dressing in the anonymous clothes of her sick self: sweatpants with drawstring waist and the metal eyelets cut off, soft sweatshirt and Ugg boots. She would take off her jewellery, remove the earrings and the piercing she did herself. She became a blank. Ready to be looked through and cut into readable slices of black, white and grey matter. Everything my daughter was, distilled down into a series of flat monochromatic images. Each scan would determine our next move: advance one space, or down the snake all the way back to where you started from.

On scan days we tried to remember what we wore last time it was stable. Gracie searched for her lucky knickers, we wore our clothes accessorised with superstition. Nobody talked in the car, all lost down the rabbit hole of our darkest fears.

A phone call wasn't quite as reassuring as a sit-down meeting with the oncologist, but once again the scan remained stable and we were grateful for the reassurance in his call.

It was the relief of knowing that you hadn't drawn the short straw – but with the understanding it would soon be your turn to pick again.

Laura was also showing a strong immune response to the vaccines. We didn't really understand the finer details of this, but it was enough that Professor VG seemed delighted. German clinics like this one were strictly regulated and only permitted to operate on a 'not for profit' basis. That's not to say the treatment wasn't hugely expensive, but the levels of complexity, especially in terms of analysis, were what we paid for, and the state-of-the-art, in-house laboratory that operated from the floor below.

Laura was definitely one of the professor's star pupils and he was fully invested in her survival. He just wanted to see her happy and thriving.

In our regular monthly meeting, he would ask cheerily, 'The life is good?' and, 'How is everything with the family Noottall?'

We'd grown quite fond of him over the past year. His office was a chaotic jumble of conference lanyards, papers, and scribbled diagrams, but he really knew his patients. He had one of those intrinsically happy, round faces and managed to maintain a level of jollity which couldn't always be easy in his line of work.

At the end of the month, both girls packed up their suitcases and plastic crates of books (Laura) and makeup (Gracie) ready for university.

Gracie left for Salford first, Mark's car so ridiculously full it was borderline unsafe. I had a rolled-up duvet balanced on my head but couldn't move as my lap was full of pot plants. She was really anxious, terrified that her flatmates wouldn't like her, or she wouldn't like them or that she'd just be horribly homesick. By the time we arrived, I was almost as nervous as she was, but we needn't have worried; her flatmates were lovely, and they all instantly became the best of friends. Within eight days of their arrival, however, two of the girls tested positive for Covid and so the flat was placed in immediate lockdown, with nobody allowed in and nobody out. Fortunately, neither had severe symptoms and the virus wasn't passed on, so the six flatmates just spent their time eating, drinking, playing games, and watching films. Gracie organised a Tesco delivery but forgot to change the address, so it all arrived at home, confirming my suspicions that they were living off vodka, diet lemonade and Super Noodles. By the time they were released back into the wild, they'd formed a strong bond and decided they'd like to live together again next year. Gracie had found her new tribe.

She had decided not to tell them about Laura straight away, and it was good for her to move out from the long shadow of her sister's diagnosis; she could be herself again, away from the well-meaning but awkward sympathy of friends who had no idea how to treat the sister of a girl with terminal cancer.

Laura left the following week. She packed less than Gracie, but the car was still full. She'd decided it was easier to live in halls again and returned to the same room in the same hall, with the same next-door neighbour that she'd had the year before.

As restrictions relaxed, Giddy Kippers could finally reopen. Nothing was especially normal; capacity was strictly limited, and we had to introduce lots of new systems, but it was lovely to see our customers returning, even if the entire country was back in lockdown within the month.

The Covid pandemic changed the world dramatically. The fear and uncertainty we had experienced in the last two years was now woven into the fabric of everyone else's life. We'd just got there early.

The novelist Susie Steiner, who also had GBM, reflected on this in a piece she wrote for the *Guardian*: 'It has been easier, weirdly, to cope with my illness during lockdown, because I'm not the only one whose life is on hold.'

In some ways I'm glad we did get there early; as Laura continually told me, we had been incredibly lucky.

At the back of my mind, I had a nagging worry that if Laura become seriously ill with Covid and resources were in short supply, another patient may well be given priority over her. I understood that ethical and economic decisions had to be made every day, especially with a limited number of ventilators, but if medics were aware of her prognosis, they might focus on someone expected to live at least another twenty or thirty years. It was completely logical, but we never wanted to find ourselves arguing for her life: we needed her to get vaccinated as soon as possible.

Glioblastoma rarely made the news but that month it was announced that The Wanted's singer Tom Parker had received the same diagnosis as Laura. He was thirty-two, with a toddler and another baby on the way. My heart went out to him and his fiancée – I recognised those blank and bewildered expressions in the photographs they released to the media.

In light of Tom's diagnosis, The Brain Tumour Charity asked if Laura would talk to Radio 1's *Newsbeat* about what it was like to be diagnosed with GBM. As a young ambassador she felt a responsibility to share the work of the charity and was also keen to highlight the symptoms people should look out for. My favourite comment in the interview was, 'They might know what I have, but they don't know who I am'.

On the anniversary of her diagnosis, Laura wrote a post on Facebook.

'On this day two years ago, my life went from worrying about essay deadlines to worrying if I'd still be alive for Christmas. The diagnosis of brain tumours made me consider the life that I'd had up until that point and I realised how lucky I'd been and how much I'd taken for granted. My sister and all the time we've shared doing stupid things that no one else would understand. My mum who would climb mountains and wrestle bears to make me safe and happy. My dad who was always there to give me advice and his coat when I was cold. My family, always by my side no matter what. My friends, always there to hear my mundane problems and make me laugh. All the things I'd done over the years and all the people I'd met along the way. It was then that I decided that I was not going to let this diagnosis get the better of me. I had an army behind me, these tumours didn't stand a chance.'

Gracie (3, *right*) dreaming about joining Laura at school, and Laura (5) devising dramatic storylines for her sister's dolls.

I love this photo, taken on a beautiful summer day at a family celebration in Norfolk, 2010.

Porthleven, Cornwall. Tanned, happy and obsessed with crabbing. Gracie would have been 9 and Laura 11.

Celebrating the end of 2010 with the best of friends. *Left to right:* me, Laura, Leo, Iona and Lorraine.

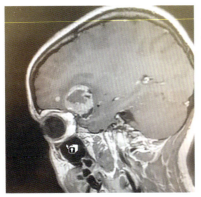

The first scan, taken on 24 October 2018 – life would never be the same again. The largest tumour can be seen just behind Laura's eye socket.

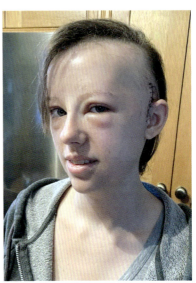

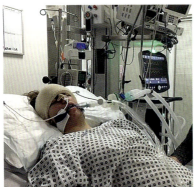

ICU, 7 November 2018. Laura was kept in an induced coma post-surgery, and we had no idea how she would be when she woke up.

The swelling, bruising and stitches from surgery number two, April 2021.

Waiting to go down for brain surgery number three at Salford Royal and rocking the green compression stockings, 22 December 2021.

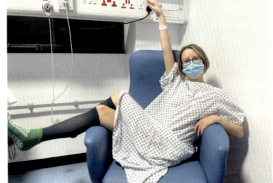

On board HMS *Charger*, with Laura captaining the ship down the Mersey, January 2019.

Showing off her skills as a marksman with the Greater Manchester Police firearms unit, March 2019.

Looking effortlessly cool as she played bass with The Switch at Blackstock Music Festival, June 2019.

Travelling at 158 mph on the back of 'Rocket' Ron Haslam's bike. Donington Park, August 2019.

Laura with Kate McKinnon at the London premiere of *Yesterday*, June 2019.

The T-shirt that said so much more than words. Manchester Pride, August 2019.

London Marathon, October 2021. The names of those lost to a brain tumour on blue ribbon, and those still fighting on red – we've lost half of those now. Note the classy flip-flop/plaster combo.

Laura and Gracie as beautiful bridesmaids for Georgina and Neil, just nine days after Laura's third brain surgery, 31 December 2021.

A fabulous day spent fishing on the River Eden with Paul Whitehouse and Bob Mortimer, August 2019.

ABOVE: How incredibly lucky were we to be able to fly in a private jet to Cologne? Ryanair has never felt the same since! May 2020.

LEFT: The new family joining *Hollyoaks*? August 2021.

LEFT: Beautiful Laura glowing with happiness in front of a giant 007 at the *No Time to Die* premiere at the Royal Albert Hall, September 2021.

ABOVE: Wonderful, ordinary things. Throwing pots in Heskin a week before Laura's fourth brain surgery, October 2022.

A day never to be forgotten: watching the Lionesses win the Women's Euros, Wembley Stadium, 31 July 2022.

A bird's eye view of Oldham, thanks to White Watch, Greater Manchester Fire and Rescue Service, December 2022.

A fabulous night at Peter Kay's *Dance for Life* show, Manchester Central, April 2022 (and no trapdoor required). *Left to right:* Dad, Peter, Mum, Georgina, Mark, Vicky, Laura, me, Gracie and Neil.

The fake Christmas balloon arch, 13 November 2022! *Front to back:* Mark, me, Gracie, Alice, Mum, Beryl, Laura, Neil, Alfred, Dad and Georgina.

Christmas 2022 in Manchester, smiling as if our lives depended on it.

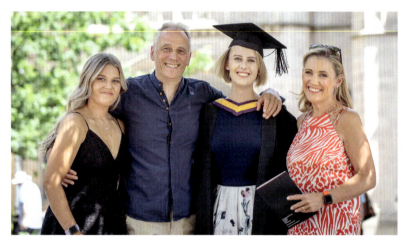

ABOVE: Just look at those smiles – I don't think we could have been happier or more proud that day. Laura's graduation from the University of Manchester with a 2:1 in Politics, Philosophy and Economics, July 2022.

ABOVE: Spoiling Alice something rotten on a trip to Gulliver's World, August 2022.

LEFT: Mark and Gracie modelling the T-shirts she designed to raise funds for Laura's foundation #BeMoreLaura, June 2023.

The Queue

November

Since they were both tiny, one daughter has always rushed into the other's room on the first of the month to administer a sharp punch on the arm of their sleeping sister.

'Pinch, punch, first of the month!'

The loser might have been caught unaware by the flip of the calendar but would resolve to get even next month. On days when they weren't in the same house, the physical punch was replaced by a text, but the score was still kept and one of the girls would declare themselves the winner at the end of the year.

'Mum, it's just hit me that one day soon, I'll go to message Laura on the first and there'll be nobody on the other end to reply.'

It was small things like these that crushed my heart.

Laura was often mildly irritated by her noisy sister – standard stuff for little girls born less than two years apart. Gracie wanted nothing more than for her big sister to play with her and, ever the opportunist, Laura started charging 20p an hour until we found out and put a stop to it.

There was, of course, so much love between the girls. Once, Laura had been left in charge for an hour, both girls strictly forbidden from going outside until we returned home. Gracie, always the rebel, had gone next door to see William, fallen over and ripped her trousers. She flew home in a tearful panic and Laura calmly ran her a bath, cleaned and dressed her grazed knee and hid the ripped trousers deep in the bin so we'd be none the wiser.

Laura's love wasn't found in showy demonstrative gestures – it was the gentle, practical kind that knew exactly what was needed.

* * *

November was a tough month.

We had grown a small online community of parents and partners caring for a loved one with a brain tumour. When Laura was first diagnosed, I looked for people who might share some knowledge, hope, or even just kindness with me. Like a lifeboat to a drowning man, I was hooked out of the water and joined the wretched souls already shivering in the boat. These days I was helping others out of the sea and handing out the metaphorical blankets.

In November, we lost a husband, and three precious children – the youngest just fourteen and the oldest twenty-four. These were families we'd got to know and tried so desperately to help, sharing everything we'd learned in the hope that we could save them some time. It felt like I had failed: they had died regardless. We lost Charlie, who we'd met with his mum in Cologne, Grace, Daniel, and Tom. It was just heartbreaking – all those lost decades of life and those poor, broken families.

Laura told me that when someone else died it felt like she moved closer to the front of the queue, that she could feel the sand running down in her hourglass. I felt that way too, but I wasn't going to admit it to her. She shared an image from Facebook of a long queue of people in a woodland scene; they were moving forward slowly and the ones at the very front were disappearing skyward, happily going off to heaven, I suppose.

Losing a child is horrific and there are no words of consolation or comfort that can possibly help. I messaged Grace's mum to tell her how heartbroken I was at the awful news, and she replied, 'We are lost without her. She was and still is my world. What do I do now? I try every day to just be, but it's so hard.'

We all shared the pain. It was agonising to see a family just like ours, suffering the worst horror imaginable, knowing that at some point, that family would be us, unless a new miracle treatment suddenly became available.

The speed with which scientists and researchers had developed a range of Covid vaccines only served to illustrate what could be achieved with money and motivation. Within ten months, people were lining up to receive a Covid jab; yet it takes an average of fourteen *years* for a patented cancer drug to be approved by NICE.* We really could move mountains if we tried.

One night we watched an item on the national news about poverty in east Lancashire. It began with the shocking fact that 18,000 children in Burnley and Pendle alone were living in poverty – the pictures looked like something from the Great Depression.

Laura was horrified to see the level of deprivation just down the road. 'Right, what are we going to do to help?' she demanded.

Soon we were part of the Curry on the Street team, helping to set up outside an empty Farm Foods shop. Trestle tables were laid out with huge vats of curry and rice, ready to be spooned into individual trays, alongside a pop-up food bank of basic groceries and donated clothing. Volunteers wore high-vis tabards and made sure that the queue of customers left with everything they needed.

Laura became a fixture, sorting the jumble of clothes and filling carrier bags with loaves of bread in waxed paper, bags of biscuits and sachets of instant rice.

I wished there was a way to download all of my memories onto a hard drive somewhere. I was so scared that I would forget some of the things most precious to me. The smiles, the laughter, the sound of her voice, the ordinary and the banal. I wished there was a way to remember everything.

I still do.

---

* https://www.icr.ac.uk/news-archive/new-cancer-drugs-taking-longer-to-reach-nhs-patients

As Good As It Gets?

December

It was comforting to wake up knowing everyone was safely home. I wondered if all parents had a similar internal version of Mrs Weasley's clock, with hands that pointed to the whereabouts of each family member. It was my first, semi-conscious thought every morning. In a pandemic, it was especially reassuring to know exactly where, and how everyone was: I bought a pulse oximeter so I could double-check.

In the quiet days of the second Covid lockdown, we were content to be insulated from the outside world, secure and safe in our family bubble. Like everyone else we experimented with sourdough (sometimes delicious, often inedible), walked whenever we could, and Laura and I tried to maintain a daily online yoga practice.

Unlike her double-jointed sister, Laura had never been very flexible, but before steroids and sickness she'd been strong, even competing in taekwondo events to qualify for her black belt.

I'd found the experience a bit traumatic: she looked so small in the red headguard and gum shield, bouncing on her toes in a cavernous sports hall while her opponent's mother screamed, 'Kick her in the head!'

Lockdown hadn't reduced the messages I received every day via Facebook and Twitter. Almost without exception they began: 'I hope you don't mind me contacting you, but my friend/partner/child has just been diagnosed with glioblastoma and I wondered if you could give us some advice?'

I was cutting and pasting pages of tips and links so often that a website became the only practical solution. With Gracie's technical support we created doingitforlaura.com and filled the online pages with helpful information. We also created an online support group on Facebook called Strength in Numbers, and each time someone contacted me, I would offer to add them to our little community, more than happy to share everything we'd learned in the hope that it could save another bewildered family some precious time. Each story was horribly familiar and utterly heartbreaking. We were rank amateurs, fumbling around as best we could, but there was so little information out there, we were regarded as experts.

I was also providing advice on negotiating entry to Germany; by now, we were on first-name terms with our consular officer, and her familiarity with our story definitely made the process a little easier.

Laura made it to twenty-one, a cause for celebration, had we been allowed. Obviously, it wasn't enough, it never could be – but it was more time than she had originally been given. She was currently well, and I was touching wood, naturally.

Covid made so many things impossible, but nothing said Christmas like a drive-in carol service in the underground car park of a Morrisons supermarket. Even for heathens like me, there was always something spine-tingling about singing carols.

I missed seeing the girls in their school nativity plays: Gracie dressed in a homemade donkey costume, the one that I forgot to cut holes in for her arms; and Laura, always the narrator because she was a good reader, dressed in robes of scratchy red curtain material, with a tie-back doubling as a belt. Not content to read from the script, she made a point of learning every word, her small voice filling the chapel, my heart bursting with love for them both.

I knew most people were going to be delighted to see the end of 2020 but, I couldn't help wonder, *What if this year is actually as good as it gets for us?*

Laura still had a terminal diagnosis. But wasn't being human a terminal condition in itself? I knew that there were dark times to come, but right then we were choosing hope, choosing happiness, and choosing love.

2021

The Cost of The New Normal

January–February

Travelling to Germany was still fraught with anxiety. In January we arrived at the airport with a plastic folder packed with documents to prove to the Ryanair check-in staff that we were permitted to travel: letters from the clinic, emails from the consulate, Covid test certificates and the passenger registration documents required by the German federal government.

We watched nervously from our place in the queue as passengers presented their documents to the check-in staff, wincing for those whose papers were met with a non-negotiable shake of the head. All documents were scrutinised a second time at the gate and a young mother, holding the hands of two toddlers, was refused boarding because her tiny children didn't have Covid tests. It was unbearable to see her sobbing and pleading to be allowed on the flight, her last opportunity to get home before borders were sealed again. It was like living in a war zone and we both felt inexplicably and horribly guilty as we climbed the steps into the plane.

By February, commercial flights were cancelled entirely, but ferries were still carrying essential freight across to Europe. Mark made plans to drive via Hull, overnight on the ship to Rotterdam, then travel through Holland across the border into Germany.

They set off on a snowy Saturday afternoon, and with the house empty I laced up my boots and hiked up Pendle Hill with Ziggy to watch the sun set. I was pulling out a torch to light up the path down as my phone lit up with Mark's name.

'How's it going? Are you on the ferry now?'

'Nope, we're on our way back.'

'Please tell me you didn't miss it—?'

'We were there in loads of time; they just wouldn't let us on the bloody ship. Apparently, Holland won't accept an NHS test, so we have to get a private one done and have the results for tomorrow, if we want to catch the Sunday afternoon crossing.'

I spent the evening searching for a testing centre that was reasonably local *and* open on a Sunday *and* could get the results back within six hours. Twitter friends suggested a clinic in Liverpool, and they were kind enough not to charge us. The additional costs of providing Covid tests was becoming the most expensive part of travelling: with pre-departure testing, daily tests at the clinic and day two and eight tests on return to the UK, it was as much as £1,600, but we knew we were lucky just to be allowed to travel. The test results came through just as Mark and Laura arrived back at the terminal in Hull and, this time, they were allowed onboard. Laura said it was like a ghost ship, the vast parking deck empty but for a handful of lonely trucks.

While Covid caused our costs to increase, lockdown also made fundraising more difficult. Laura's cousin Lanna helped by challenging herself to walk 32 miles every day for five days: a mile for each person diagnosed with a brain tumour in a single day. She would start in the gloomy early morning and it would be dark again by the time she finished. Sometimes she walked alone, or with her dad John, mum Jo or sister Jenny. Gracie kept her company twice, and on the last day I walked too, with Laura,

Mark and the rest of the family joining us for the last thirteen miles. Poor Lanna's feet were painfully blistered and she was exhausted by the end of the week, but our girls shared their stubborn determination as well as a surname.

Laura ploughed through assignments on ethics and jurisprudence, but it took her an age to finish an essay. Every meal, even a bowl of porridge, lasted at least an hour, longer still with a handful of tablets to swallow, one by one. Sometimes she would still be eating lunch when I began preparing dinner. Usually she was watching *The Office* or *Saturday Night Live* on her phone at the same time, stretching out each mouthful to delay the inevitable return to her desk.

Mark would pass through the kitchen and ask, 'Laura, how on earth are you STILL eating?!'

She was a procrastinator and could be easily distracted by an interesting fact, which would send her down an internet rabbit hole. Or she'd be compelled to rearrange her sock drawer *again*. In her defence, we didn't always get the cannabis dose quite right and being high was not conducive to academic work. Sometimes we'd find her absorbed by patterns in the table mats and fascinated by the letters she could see in the laminate kitchen flooring, or emptying out a packet of Pom-Bears to compare the arm position of each teddy-shaped crisp. Another time she announced, 'My mouth tastes like Ikea.'

Laura was desperate to get her driving licence (and her independence) back and petitioned the GP to write the necessary supporting letters. The cannabis would soon have to be a thing of the past, but it would be a fair exchange. Things felt like they were returning to a level of normality, albeit in a brave new Covid world.

Freefall

March–April

We took Laura for an early morning scan. She was high and hungry afterwards, so we stopped at the M&S café for pain au chocolat, ginger beer and prawn cocktail crisps – the breakfast of champions.

When we got home, she went for a sleep. Gracie called me in a panic from Salford, frantic because she'd forgotten to wear her lucky knickers and thought she might even have left them at home. I could hear her, rummaging through drawers with the phone wedged between ear and shoulder, then a sigh of relief as she found them and changed immediately.

By the afternoon Laura was taking part in a Zoom meeting organised by The Brain Tumour Charity. It was a session with some of their important donors and Laura was helping to explain the impact their generosity had on young people like her. I was on hand to help in case she needed a prompt or to be reminded of a word. I didn't want to distract her with eye contact, so I was playing solitaire on my phone when Mark slipped into the room.

'Dr C just called. Wants to see us tomorrow,' he whispered.

My heart plummeted like a lift in freefall.

For once, I hadn't allowed head space for the idea that the tumour could be growing. I hadn't even given it a thought this time. I'd taken my eye off the ball and, by not worrying, I had allowed this to happen.

If it was good news, it would have been given over the phone. This was unquestionably bad.

I watched Laura talk about how well she was doing, smiling brightly into the camera on her laptop which was balanced precariously on a stack of books. She looked over and caught my eye. I smiled back, delaying the inevitable.

'Uh, oh, she's going to be so crushed by this. You've made her feel invincible, she's going to be soooo angry with you,' Siobhan gloated.

Laura was livid. She wanted to hit something, so I dug out my old boxing gloves and held out the pads. Her punches were surprisingly powerful, and I was knocked off balance as she pummelled, a glossy film of tears covering her eyes as she furiously refused to cry.

Gracie was distraught because of the knickers, and I was dwelling on the fact that I'd forgotten to put on the small silver compass necklace Laura and I both wore, wondering irrationally if that made me responsible for the bad news. Or maybe it was because I had been too proud of her.

Mark and I lay in bed for hours that night, but it was clear that neither of us were finding sleep: he was restless, all tangled up in fear and sheets, the wind howled outside, and it sounded like my wounded heart. We couldn't speak because this fear went beyond words, and we couldn't comfort each other because we were both too scared. I started work on a hard, brittle veneer to protect myself from what would come next.

Laura's fury had dissipated quickly, and she resumed her usual pragmatism, wanting to get on with the practicalities, planning for next steps and looking on the calendar for a window of when surgery might disrupt her life the least.

The thought of a second operation, a relapse, a recurrence, left me feeling hollow. We had tried everything, and it had still come back. We weren't being called in for a friendly catch-up: this was the bad news that had been hanging over us for the last two years. I felt nausea rolling in my stomach and couldn't stop my hands from trembling.

In the early hours I had a call from Gracie, who was sobbing uncontrollably. 'I shouldn't be at uni when we don't know how long we're going to have Laura, but when I'm at home I feel guilty because I'm not at uni. I don't know what I'm supposed to do.'

And after a pause, 'She's not going to grow old with me, is she, Mum?'

We'd been complacent, blinded by how brilliantly she'd been doing, but the cancer was going to come back and claim her; this dreadful, choking uncertainty would be ours for as long as she lived. Laura didn't have any magical protection against this bastard disease after all.

'I can't go through this again,' Gracie sobbed. We all felt the same.

Covid restrictions meant that Mark couldn't come to the meeting with Dr C, but he could take part via FaceTime from the car park. I positioned my phone on the desk with anxious fingers and completely forgot how to make a video call. I was so frightened I couldn't think straight, and Laura had to take the phone from me to connect with Mark, his phone balanced on the dashboard of the car.

Before the meeting I'd asked him: 'What questions do you have for Dr C?'

'What?'

'Do you have anything you want to ask him?'

'Yeah,' he'd replied defensively.

'Well, what are they?'

'I don't know. I'll know when he says what he has to say first.'

'So, there's nothing you've actually thought of in advance of the meeting, then?'

'Pack it in with the arrogance, Nic.'

'It's really starting to piss me off. I'm doing all the heavy lifting here, Mark! It's not some domestic chore – it's not the bloody ironing. This is our daughter's life, and I'm not carrying all the weight and the responsibility; it's too hard, and I can't do it on my own.'

Mark's fear looked like indifference to me, and he'd retreated into his shell. I was poking him with a stick to get a reaction, but it only pushed him further away. And the stick will have hurt, filed to a sharp point with my resentment.

'What's the point in me being upset? What use will I be to you if I show you how worried and scared I am?'

'What use are you to me if you're just a shell?'

There was, of course, a new tumour.

It was on the periphery of the brain and looked a bit like a meningioma, possibly caused by radiotherapy … or it could be the GBM back on the offensive. It was unlikely to be good news and a cloud settled upon us.

That night we walked up Pendle Hill, taking regular stops to let Laura catch her breath, and watched the sky darken from a soft blue to peach to inky black, pointing out stars as they appeared one by one and trying to identify constellations using an app on Gracie's phone. Laura talked about how inconsequential we all were and made casual references to her funeral, which froze my insides.

Nobody wanted to engage with the subject. If we didn't mention it, it couldn't happen. The bad news made me irrationally obsessed with the fact that we didn't have any good photos of the four of us – just selfies with half Gracie's face missing or combinations of three with the fourth acting as photographer. It seemed so frivolous in the circumstances, but I wanted a record of how we once were.

I tried to blur the connection between the bad news and the photoshoot, but everyone knew that I was just desperately trying to freeze time and save what I could from the approaching bin fire.

We looked really happy on those photos, a perfect study of casual family life, everyone sporting jeans and anoraks. Even Ziggy got involved. I'm smiling as if my life depended upon it.

* * *

Mr L now specialised in spinal surgery, so we had an early evening appointment with our new surgeon, Mr D, who was Italian and had a gentle, reassuring manner.

He wore a soft grey jumper over a shirt and tie with smart grey trousers. He looked freshly showered and, if we had been sitting closer than the requisite two metres, I expect he would have smelled nice – perhaps a lemony cologne. His tanned wrist showed an Apple watch, and I wondered if he'd already reached his 10,000 steps that day.

His hands were neat but not delicate. I imagined a brain surgeon would have the elegant fingers of a pianist, but these were short and if not quite 'workman-like', then certainly the hands of a craftsman: hands that should produce something beautiful rather than pick away at cancerous tumours.

He came out to collect us from the waiting area and somewhere in his face I could already see bad news.

I tried to be brave. The blood pounding in my ears made it hard to hear, but his solemn expression told me what I already knew: it was another glioma. The cancer was back.

Tears dripped down my face to be absorbed by the standard-issue blue facemask – helpful, as I couldn't find a tissue. I didn't want either Mr D or Laura to know that I was crying, grateful they couldn't see my face crumpled in misery.

Mr D would schedule a second operation on Laura's brain and remove as much of the new growth as he could. He explained that recovery would take longer this time, that each subsequent surgery increased the risk, but he felt reasonably confident this new tumour could be removed safely.

Gracie went back to Salford, but called me in the small hours, inconsolable. 'This is going to be our life, isn't it? We are going to have to go through all this, every three months, and if we're not … that means she's dead.'

I tried to think of something to say that might help, but my head was too fuzzy and dull. I shivered in the dark bedroom; the only light came from my phone, which displayed a photo of Gracie, smiling in a blue hoodie on a bright spring day when we'd been on a speedboat ride down the Thames and things like this happened to other people.

'Oh, my darling, we're trying everything, aren't we? There's probably only Laura in the whole world on this combination of treatments. Maybe she'll be the one?' I hoped that I sounded more convinced than I felt. It was a struggle to keep positive – once again it felt as though we were teetering at the edge.

My heart would begin randomly hammering double time in my chest, leaving me gasping for breath. I went out for a run but cut it short: my legs wouldn't hold me up and I felt bloodless and empty. I ended up walking home and fell fast asleep on the sofa. Laura gently prised a cup of tea out of my hand and took me up to bed.

The day before surgery I cleaned the house from top to bottom while the girls watched the entire series of *Britannia High*. They'd both loved it as kids and knew all the songs by heart. Laura had bought the boxset on eBay, and it had been saved for the perfect uninterrupted day together. In the evening we had an impromptu game of cricket in the garden. Ziggy was an excellent fielder but kept running away with the ball. We played until long after it had gone dark, delaying the end of the day.

It felt like the night before a difficult exam, or some long and dreaded journey.

Returning to Salford hospital and walking down the same corridors with the same paintings on the walls brought back all the trauma of last time. But things were different now: patients for surgery were dropped off at the door with a small overnight bag, only to be collected once they were discharged – no visitors permitted on the wards.

I couldn't bring myself to just abandon Laura with a bag and a label like an evacuee and pleaded with the admissions team. 'Please can you let me stay? Just till she goes down to theatre? Look, I did a Covid test last night.' I brandished proof of my negative status on my phone. 'Sometimes, she gets confused and needs a bit of extra help with things.'

It was only the slightest exaggeration: as it happened, she did need help with the green surgical stockings, the grippy socks and paper knickers, and when asked by the pharmacist for details of her medications, Laura only had a very loose idea about the capsules and tablets that filled her daily meds box.

When the time came for her to be wheeled down to surgery, I waved her off cheerily, then as she disappeared behind the sliding doors of the lift, I burst into tears and had to be consoled by the nurses.

I was not ready to let her go.

I sat on the picnic benches outside the hospital, while members of staff in various shades of blue unclicked Tupperware lunch boxes and a couple had a loud and heated argument about his 'bloody' sister, dragging angrily on cigarettes with paper face masks under their chins.

Mark came to collect me. I cried all the way home, while he made positive noises and patted me on the knee in a way he hoped I would find reassuring. I didn't relax until we had the phone call just after 7 p.m. to say things had gone well. Mr D even put Laura on the phone: she was croaky from the anaesthetic tube and made little sense, but she'd come through and he was happy and therefore so were we.

Last time, Laura had spent a full five days in hospital, which made wheeling her out to the car park 24 hours after surgery seem reckless. Quite honestly, this felt way too soon: she was sickly pale, her face swollen, her eyes puffed and blackening, her head lolling heavily onto her chest like a zombie. I worried about the risk of a bleed, or an infection: we were a good thirty miles from the hospital if something did go wrong.

She woke every four hours, incoherent with pain. I made a chart so we didn't accidentally overdose her on codeine and paracetamol. The next few days were spent trying to persuade her to eat and then rubbing her back and passing tissues when she was sick. I slipped into her room at regular intervals to check she was still breathing; she was so bruised and fragile.

Mr D confirmed that, despite initial optimism it might be something less insidious, it was indeed glioblastoma. The black eyes faded and the bruising turned from purple to green to yellow, ten new spidery stitches made a question mark in front of her left ear. Convalescence was a cocktail of sleep, *Harry Potter* films, and egg mayonnaise sandwiches.

I went for a run and fell over, tripping over my own clumsy feet and sprawling across the road in a spray of gravel. Tiny pearls of blood oozed from my knees and the palms of my hands, where I'd tried to break my fall. An elderly man came across to ask if I was OK and needed a lift, but I quickly assured him I was fine and limped home. I fell again a couple of days later, ripping away the all the newly healed skin. I'd only just set off, so stubbornly refused to cut the run short. When I eventually returned home, I realised I'd cut my head and had an alarming streak of blood down my face; no wonder I'd had so many funny looks. I was unravelling; I couldn't even stay upright.

But at least when I was on the ground, I couldn't fall any further.

I'd Just Like to Be Old

May

Just days before, Laura had confirmed her course options for the final year of her PPE degree, and now she was waiting for a CT scan to see if the cancer in her brain had spread to her spine.

Unfortunately for us, the blood analyser wasn't working properly, which meant five hours in the waiting room, during which time we watched the lunchtime news followed by a slew of afternoon quiz shows, then the same news repeated at tea time. Down the corridor, someone was celebrating a birthday with hip, hip, hurrays and three jolly cheers.

The machine couldn't be fixed, and we were apologetically asked to reschedule the appointment. It couldn't be helped but I cried tears of frustration at the waste of an entire day. I was stretched so tightly, I could snap at any moment. It was the closest I'd ever felt to breaking down.

Laura was hungry and I had promised her a chippy tea as compensation for the wasted day, but it was late and every chip shop we tried was already closed. We arrived home at the same time as the Sainsbury's food delivery, just in time to see all the plastic crates topple off the back of the truck.

The driver was remorseful. 'I'm not having a good day,' she said. 'My dad died last week.'

We both looked at the broken eggs on the tarmac as if they said it all.

Later, I dragged the bin down the driveway, leaving it ready for morning collection and just carried on walking, only a mile or so. I could have walked all night and right through the following day and slept in a bush, but I imagined they'd have to report me as missing, wearing a long green skirt with Gracie's anorak and only dog poo bags in my pocket, so I walked back home before anyone even missed me.

Next day in the car, Laura was eating mint choc chip ice cream and Radio 6 Music played, 'Here Comes The Sun'. She was completely happy and living in just that moment: a favourite song and her favourite ice cream flavour. It felt like we were riding a white-knuckle emotional roller-coaster of highs and crashing lows. It was exhausting and I wondered just how long we would be able to hold on for.

Walking down the canal on a Sunday morning, talking to Laura about the things we were grateful for, we crossed paths with a friend from parkrun and stopped for a short (socially distanced) chat. Mo was an elegant lady in her sixties who was once an actress.

'She used to be in *Coronation Street*, you know,' I told Laura, as we walked on in opposite directions.

'Really? Who was she?'

'Well, nobody you'd know. I think it was in the seventies.'

'Wow, you'd never guess.'

'It's funny, isn't it? How we're surprised that old people once did all these amazing things that you'd never expect.'

'I'd like to be like that.'

'You've done lots of amazing things.'

'No, I'd just like to be old.'

A Notice of Intent

Summer

Laura decided that she didn't want to restart chemo immediately. She knew it was likely to make her sick and her main priority now was to complete her degree.

Further chemo could also have implications regarding future fertility, but we were better prepared this time and, following a number of consultations, it was decided Laura should begin a series of hormone injections to stimulate her ovaries and any useful eggs could be harvested and stored until needed. A scan had shown that the number of available eggs was already small so it was now or never.

In the months to come, Laura would squeeze the soft skin of her stomach into a small pouch and inject herself daily with a short, sharp needle. This was followed by periodic ultrasound scans to ascertain the maturity of the eggs and, finally, surgery to remove them.

I wasn't allowed to go with her. Instead, she sat alone in the waiting room alongside couples holding hands and discussing favourite names for longed-for babies.

But for Laura, this was a notice of intent, a promise to her future self that she would still be there, and had given herself the best chance of being a mum. It felt like a beautiful pipe dream, but sometimes an imaginary future is the thing we need most.

Do you know what the definition of optimism is?

Buying your terminally ill daughter a three-year, rather than a twelve-month disabled railcard.

We were far from finished, there was still so much to do.

In July, Laura was invited to Wigan to drive a crane so big that it took sixteen trucks to move and another crane to reassemble. Then she was off to Cumbria, where she operated a big pink digger, and managed so well they left her to it, scooping and shifting full buckets of peaty earth from one part of the site to another.

She was unexpectedly gifted last-minute tickets to the men's Euro finals at Wembley. I stayed up late to sew a George Cross of red sequins onto her white face mask.

Our local BBC radio station nominated her for their Pride of Lancashire award, and she was sheepishly thrilled to be voted 'Young Ambassador of the Year' by her peers at the Brain Tumour Charity.

Professor VG agreed that we should save chemo for when we'd run out of other options and, in the meantime, begin production of a further dendritic cell vaccine, using tissue from the new tumour. He also recommended a promising checkpoint inhibitor, Keytruda, which was available on the NHS for a number of specific cancers but not yet licensed for brain cancer. We could access it privately in London, but it wouldn't be cheap.

Mum and Dad generously offered to release some equity from their house, they were so desperate to help, and we launched another fundraising campaign, but it was going to be a massive job to raise so much money again. It was awkward and humiliating to have to crowdfund in the hope of keeping your child alive, and I wished it didn't have to be so hard.

Mark's friend, the comedian Peter Kay, came over for lunch and cheered us up. They had worked together briefly at Granada fifteen years ago. When Laura's story first made the local news, Peter had given Mark a call and had maintained regular contact ever since. We were a tough audience, loaded down with the worry of what was ahead, but he was generous with his time and unshakeably wonderful. If he hadn't been so kind and lovely, I wouldn't have been brave enough to send him an email a few weeks later asking if maybe he'd consider doing a ten-minute slot at the fundraising ball I'd been planning.

I wrote the email, giving Peter as many get-outs as I possibly could and apologising profusely for being so forward as to ask. I knew Mark would have tried to talk me out of it, still squeamish about asking for help no matter how much we needed it. I pressed send and cringed at the horrible, pushy person I'd become.

Minutes later my phone rang. 'I could do you ten minutes at your ball, or ask them at Burnley Mechanics Theatre, but what I could also do is phone up the Manchester Apollo and see what their availability is like.'

I almost dropped the phone. Within a week, we had a matinee and an evening show booked at the Apollo, one of the biggest venues in Manchester. Peter hadn't toured for many years, and I knew that there would be press interest – but once the details were released, the world went mad.

We were thrust into the spotlight, and every day seemed to bring new requests for interviews. We popped up on television, radio and in print, explaining Laura's diagnosis and – much more interesting to the press – our friendship with Peter, again and again, as new outlets sought different angles. We stood in the rain in the garden under a golf umbrella for ITV and round the kitchen table for the BBC; we sat on sofas with Eamonn and Ruth at *This Morning* and Louise and Charlie on *BBC Breakfast*.

One evening, we had to watch two stations simultaneously as a local regional interview was broadcast at the same time as one on national news. Little Alice found this most confusing.

We were interviewed for an article in *The Telegraph*, which ran with the headline: 'Why Peter Kay is getting back on stage to help my sick daughter.' The accompanying photograph made us look like we were a new family joining *Hollyoaks*.

When the tickets finally went on sale, they sold out completely within six minutes.

Hours before the show began, there was already a long queue of people snaking round the side of the building, holding coats over their heads in a summer rain shower. Nobody was complaining, though – they were just excited about the show, delighted to have been lucky in the frantic scramble for tickets.

Arriving at the theatre, we were even 'papped' by photographers shouting Laura's name as Mark parked the car. It was so unexpected, she couldn't stop laughing at the ridiculousness of the situation.

Thirty minutes later the photos appeared as online *Exclusives!*

Gracie had surprised me by asking, 'Do you think it would be OK with Peter if I introduced him on stage and said a few words about Laura. You know, to explain what we're raising money for?'

'We can certainly ask him, and I don't think he'll mind. But are you absolutely sure, Gracie? It'll be terrifying, on your own in front of all those people.'

I thought she'd change her mind, but I should have known better than to underestimate our Gracie.

She tried on every dress in her wardrobe before deciding it contained nothing suitable. Pillowy white packages promising *pretty* and *lovely* began to arrive from online retailers. Most of the dresses went straight back to the post office resealed with a slash of brown parcel tape but she held on to a dark blue playsuit with thin straps and bought new white trainers to complete the outfit – I'd talked her out of unfamiliar high heels, which would have made the walk on stage clunky and awkward. She needed to have her feet firmly on the ground.

I waited backstage with Peter and Gracie as the noisy audience quietened and settled down to be entertained. She walked out and found her mark in a pool of light; she looked like an angel, so small and vulnerable. I was trembling with the nerves she seemed to be controlling perfectly. Peter put his arm around me and assured me that she would be absolutely fine.

The theatre filled with a shriek of feedback and my heart lurched for her.

She took a deep breath and lifted the microphone to her lips with a small smile. 'Hello, my name is Gracie,' she said. 'And Laura is my big sister.'

There was a collective 'aahhh' from the audience.

Peter was right, she was absolutely fine. A euphoric Gracie returned to her seat and Laura looked at her sister with love. 'I'm so proud of you Gray, you were brilliant,' she whispered.

It was an extraordinary day. The audience cried with laughter and after the show people lined up to take selfies with the girls, and to tell Gracie how brave she was. Our faces ached from smiling and we felt lifted by the wave of love and the incredible kindness that surrounded us. Friends shook collection buckets for The Brain Tumour Charity and people emptied their pockets of loose change as they left the theatre, still laughing at Peter's jokes.

The media attention continued into the next day, and we were invited to the *BBC Breakfast* studio to talk about how brilliant the night had been.

As we handed in our security passes and found the taxi home, Laura turned her phone back on and a Facebook notification flashed up.

She looked at me, her eyes filled with tears, and said, 'Ria'.

I'd known the day before but had waited to find the right moment to tell Laura that her friend and fellow GBM warrior, Ria, had died, aged just twenty-five. I'd missed my opportunity, and she was heartbroken and furious that this vile disease had stolen yet another young life.

I also had a notification on my phone, from someone who'd been moved by Laura's words on *This Morning* the previous week: 'I don't want to spend the days wasting my life away,' she had said. 'I want to seize life and get as much out of it as I can.'

He owned a big house in France and thought it would be ideal for a family holiday. He had left a phone number for me to call.

'Might be a scam,' said Laura suspiciously.

'Call him right now!' ordered Gracie.

I tentatively dialled the number, and a lovely Irish voice explained how he'd seen us on TV and just wanted us to have a nice holiday on him. He sent me a link to a booking site with photos of a palatial French farmhouse with a pool and tennis court; a house that previously had been the country residence of the American ambassador to France.

'It's a great place,' he said. 'Ideal for parties, needs plenty of people. Ask all your friends and family ... fill it.'

Fabulously Normal and Ordinary Things
September–October

We really did fill it, as thirteen of us travelled to France.

By the time we arrived, it was dark, but the majestic house had been lit up for our arrival.

We were spellbound. If I could have bottled that unforgettable feeling, I would take the smallest sip every day and make it last a lifetime.

We ran from room to room, gasping with delight and shouting to each other, 'Come and look at this one!'

'Bagsie this one!'

'Come and see the size of this bath!'

Mark and Laura arrived a day later as she'd been keen to attend the BBC's *Pride of Lancashire* awards ceremony in Blackpool. We'd been given a nod and a wink that she'd won, but Laura was completely stunned when they announced it.

She was interviewed on camera, proudly holding her award. 'It's not just me that has a brain tumour, it's not just me that's got a terminal cancer diagnosis. What sort of legacy am I going to leave if I just focus on myself and not on others?'

The house was in a very rural part of south-west France and when night fell, there wasn't a single light to be seen from the veranda. We took turns cooking and had the occasional trip to town, but mostly we sat around the pool or at the long dining table and talked, appreciating that we may not get such an opportunity again.

For lunch we ate baguettes, crisp and brittle on the outside, soft as clouds on the inside, with a slick of salty butter and soft creamy cheeses that stuck to our teeth. We borrowed bikes with clunky gears and rode four abreast on empty French lanes lined with poplar trees.

In the evenings we played Hi Harry, a ridiculous game that involved those with the worst memories (or the lowest alcohol tolerance) ending up daubed with a blackened cork. We played cards, had a quiz night, a scavenger hunt and swam at midnight.

We were a million magnificent miles away from reality.

The bucket list had been extended to include new cultural elements: Laura wanted to experience both the opera and the ballet, and we were generously gifted tickets to the magnificent Royal Opera House for a performance of *The Magic Flute*.

This gave us a perfect opportunity to dress up, and Laura got me to take lots of photos of her looking elegant in a long black dress against the baroque red and gold of the theatre. I can't say that I entirely understood the plot, but it was still amazing. Laura loved every minute and I managed to stay awake for almost all of it.

I also had another surprise planned for Laura just a few days later, which would require further dressing up.

Some ideas took more legwork than others; firstly, it was a matter of online research to identify the decision makers, then searching for an email address in the hope of dropping into the right inbox (sometimes a process of trial and error), then writing a letter that would be suitably persuasive. I wasn't always successful, but I was creative and tenacious in my attempts, and it definitely helped that I could share links to newspaper articles and now clips from TV.

It took many emails, and some handwritten letters too, but eventually a message arrived to say we had tickets for the premiere of the new James Bond film, *No Time to Die*, at the Royal Albert Hall.

Laura was beside herself with excitement. We waited in a long queue of beautiful people, many shivering in flimsy dresses and strappy heels as the autumn drizzle flattened their curls or frizzed out carefully straightened hair. Security staff with clipboards rushed up and down the line checking Covid passes and tickets, and then we were in. Laura wore her dress from the *Yesterday* premiere (Bruce Oldfield – John Lewis sale – bargain) but now she had longer hair and a slight tan from France, and I'd not made too bad a job of her makeup. She almost glowed with happiness. I took her photo in front of an Aston Martin covered with bullet holes, and then one with Phoebe Waller-Bridge in the background being interviewed on the press stage.

Our seats were below the royal box and we stood solemnly to welcome Charles, Camilla, William and Kate before a rendition of the national anthem, but the real stars were the cast of the film, who were introduced one by one to the audience with escalating levels of whoops and cheers until Daniel Craig finally appeared in a raspberry velvet suit.

The film was, of course, fabulous, we were thrilled just to be there and, unlike the rest of our row, in no rush to head straight out when the credits began to roll.

As the recently vacated seats flipped back up and the lights came on, it became apparent that not everyone had realised there were packets of dry martini James Bond popcorn under each one. Laura and I scooped up as many as we could carry, because, well, you would, wouldn't you?

*   *   *

Covid put a stop to many mass-participation events, causing deep financial anxiety for the charities that depended on the income they generated. So, five days later, it felt like a privilege to be back on the start line of the London Marathon in a Brain Tumour Charity vest, even if I hadn't managed sufficient training. I wanted to run for the people I knew and honour those we'd lost, so I decorated my running vest and matching tutu with ribbons. Around my top were the names of those who'd died from a brain tumour, written in silver on turquoise ribbon, and on the skirt those who were still fighting, their names on red ribbon. I felt the weight of their legacies as I ran, not very quickly, through the streets of London looking like Upsy Daisy escaping from *In the Night Garden*.

Laura and Gracie came down to cheer me on, and I never wasted a chance to stop for a quick word and a tearful hug. I sobbed when I finished, and again when I met up with Uzmah, a friend I'd met online, who'd travelled down to watch because she knew I was wearing her late husband's name.

In the recovery centre we cheered each runner as they arrived, between stuffing our faces with sandwiches and cake. Many of those taking part had chosen to raise funds for the most personal and heartfelt reasons: Claire ran for her husband, Con; Iain for his son, Duncan; and all of us because we didn't want other families to go through the same trauma and heartbreak that we'd experienced.

On the third anniversary of Laura's diagnosis, we ate eggs, beans and sweet potato cakes and watched Wallace and Gromit and then *Ghostbusters* on a soft rainy autumn afternoon, so glad that she was still with us, doing fabulously normal and ordinary things.

Please Don't Keep in Touch

November

I often felt like Haley Joel Osment in *Sixth Sense*: I saw dead people. Only I didn't – I saw the grieving. They approached me tentatively from the grey, shadowy corners of social media and held out the person they'd lost like a small animal cupped gently in their hands, lifting them up as if for a blessing.

'You bring this on yourself, sharing so much on Twitter. Just explain that you can't answer every message,' Mark said.

Sometimes it took me by surprise, the number of people who got in touch, but I knew that I'd swapped our anonymity for a platform on which to raise funds and awareness.

'I know, but I can't and I'm not complaining. I get it. They just need to be seen, for their pain to be acknowledged. It's not a lot to ask, is it?'

It wasn't a big deal but every single one was a shell or a button: it didn't weigh very much alone, but too many could bury you.

We lost so many people from our GBM community that November: Dave, Stu, Ethan and Lisa, names I'd been proud to wear on my marathon tutu.

Another four families devastated.

'Mum, you've got to stop going on your phone,' Gracie said. 'It's just making you so sad.'

When you share your story on the radio or TV, you have no idea who might be listening. Somewhere in London, an artist called Rosalind Wyatt was working on a project for the Institute of Cancer Research and heard Laura speak on BBC5 Live. She was producing an art installation – a series of lab coats embroidered with the words of people dealing with cancer – and asked if Laura could send a contribution. She was happy to oblige.

Dear Cancer,

I'm Sorry I ruined your plans with my positivity.
I Know I was supposed to start to prepare to die
but I decided to give that a pass and live my life
instead. You unintentionally changed me into a more
generous, fulfilled and strong Person, and for that,
thank you.
Please DONT keep in touch,

Laura ☺

It was true, Laura had definitely been changed by her diagnosis.
She'd found a new empathy and compassion, and just seemed to
feel things more deeply than before.

In between assignments I would find her busy on her laptop.

'What are you working on now?'

'I'm helping to map Uganda.'

I looked confused.

'We're using GPS to mark up roads and buildings, because
unbelievably, there aren't any proper maps of northern Uganda.'

'Is this part of your course?'

'No, it's just volunteering, really, but the cool thing is that I'm
helping to get free prosthetic limbs to people who've lost arms
and legs in the civil war. Without maps, the mobile clinic can't
find them.'

'Pretty cool,' I agreed.

Unfortunately, arms and legs were becoming an issue for Laura
too.

The problem with immunotherapy is that it stimulates the
entire immune system, which means it can cause inflammatory or
autoimmune issues to any part of the body. Basically, there's a risk
of anything ending with 'itis' and, unfortunately for Laura, it was
arthritis in her knees and ankles.

I ordered a folding stick from Amazon, black with pink flowers, to help with walking, but she was in a lot of pain, especially

at night, and it left her feeling miserable. If the checkpoint inhibitor Keytruda was working – and we couldn't really tell – was it worth the discomfort? But then what was the point in living if you couldn't participate in life?

Laura called one night from uni, almost in tears because her fingers and hands hurt so much that she couldn't write notes in her lectures and was struggling to manage the stairs.

'It will probably stop once you're off the Keytruda,' I tried to reassure her, but with little confidence.

'But what if it doesn't. What if this is permanent?'

Nobody had an answer, and I was reluctant to stop treatment early, still hoping the new drug was working its magic – but that was easy for me to say, as they weren't my knees.

The best kind of Friday night was when I arrived back from work to find both the girls home from uni and Mark cooking something nice for tea. The full washing basket I could cope with – it was just wonderful to have us all in the same room, talking over each other and teasing Mark about his dubious chicken casserole.

Looking around the kitchen table, I knew without doubt that I wouldn't want to be anywhere else, with anyone else, in the world. These were my people, and we were so much stronger together.

A storm surprised us with a blanket of heavy snow, and the girls, wrapped up with coats over pyjamas, took Alice into the garden to build a snowman. Gracie made the head, rolling a snowball around the lawn, and Laura found sticks for arms and relinquished one of her carrots for a nose. They named him Ronnie for no good reason and Alice was delighted.

That night we put up the Christmas tree, even though it was a bit early. But what was the point in waiting and being cool about Christmas when life was short, and it was actually snowing outside?

Crack On

December

We held our annual 'Breakfast with Santa' event at Giddy Kippers, which involved my dad in a red suit and white beard, sitting with a table of toddlers eating pancakes and mini cooked breakfasts.

Laura's scan had been the day before and the wait for results flipped my stomach.

'Don't be reading anything into it,' Mark warned, conscious of my grim expression, in spite all the festivities.

The call came at 3:30 p.m. and Mark and I retreated to our Blue Sea party room so we could hear properly. But by then I had no doubt it was bad news.

'It looks like an area of regrowth,' Dr C said. 'But obviously we'll have to wait for the full radiology report and the MDT next week.' I stared at the mural of smiling fish as my eyes swam with tears.

How had we not known? What clues had we missed again? Could they even operate so soon?

We were back at square one for a third time, and barely nine months since Laura's last surgery.

The next morning, I came down to find both girls squeezed into Gracie's single bed, laughing at 'epic fails' and YouTube compilations of clever dogs on her phone. By unspoken agreement we'd all decided to just crack on – no point in thinking too hard about the next few weeks, let's get the most out of the day.

I took the girls out for hot chocolate, we bought bargains in a charity shop and blew kisses to a bus driver in a Santa hat. If you'd driven past or been sitting next to us in the café, you'd have never known that our hearts were completely shattered.

Laura was always a thoughtful gift buyer, but never more so than since her diagnosis. She knew opportunities were numbered and made every one count.

For Gracie's birthday, she wrapped two boxes. In the first was a trip down their childhood memory lane with all the toys she'd loved as a child: a Tamagotchi, luminous slime, sea monkeys … she'd also assembled a film with the opening sequences of the TV shows they'd watched as children. It must have taken Laura ages to find and edit the clips together. Both girls were singing along to the opening credits of *Tracy Beaker*, but Gracie's eyes were full of tears at the love contained in her gift.

It was beautiful; it felt like an ending.

A second box contained all the things that Gracie needed now she was a grown-up: a Swiss army knife, a glass nail file, and a personalised bottle opener so she'd stop using her teeth.

'I'm also gifting you the benefit of my free financial advice. You're twenty now, so it's time you stopped buying crap and got yourself a help-to-buy ISA.'

I couldn't shake the feeling that Laura was trying to condense a whole lifetime of big-sisterly advice for Gracie into whatever time she had left.

Nobody really wanted to hear what Dr C had to say: we knew it wasn't going to be good. Our lovely new nurse specialist Hanna was at the meeting too, which seemed consistently to be a sign of bad news.

There was a new two-centimetre tumour, this time on the top of Laura's brain. Mr D had said he would be prepared to operate again so that was a good thing but still, another brain surgery, FFS? How can that ever be good news? She was so close to finishing uni too, and her birthday, and Christmas, and Neil and Georgina's wedding, which was now on its third date as a result of the pandemic. She was so close to getting on with her bloody life, but here we were again.

Laura was typically sanguine, but Gracie and I cried quietly as we parked outside Laura's uni halls to bring her bags home for Christmas, hoping that she'd still have the chance to return in the new year, but knowing nothing was promised.

The new tumour was deeper in the brain and not as easy to access as the previous two. Realistically, surgery alone was only going to buy us an extra six to twelve months, so she would need to go back on chemo again, but there was more. 'I'm afraid, Laura,' Mr D said, rolling the r with his soft Italian accent, 'because the location of the tumour is so close to the blood vessels that control movement, there is probably a one in ten chance this operation will leave you permanently paralysed.'

'So, what happens if I don't have the operation then?'

'Well, then, I am afraid you will die.'

'OK, if I'm paralysed, will it be both legs?' she asked, and I wondered where she was going with this.

'Perhaps it will just be your left side that you will lose.'

'That's fine then,' she replied. 'I kick with my right foot.' And as she reached for a pen to sign the consent form: 'And then there's always the Paralympics. I'd probably qualify for those, wouldn't I?'

Mr D smiled at her. 'I have a space in my diary for December 30. Is that OK for you?'

There was an awkward silence. 'If that's the nearest available time, that's fine,' I said. 'It's just that Laura and Gracie are bridesmaids for my brother on the 31st, so if there was any possibility of sooner …'

'Leave it with me and I'll see what I can do.'

Laura and I spent the next hour in the pre-op waiting area. The radio was tuned to a local commercial station playing every single Christmas song there had ever been, interspersed with irritating adverts. I longed to snatch a crutch from the man opposite and smash the radio into smithereens screaming, 'Just fuck off with your shitty Christmas songs!'

Instead, I played solitaire furiously on my phone while Laura completed her daily German Duolingo practice, then listened to music through her headphones.

'I think they're giving up on me, Mum,' she said sadly, as we walked across the car park.

I turned to face her. 'No, they're not. If there was no hope, they wouldn't waste all that money on an operation, would they? They must think there's every chance it will be successful. We need to stay positive, chick.'

I cried all the way home, quietly, so Laura in the passenger seat couldn't hear; my bag a soft nest of wet tissues and me a massive hypocrite.

We were meeting Peter Kay later for tea. I don't think he could have seen many audiences as miserable as us in his time as a stand-up comedian, but he had an incredible knack of getting smiles from the saddest faces. 'You should come to *Dance for Life* next year. I'll get you up on stage with me,' he said. 'You can come up through a trapdoor in your wheelchair, Laura.'

Only Peter could make us laugh with a line like that.

We all felt a hundred times better by the time we left. If you could cure someone with laughter and a good bear hug, Peter could heal the world. We were so grateful for his support and generosity; things were grim but at least the funds he'd raised would allow us access to further vaccine therapy in Germany, and we knew how lucky this made us.

Mr D did manage to find an earlier space on his list and Laura's surgery was scheduled for 22 December. We tried to keep things as normal as possible, buying and wrapping presents for the Boxing Day event – which couldn't really have come at a worse time.

'Do you think maybe we should cancel?'

'Absolutely not.' Laura was adamant. 'We've promised a Christmas dinner to 250 people, and you've got all these presents and the food and volunteers. We're not cancelling anything.'

Later I dropped the first car full of presents down at Giddy Kippers.

'How's Mark?' Michael asked.

'Fine, I think. He's not said that much, to be honest.'

'I don't think he's fine, Nic. He was really upset when he came down here earlier, but he's trying to keep it together – he thinks he has to be strong for you and the girls.'

I felt horribly guilty for not noticing. It's easy to share happiness: it radiates warmth and light and joy, and people are happy to bask in its reflected glory; but misery is best kept to yourself – it doesn't translate well into words; better to seal it up like a Ziploc bag. We were all tense and angry and frightened. To be here, again, felt like a cruel and inhumane punishment.

We brought Laura's birthday forward so it was the right side of the surgery, and woke her up with Taylor Swift singing '22' – she'd given Gracie permission to play it for one day only. Covid protocols were still in place, and she was confined to home for the 48 hours prior to surgery, so the four of us watched films and ate birthday cake. Gracie organised an All About Laura quiz, then a scavenger hunt, and we rounded off the night with a murder mystery bought from Amazon for the occasion. Laura insisted on reading out all the evidence like Helen Mirren in *Prime Suspect*, and was triumphant when we finally cracked the case.

But when she was tucked happily into bed, we cried.

* * *

Another early morning with the sick feeling of dread; a hospital gown; a wristband that told the world she was allergic to cats and prawns; green surgical stockings and matching grippy socks. Mr D came down to say hello and with a Sharpie he drew an arrow on the right side of Laura's neck, like This way up printed on a box.

We had a few hours to kill and watched videos on my phone until I heard the trolley rattling down the corridor to collect her. I began to panic, too hot, and I couldn't catch my breath.

I didn't want it to be time, I wanted to keep her here with me, always.

I held Laura's hand as the porters pushed the trolley to the lift doors. 'Please take good care of her. She's really special to us and it's her birthday tomorrow.'

'We will, love.'

'See you soon, Laura. Love you.'

The doors closed and I shattered into a thousand pieces.

The nurses were kind and reassuring. 'She'll be absolutely fine, I promise.'

'Yes, but for how long?'

I cried my way through a half-pack of tissues on the walk from the hospital to Gracie's student house, drowning out the voices in my head with *The Archers* omnibus. We played Dobble and waited, then drove to Neil's and waited some more while Alice did her best to distract us with sofa gymnastics.

Time slows to a glacial pace when all you want is for a phone to ring with good news, which it finally did at 4 p.m.

The operation had gone well, and Laura still had the use of both legs.

She messaged me at 5 a.m. because the tubes and catheter were making it difficult to sleep and I wished her the happiest of happy birthdays. I was so relieved she'd made it to twenty-two, she would have hated to be #Forever21 – far too much like the tacky fast fashion chain.

When Laura woke a second time, the nurses had left chocolates and little bottles of shampoo and conditioner, handy as her hair resembled a bird's nest with ten neat stitches dividing the parting. Neil's friend, Michael, had popped up to the ward in his police uniform and with an evidence bag filled with more chocolate, causing something of a stir on the ward.

Laura walked out of hospital like a rock star, in jeans and her favourite Beatles T-shirt, with a good few hours of birthday left to celebrate.

'In your face, Siobhan,' I whispered under my breath.

We watched *The Muppet Christmas Carol* and ate pizza in front of the fire. The relief was palpable – how lucky were we?

The next day, Laura got up and washed her hair, fed Ziggy and was fully functional until she crashed out after the traditional Christmas Eve viewing of *It's a Wonderful Life*.

'You know, this is a bit like us,' Laura said, as Donna Reed arrived with a laundry basket full of dollar bills and snowflakes in her hair. 'Not the bankruptcy or the suicide attempt – or the angel, obviously – but just the way everyone pulled together to help us.'

We knew how very blessed we were to have Laura pulling crackers on Christmas Day. The half-life of anaesthetic had fizzled out, leaving her with a little pain and some itchy stitches, but she was better than we had any right to expect three days after surgery.

Meanwhile, over in Liverpool, a family just like ours was saying a final goodbye to Owen, another glioblastoma warrior, aged twenty-one.

Boxing Day was our chance to give something back, and despite losing a year to Covid, our team of enthusiastic volunteers had only grown. The grotto was stacked with presents, the brass band played, and 250 people had the choice of traditional Christmas dinner, curry, or pizza and chips.

Before we opened Giddy Kippers' doors, Laura gave a speech explaining why this event was so important to her and thanking everyone for giving up their precious bank holiday.

'What y'on about?' said one volunteer. 'It doesn't feel like proper Christmas 'til we've done this. We should be thanking you.'

She was on her feet all day, helping to serve food and cleaning up – I had to take the dustpan and brush out of her hands to stop her from sweeping underneath tables. When the last guests were bundled into taxis with carrier bags full of presents, clothes and food, we took all that remained up to Curry on The Street: not a thing was wasted.

Laura was understandably shattered, and we were all enjoying a well-deserved lie-in the next day when I received a message from Nicky Fishwick, asking if Laura would like to come and fly in Dave's helicopter.

We got ready as quickly as we could and drove out to meet Nicky and 'Bank of' Dave outside their fabulous house on the other side of Pendle Hill. The shiny blue helicopter had once belonged to the Duke of Westminster and was Dave's pride and joy.

The plan had been for just the girls to go, but I didn't take much persuading to fill the spare seat. We flew low over the green Lancashire plain and out to the Fylde coast, landing on an inaccessible sand spit where we wrote Laura's name with a shell in the sand.

On the way back, Dave said: 'Have you been paying attention, Laura?'

'Yes, absolutely.' And of course, she had.

'Do you want to take the controls and fly us back?'

'I'd love to, if you're sure that's OK?'

Gracie and I turned to look at each other, our mouths made matching Os. Was he serious? She'd only had brain surgery five days ago, and now she was flying four people in a three-million-pound helicopter.

But Laura had been following intently and took to it like a natural; even Dave was impressed by her ability to handle the controls and maintain her line towards Pendle Hill.

Another vehicle ticked off the bucket list.

With every lockdown cancellation of the wedding, it seemed less likely Laura would have the chance to be Neil and Georgina's bridesmaid. Eight days after brain surgery it looked almost impossible.

She woke up feeling sickly. 'My brain feels all dehydrated, like there's loads of pressure. I think I might be sick. Have I got time to go back to bed for a bit?'

'Not really, you and Gracie are meant to be having your hair and make-up done at ten. But, listen, we don't have to go, and nobody expects you to be there. I'll stay here with you, it's completely fine.'

'Tell Gracie to go on ahead, I'll catch up. I just need a nap.'

I dosed her up with painkillers and anti-sickness meds then closed the curtains.

Laura woke with less than an hour to go, pale and shaky, but determined. There was no time for professional hair or makeup, so Gracie and I did what we could with some sparkly clips and a blusher brush before zipping her into her long navy dress. Before surgery, Mr D had asked what colour she'd be wearing, and his neat little stitches matched the dress perfectly.

We arrived at the venue with only minutes to spare before the ceremony, but you'd never have known. Both girls looked radiant as they walked down the aisle, followed by the beautiful bride. I tried to record it on my phone but couldn't see clearly, my eyes blurry with tears. Laura made her way to the lectern to give her reading and I wasn't the only one rummaging in a clutch bag for a packet of tissues.

The evening, and the year, finished with a spectacular firework display. We had made it to 2022, but the joy of a new year came with the familiar cold stomach chill of anxiety: who knew where we'd be a year from now?

2022

See How Lucky We Are!

New Year

We started the year with a weekend in a London still dressed in Christmas lights that glittered and reflected in puddles of bitter January rain, a rare trip as a family of four. The weekend had been gifted to us by way of apology for an excruciating evening the summer before, back when Laura was having infusions of Keytruda at the London Clinic.

I'd tried to cheer her up with a last-minute theatre trip to see *Constellations* with Anna Maxwell Martin and Chris O'Dowd, smugly delighted with myself for bagging the last two available seats for the midweek performance.

'How good is this?' I grinned at Laura as we clinked our glasses of complimentary fizz.

It was a magnificent piece of theatre, and we were enthralled by the acting and the stunning set design until, about halfway through, my stomach lurched and I realised with crushing inevitability where the story was heading.

The female character had been diagnosed with glioblastoma and was arranging to travel to Switzerland to end her life.

The hairs stood up on my arms and the fizz burned my throat like acid. There was no interval in which to escape, and we were squeezed into the middle of a row. I prayed for a fire alarm or for the seat to just swallow me whole.

'I'm so sorry,' I mouthed to Laura. 'Shall we go?'

But she brushed me off and stared straight ahead, her mouth a grim line.

She was horribly quiet on the walk back to the hotel.

'I do get it.'

'What do you get?'

'I get why someone with this would want to end their own life. It's the only control we have.'

Instead of cheering Laura up, I'd forced her to confront the most brutal depiction of her future. 'I actually think you've outdone yourself here, Nicola. Really, this is top drawer mothering,' Siobhan sniggered.

Ordinarily, I would have at least read a couple of reviews, but the booking had been made at the last possible moment and I hadn't looked beyond its stellar cast.

As Laura slept, I searched the theatre's website to see how I could have missed something so momentous. In my defence, there were no clues as to the content, so as a way to assuage my own guilt, I sent an email, suggesting the addition of an advisory note on the booking page to avoid the same thing happening to someone else.

I didn't like that I was becoming the kind of person who sent grumpy emails.

Within days a contrite reply popped into my inbox with an invitation to see another show and spend a couple of nights in the city. It was unnecessarily generous, but we had a fabulous weekend; it was the perfect distraction. Laura and I bought T-shirts from John Lewis with OPTIMIST in bold red capitals: a statement of intent, or our version of magical realism. I was desperately trying to enjoy every moment, chewing each one twenty times before swallowing.

Once we were back home, I took Laura into Manchester to meet up with a friend. As we walked back to the car park, she fell over crossing a busy road and lay motionless as the cars revved their engines and the traffic lights prepared to turn green.

A man shouted through his window to see if we were OK, and I struggled to get her back on her feet, my heart pounding. We joked about it as she limped back to the car, and she promised it hadn't hurt, but we were both shaken up by how close we suddenly felt to disaster.

In the early hours of next morning, Laura rang her bedside bell because her lower lip felt weird, and she couldn't feel her fingers. She went back to sleep eventually, but I stared at the ceiling for hours. This level of constant worry must be shortening our lives by years.

The bell was a godsend, but it was no help to Laura when she woke up in the middle of a massive nosebleed, staggered to the bathroom then passed out. She lay on the floor for half an hour, unable to stand or shout for help. I ordered a hand bell.

Gracie came home for the weekend; she was so very low. 'How can I live without her, Mum?'

I didn't know the answer, it was a question I often asked myself, but I needed to give her something. 'You have to be here for Alice, Gracie, you have to be here for me, because there will be better days ahead. Not the same, but eventually we will have good days.'

'I won't have good days without Laura in the world,' Gracie said. 'How could I?'

The weeks spent in Cologne gave me precious time with Laura. I'd even mastered the art of German online food shopping, timed so the order would be delivered in the gap between our arrival and the first appointment at the clinic.

Laura would go for a nap, and I'd stand by the window waiting for the bike with its little trailer to pull up outside. I never knew what the name on our doorbell might be, so I'd rush down to collect the paper sacks of groceries and by the time Laura woke up, I'd have lunch ready – or at least apples and carrots and Pringles and cheese.

The money raised by Peter's shows meant we could afford to fund two more dendritic vaccinations, and this time the clinic was also able to use tumour tissue removed in the last surgery, which had been flash-frozen as we'd requested.

Laura used the time between treatments to apply for graduate jobs, but so far without success, she found it difficult to know how much to reveal or conceal.

'Am I ever going to just be normal again?'

It was physically painful to see her rejected. How could it not be obvious on paper how fantastic this girl was and how hard she would work if only given a chance?

'So much for saying I could just be like anyone else.'

Although the search for a job wasn't going well, Laura's love life was at least showing signs of improvement. She went on a first date to a bowling alley and called me to tell me how it had gone.

'You'll really like her, Mum. She's doing a masters and she's so smart. I even told her I had cancer.'

'You did? Wow, what did she say?'

'She just kissed me.'

I was so happy for her. But while I still really wanted Laura to fall in love and be loved back, I was also terrified that someone would hurt her. Strong as she appeared on the surface, that might break her. She was always slow to make herself vulnerable, but especially now when life was so precarious.

Gracie was not altogether happy about it – another person in Laura's life meant she'd have less time to spend with family, and this seemed particularly unfair when Gracie had steadfastly avoided romantic entanglements for the same reason, putting that side of her life on hold so she could maximise time with Laura.

'She'd better not just drop us now she's got a girlfriend.'

I could see both sides.

In the jumble of soft warm laundry that tumbled out of the drier and into the basket, I noticed a hand-drawn star on the label of a pair of Mark's pants. He'd found a Sharpie and carefully drawn an asterisk on the silvery label that once gave washing instructions before the words faded away. He must have decided that these were his lucky underpants.

Maybe he had worn them on scan days when everything had gone well or those hospital appointments when we could exhale and rejoice at the word 'stable'. Mark had endowed those pants with mythical superpowers, and under no circumstances could they be confused with other, more ordinary pants – siblings from a Next multipack.

We weren't done with that magic yet, and he needed to be able to find those lucky pants every three months for the rest of time.

Amani's parents were just like us, desperately trying to find a way to buy more time with their daughter. She was beautiful and smart and deserved a life, but another family had lost its light.

I knew this awful news would upset Laura and I didn't want to rattle her.

'Amani,' she said, quietly.

'I know, my darling. It's devastating, isn't it? I'm so, so sad for her family.'

'Mum, how come I'm still alive?'

'I don't honestly know, Laura. I'm glad that you are, though.'

* * *

At the end of February, Russia invaded Ukraine and we gathered to watch the evening news, horrified by the footage of desperate families crowding into train stations, carrying small children and bulging suitcases in the search for safety.

Laura came down from working on her dissertation and stood in the doorway. 'This is absolutely awful. What can we do to help?'

The next day we bought hundreds of pounds' worth of toiletries, nappies and baby products and took them to a donation centre where they were to be consolidated and driven to the border.

'It's not enough though, Mum. We need to offer a family somewhere to stay – we've got a spare room and I don't mind sharing the bathroom.'

Laura was back on chemo again, and back to being sick almost every day for a week each month. The idea of sharing a house with strangers, when she was at her very weakest and most vulnerable, seemed impractical and maybe even reckless, but she was resolute.

'See how lucky we are, living in our nice house in a safe country? It's our duty to help where we can.'

Mark took a little persuasion, but Gracie looked at me, incredulous.

'You want to bring refugees into our house while Laura's so sick? That's insane! Do we not already have enough to cope with?'

With three votes for yes, it was a majority decision, and we submitted our interest in hosting a Ukrainian family.

Fun-draising

March

We'd been planning a fundraising ball at Giddy Kippers before Covid scuppered everyone's plans. Adults and alcohol in a children's play centre, what could possibly go wrong?

One of our suppliers, Birchalls, provided us with all the food, and Courtney Birchall was on hand to manage every detail. Mark had been sent out to collect a list of raffle prizes; he was so bowled over by the incredible generosity of local business owners that he came back looking uncharacteristically emotional.

Luke, who'd previously worked as our chef, teamed up with Michael to run the cocktail bar, and radio presenter Tony Livesey acted as our auctioneer.

On the night, Laura gave a speech to thank everyone for coming, smiley and elegant in her long black dress. Then when everyone was sufficiently giddy, we opened the play equipment for half an hour and men in black tie flew down the slide and ladies in long dresses swung across the play frame on zip wires. It was an unforgettable night and although many probably woke with unexplained bruises the next morning, everyone seemed to have a wonderful time – when the lights came back up, nobody wanted to go home.

Laura continued to stay at uni during the week, and we'd try to tempt her home at weekends to check she was eating properly and taking her tablets. Uni life was different after Covid and either there wasn't much socialising at weekends, or Laura just wasn't that interested. It's not the same experience when you tire easily and can't drink. Mark coaxed her back by promising her a day with power tools, cutting down branches to make a bonfire – he knew she'd find that impossible to resist.

The routine three-month scan was described as 'essentially

good', but there was some 'enhancement' which in a best-case scenario could just be the cavity left by the tumour collapsing in on itself. The next one would be crucial, though. People with brain tumours like Laura lived their years in quarters – dissected by scans. It's impossible to comprehend the level of stress unless you experience it. When well-meaning people said, 'I honestly don't know how you cope – I know I couldn't,' I'd smile understandingly.

If their lives imploded like ours they'd cope just fine, because they wouldn't have any choice. And that's the absolute truth.

We organised another get-together for our Strength in Numbers family. This time I brought stickers: pink hearts for those who'd lost someone, gold hearts for carers and silver stars for those with a tumour. Gracie made a point of jumping up to greet each guest as they walked hesitantly into the restaurant, searching for a familiar face. Some were buoyant, others emotional and overwhelmed, and I watched as Gracie gave a pink star to a young widow in tears, comforting her as she ordered her a drink from the bar. We'd brought along some craft supplies for the children and later I spotted Gracie colouring with a group of girls – two teenagers wearing gold stars for their dad, Liam, and a little one with a pink heart for her grandma. She had them all laughing, and I almost burst with pride. She'd always been kind, but this new maturity and compassion for others just melted my heart.

In the Easter break, Laura travelled to Basingstoke to drive tanks. Wearing her dad's jacket on top of her own and a beret at a jaunty angle, she beamed down from her position, high in the turret.

Captain Dave invited us to spend a day with the Red Arrows at RAF Scampton; not up in a jet, obviously, but we did get to watch the team practise, sit through the debrief, and take lots of photos. We had a tour of the hangar where the planes were maintained and Laura got to sit in the tiny pilot's seat, grinning in her *Top Gun* aviator sunglasses.

I finally agreed to play Mario Kart with the girls and was just as bad as expected, giving them both many reasons to laugh at me. The laughter stopped when we heard on the radio that Tom Parker from The Wanted had died. He'd been having treatment in Spain and his last scan had been stable, he'd spoken about brain tumours in Parliament just months before, and seemed to be doing so well. It was dreadful, shocking news.

Glioblastoma is an absolute bastard. It doesn't care whether you're a pop star, Joe Biden's son or thirteen-year-old gorgeous George who also died that month. It's as relentless and devastating as a forest fire.

Dancing and Swimming
Spring

We made it to Peter's *Dance for Life* show and Laura had no need of a trapdoor; in fact, she danced all night. The whole family was out in force, wearing blue tutus, legwarmers and red Brain Tumour Charity T-shirts. The music was straight from the school disco and the audience loved it. Gracie showed off her cartwheels and my dad got in trouble with my mum for chatting up other women (he really wasn't). Peter got us all up on stage and we joined him in a 'Love Train' conga in front of 10,000 people.

Laura was on great form, having just submitted an essay she'd wrestled with for months. My favourite moment of the night was watching her belting out Katie Perry's 'Firework' with everything she had, hands in the air, eyes sparkling and a crescent of turquoise glitter on her face.

When the lights went up, Neil made snow angels in the rain-bow-coloured confetti that had fallen like feathery snowflakes to the floor, and we joined Peter for backstage drinks – until we realised that Laura had fallen asleep with her head on my dad's shoulder.

The chemo was once again accumulating in Laura's body, leaving her sick and listless. The fatigue made it harder to face the remaining essays and the dissertation she still needed to complete. Her appetite had disappeared too, meaning that eating the smallest lunch would take hours, and she'd need a nap to recover.

I was trying to motivate her to get the work done, and also make sure she rested. I was walking the finest of lines: the girl deserved a medal as well as a degree.

A kind friend offered the use of her beautiful converted boat-house on Windermere, and we had a lovely weekend of respite in the soft, drizzly Lake District. We walked, played Scrabble, and sat on the jetty watching boats. Ziggy was chased by an angry swan, and we zoomed round Grizedale Forest on segways. Suffice to say, Laura was a natural; while Gracie and I crashed into trees.

We had talked about wild swimming, but April was chilly, and it seemed a bit rash. Laura was still up for the adventure, though, even if she was always first to feel the cold.

'I don't think you should, Laura. You know what you're like, and we don't want to ruin the rest of the trip with you getting hypothermia or something,' Gracie said.

She had a point: years before, the girls had tried surfing in Cornwall and even in a wetsuit Laura emerged from the sea frozen. We'd had to cover her in a mountain of our coats until she eventually returned from blue to pink.

Laura looked at her sister with narrowed eyes, changed into a swimsuit and laced up her trainers, walking into the icy lake without hesitation. Gracie and I raced to catch up with her, yelping with the shock as the cold took our breath away. All three of us swam, but not for long. Mark didn't join us – something about the male anatomy and cold water, apparently.

'Never a good idea to challenge Laura or tell her she can't do something,' I said to Gracie, as we towelled ourselves dry. 'You know what she's like.'

'I know exactly what she's like,' Gracie replied, with a complicit smile.

In some ways, what happened to our family was a bit like a football club entering the relegation zone. It made us reassess what was important, forced us to work together, rally our supporters, and gave us a sense of perspective. When you're teetering on the edge, you have the keenest awareness of what's at stake.

Were we a stronger family because we had been tested so relentlessly? Definitely. That's not to say that I wouldn't have preferred normal and ordinary, but if our team had finished mid table, it wouldn't have seen the extraordinary support and all that incredible love and passion. I guess, as a family, we were just the same.

In May, Laura was woken by yet another nosebleed, and she was tired all the time. When I came home one day to find her on the carpet in the hall, my heart froze. I thought she'd fainted, but she was OK – just resting on the floor before the exhausting task of walking up stairs.

The playwright Anna Deavere Smith wrote: 'Cancer therapy is like beating the dog with a stick to get rid of his fleas.' And she was absolutely right.

The good news was that Laura had finally submitted her dissertation, a colossal achievement in the circumstances. I just hoped that it hadn't cost her too dearly.

A lady from the local authority came to check our house was suitable for a Ukrainian family to live in. It felt like we were adopting a child and I was almost nervous.

Laura was excited at the prospect of helping, but Gracie was still apprehensive. 'Are you absolutely sure this is a good idea, Mum?'

She had so little control of her world, this was one more thing she didn't have a say on.

I felt guilty that we'd bulldozed her into going along with Laura's plan; but it wasn't just about Ukrainians, it was her whole life.

Be Kind, Be Brave, Be Silly, Be Honest

June

Our previous holiday in France had been perfect, and we worried that it could never be as good a second time, but it really was. The sun shone, and we lazed on pool inflatables, competed to solve a murder, and crammed twelve of us in a minibus to dine at a tiny rural restaurant that only served duck. We'd brought decorations and when Laura submitted her final essay, we had a little party to celebrate her achievement.

I'd asked everyone to choose their desert island discs and make a playlist of their eight songs, and after dinner we would meet by the pool, light candles, and share our choices. I stood in for Lauren Laverne, and we filmed each one. I don't think anyone could have predicted how emotional and precious this would turn out to be. It took a week to complete, and many unexpected tears were shed, but we all knew each other a little better after that. It was truly beautiful.

Soon afterwards, Laura received an email confirming that she'd passed her degree with a magnificent 2:1. We were actually going to see her graduate – something we had hardly dare hope for. It was such fantastic news, I couldn't wait to see her in cap and gown and wanted to make the whole day as special as possible for her. The Hyatt offered to host a graduation lunch in the private apartment at the top of the hotel, with its own bar and incredible views of the city – a venue normally rented out to footballers and celebrities. We just needed a dress, so on our June trip to Germany I took Laura shopping.

The changing room was full of light in the glass-walled department store. Each cubicle was occupied, mostly by young girls choosing prom dresses. In the area just outside, I watched from a stool beside a full-length mirror, where a selection of high heels waited for a reverse Cinderella to kick off her trainers. Periodically a curtain swished opened, and a girl would step out swathed in satin, embellished with jewels, tugging to keep a strapless dress up, on her tiptoes to replicate heels. Some were beautiful, some soon would be, but every girl would look gorgeous on prom night, like a dress rehearsal for a wedding day.

I remembered Laura's prom. She hadn't wanted a fuss or been particularly bothered about going. She'd bought a dress from the New Look sale – black, with gold Grecian detailing – she had looked perfect, with her long blonde hair half up, half down, falling in ringlets down her back. A flustered makeup artist arrived with a stack of palettes and a toolbelt of brushes, transforming Laura into someone we hardly recognised, her teenage awkwardness replaced by a new, elegant composure.

The curtain in front of me opened and broke my reverie. Laura was a different girl now. Her hair was shorter, but it no longer screamed cancer. She was wearing a dress with a navy jersey bodice and a full, silky print skirt. It had a fifties' vibe, and she looked beautiful. She didn't need satin and jewels now, just something classy to wear under an academic gown.

'Do you like it?' she asked.

'It's absolutely perfect,' I replied.

Still in Cologne, I took Laura to an outdoor spa for the day. We swam and read books in the sun, and felt very clever for having negotiated our way there and successfully avoided the naked sunbathing areas.

We used to hear scan results in anonymous offices, a computer screen turned around to allow us to draw our own conclusions from the black and white Rorschach image. Sometimes I could see a face or a pattern, sometimes I was too scared to look.

In lockdown we would wait for a call, the four of us gathered at the bottom of the stairs with the phone on speaker, expecting the worst, bubbling with anxiety and nervous energy.

Today we were in a café. Laura had ordered a Wensleydale and apple sandwich but when it came, she couldn't face it. Madonna was singing 'Borderline' when the phone rang. It would have been a terrible place to hear bad news, but there's no such thing when you hear the word 'stable' and can breathe for another three months.

We got home to find Mark lecturing Gracie on how she should apply for Camp America and do something useful in the summer holidays. I could see the frustration in her body language, tears threatening to spill from her eyes.

'You are joking, right? You think I could go away for three months and leave Laura? I would absolutely love to do Camp America, Dad! I could have spent a year in Chicago as part of my course – but how on earth do you think I could leave her for that length of time? You have no idea what it's like for me! I can't travel, I can't be in a relationship – I just need to be here, spending as much time with Laura as I can, while I still can. And the only way that this won't be the case is when she's dead. How are you not getting this, Dad?'

Mark's intentions had been good: he wanted Gracie to spread her wings, but he forgot to join up the dots sometimes. I'm so glad Laura got her summer in the US. At the time I'd worried about all the things that could go wrong, but she'd had the time of her life and no regrets.

I hoped Gracie would get her chance soon. Just not right now.

The next morning, she and I got up early and walked twelve miles on Pendle Hill, then refuelled with a cooked breakfast on a picnic bench outside the cabin café. We did our best talking while we walked side by side, without distractions, on the wide, open moors under clean-washed skies.

As the end of term approached, the head teacher at a local primary school asked Laura if she'd consider writing a letter of advice to the Year 6 children as they left for secondary school. She'd be following in the footsteps of Alastair Campbell and Sean Dyche, so it was an honour to be asked.

Laura thought long and hard about what the last few years had taught her, and then wrote: 'Ever since I was young, I had a plan. A sort of vision about how my life would go, as I imagine most of you do too. I got irritated when things didn't follow my plan and used every force necessary to put it back on track again. My dad constantly liked to tell me, "You can't predict life, you never know what you're going to get" and as much as I hate to admit it, he was right.

'While I was starting university, by a series of very fortunate events, I was diagnosed with brain cancer. I was lucky, because I was later told that if it wasn't diagnosed as fast as it was, I wouldn't be here to write this letter. This news turned mine and my family's life upside down and we had to start adapting to life with cancer. Much like my dad had predicted, my plan was instantly changed forever.

'Dealing with cancer and all its side effects has taught me a few lessons that I would like to share with you today.

'If you get knocked down, don't stay down. Sometimes you might need a little time to recover from bumps in the road but get up as soon as you can. That's what will make you strong. Resilience is important, because we can't always control what happens, but we can control how we deal with it.

'Don't let others limit you or tell you that you can't do something. If you work hard and put your mind to it, there's almost nothing you can't achieve. Challenge other people's expectations and make it your mission to prove those doubters wrong.

'Sometimes you will need to ask for help from those around you. This doesn't make you any less capable. We all need help from time to time and it's important to talk to the people who care about you. It's not a sign of weakness!

'My life most definitely hasn't gone to plan but there are so many opportunities and experiences that I would have missed if it had. At the time, finding out I had maybe a year to live was the worst thing I could have imagined, but in the last three years I have met incredible people, travelled to brilliant places, and lived more in a few years than many people do in a whole lifetime. It's not what I would have chosen, but I can honestly say I have made the very best of a bad situation.

'I have also learned that, although watching the news makes you think the opposite, people are really very kind.

'I hope that your life does go to plan, but if it doesn't, you might be pleasantly surprised at what's just around the corner for you.

'And so, as you all make this next step in your lives, I hope you take all the opportunities life gives you and say "yes" to things, even if you're a tiny bit scared.

'Be kind, be brave, be silly, be honest, be happy, be you.

'Love from Laura x'

'Salutation' day

Summer

Laura had always wanted to see the musical *Hamilton* and she was delighted when I managed to finesse some tickets and a night in the lovely Claremont Hotel. After the show, we bought T-shirts and danced around the hotel room wearing them. I loved these opportunities to spend time with her, talking rubbish and reminiscing about the things we'd done together.

'Hey, what about that time when we …'

'Yes, and then you did that …'

One day I'd be the only one to remember them, and this suddenly made me wonder what the point was. Memories are like a see-saw, and a see-saw with only one person is just a plank of wood pointing at the sky.

The whole family had been elated with the news of Laura's 2:1. But her own reaction couldn't have been more typical: 'It's not a first, though, is it?'

I reminded her of the nineteen weeks of treatment in Germany, the eleven cycles of chemo, six rounds of Keytruda, two blood transfusions and two brain surgeries that she'd endured during the last three years, not to mention the challenges of Covid or the tiny Airbnb apartments in Cologne with poor WiFi, or the soul-sucking fatigue she'd experienced.

'Well, I suppose it's OK, all things considered,' she grudgingly conceded.

'And now I'm going to need to get at least a 2:1,' Gracie replied, rolling her eyes. 'As if you went and managed a grade like that, with all you've had to deal with.'

We all knew how hard she'd had to work, grinding out essays when she was sick and exhausted, fuelled by a potent blend of courage and the determination to prove her doubters wrong.

As if two wasn't enough, our home was about to gain another couple of courageous girls.

Late one Tuesday night, Mark and I waited for a flight from Budapest to touch down at Liverpool airport. We weren't the only people holding cardboard signs and looking nervous. I'd decorated ours with some blue and yellow flags and translated, 'Welcome to England' into Ukrainian.

Our spare room had been emptied of accumulated junk, Mark had given it a lick of paint and we'd bought a new bed and fresh linens, yellow cushions, and Ukrainian bunting.

Mother and daughter Tanya and Yeva arrived in the UK with nothing more than hand luggage – Yeva's tiny suitcase was printed with the universal face of Mickey Mouse. And they seemed to have brought more gifts for us than belongings: airport carrier bags stuffed with sweets and chocolates, T-shirts, and a little cushion printed with the golden wheat field and the bright blue sky of the Ukrainian flag.

The following weeks were spent arranging visas and registering with the doctor, the dentist, and the job centre. I took Yeva to visit the local secondary school. She looked bewildered by the chaos and noise of hundreds of children charging between classes, but she was delighted with her new uniform, and we took photographs to send to her grandparents and dad. Six months before, he'd been working as a carpenter, fitting kitchens, but now he was on the frontline, defending his country against invaders.

Neither Tanya nor Yeva spoke a great deal of English, but we made good use of translation apps and hand gestures. Life in Ukraine didn't seem all that different from ours, but it was apparent that the division of labour between the sexes was still quite old-school.

Mark cooked tea on the barbecue one night and Tanya looked horrified. 'This is normal?' she whispered to me.

Later that night I stood in the doorway and watched Laura and Gracie pretend to be terrible at Mario Kart so that Yeva, who'd never played before, could win. It was the first time I'd heard her laugh, and I don't think I had ever loved them more.

Laura's graduation day was on one of the hottest the UK had ever experienced. I'd packed emergency meds, cool packs, drinks and cereal bars just in case Laura felt faint or dizzy, but she was so full of joy, I needn't have worried.

She looked stunning, the dress from Cologne was perfect, especially when accessorised with mortar board and gown. I smiled so hard and took a million photographs. I just wanted to burn the memory into the backs of my eyes, so I never forgot how beautiful or happy she was.

Once the graduands were seated, in strict alphabetical order, the guests filed in, grateful for the cool relief of Whitworth Hall. Mark, Gracie and I sat on the front row with phones poised to record the moment, the culmination of three tough years of grit and determination, a challenge that had often seemed inconceivable. It was hard not to think back to the day Laura had been given her prognosis and told that a return to uni was impossible. I knew on a visceral level how gruelling it had been and what it had cost her to get here.

Laura's name was read out and we whooped and cheered so loudly that people turned around to stare, but the vice chancellor went on to explain that throughout her studies, Laura had also been dealing with the additional challenges of a terminal brain cancer diagnosis.

I can't remember what else he said because I was weeping, but I heard the collective intake of breath from a hall full of parents, then enthusiastic applause that lasted ages and almost raised the roof. Laura smiled shyly, she didn't like all the fuss, but this day was hers; she was our rock star and I'm not sure I'd ever seen her so completely happy. Later, when she was interviewed on the college green, she described the day as 'pretty epic'.

Mum made her a 2:1 cake and Alice called it her 'salutation day'.

Laura sent official graduation photos to both her surgeons. She wasn't gloating, though, as we hadn't beaten the disease, just found more time that we had any right to, and without their skills Laura would quite probably be dead. It was a sincere thank you.

Her graduation generated more interview requests: it made for a good story – 'Brain cancer girl told she wouldn't go back to university, graduates.'

We gratefully took every opportunity to raise awareness of the disease, happy to join Naga and Charlie on the red BBC Breakfast sofa, although the clip they shared of Laura on the stage left me in pieces.

'That's what I've learned,' Laura said. 'If this is all you get of life, then why not say yes to everything that you get offered?'

A few days later we were back in the same studio adding another extraordinary item to the bucket list. This time Laura was presenting the weather with Owain Wyn Evans. I'd found her a T-shirt with a weather symbol on it and after twenty minutes in make-up she emerged with cheekbones we'd never seen before, her blue-green eyes luminous. Following the autocue and pointing to the right areas on the map was harder than it looked; Laura the perfectionist took at least six attempts to describe warm fronts and high pressure, not happy with the take until it was faultless. These days nothing fazed her, every opportunity was a blessing to be relished and treasured. Who else got to do such incredible things?

These bucket list adventures lived in a museum drawer, and when days were dark we could slide it open to reveal individual memories like warm stones to be handled and inhaled.

* * *

Laura had always been a Lioness at heart and played for Pendle Diamonds football club when she was younger. In an early game, she'd kicked the ball out of play and a few supporters had clapped; as a result, she did the same in every subsequent match, much to the frustration of her coach.

We travelled to Sheffield to watch the England women beat Sweden in the semi-final of the Euros. Laura was ecstatic at the win, and before we'd even made it back to the car she asked the inevitable question, her voice hoarse from shouting and cheering. 'I really, really want to go to the final, Mum! What's the chances of getting us tickets?'

'Seriously? You think I can work miracles, Laura! It's a big ask – everyone in England will want to be at Wembley. I bet the tickets sold out months ago.'

In the end, BBC *Newsbeat* made the magic happen. And not only did they secure tickets, but the England captain Leah Williamson recorded a video message for Laura, which was played to her over Zoom.

'We've been following your story and we're incredibly inspired by you and the fight that you have in you,' she began.

Laura couldn't have been more thrilled and watched the clip again and again.

We checked into the fabulous Langham Hotel and enjoyed a quick afternoon tea before we painted our cheeks with the red and white of St George's Cross and changed into our England shirts. The atmosphere was joyful and tingly with anticipation; Wembley Way packed with excited families and supporters all hoping for a great day of football.

Newsbeat had asked me to try to record as much of the experience as I could, so I captured Laura's delight at our seats above the tunnel, her joy at the first goal and misery as Germany equalised. But her face as Chloe Kelly scored in extra time and the final whistle went, was beatific. The footage was wobbly as I was trying to film Laura, watch the pitch and not get too emotional but I hoped I had captured her pure, unmitigated delight.

Laura bought a bright orange football shirt the next day – a youth's size because it was bit cheaper – and had WILLIAMSON printed on the back. She wore the shirt to Birmingham where we spent another glorious sunny day enjoying the spectacle of the Commonwealth Games.

I'd nominated her to carry the Queen's baton and she'd taken her turn in the relay between a health care entrepreneur and Gemma, who campaigned for anaphylaxis charities, having lost her daughter to an undiagnosed nut allergy. The streets of Blackburn were not exactly packed with supporters, but we brought noisy cowbells and cheered and clapped as Laura, in her Commonwealth Games uniform, took the tall silver baton and thrust it high in the air. It was heavier than it looked, and she wasn't holding it quite so high when she handed it over to Gemma with a relieved look on her face, but it was a moment in history, and she'd taken a part.

On Mark's birthday, we traipsed across fields with swimsuits on under our shorts trying to find a waterfall I'd heard about. Gracie was losing patience with my map reading and we were close to giving up when I found it in a clearing. The hot weather had reduced it to a trickle, but we tiptoed across the rocks, slippery with emerald moss, arms held out for balance, and lowered ourselves cautiously into the cool water. Ziggy was delighted to have company for a change and splashed us with his furious doggy paddle.

There was no one else around, just the five of us in the little pool shaded by overhanging branches. We could have been anywhere, and it was perfect. Only bettered by the arrival of Alfred Edward on my dad's birthday. A brother for Alice and a brand-new baby cousin for the girls.

With the chaos of a new baby at home, Laura and Gracie took Alice out to a theme park for a treat. They spun dizzily in teacups, rode horses on the carousel and Alice got shy and starstruck when she met her hero, Bing the bunny. They said yes to everything, and the toddler was awash with slush, hot dogs and donuts. She fell fast asleep in her car seat, still clutching the string of a balloon.

'I hope that I live long enough for Alice to remember me,' Laura said.

From when she was really quite young, Laura had always been clever with money: she once sold Gracie her fish tank for £30 but a condition of the sale was a mandatory tank cleaning contract, fleecing her out of a further £15 every month.

She was always looking for dropped coins too, especially around the tills in supermarkets. The day she found a £2 coin in Boots was – no exaggeration – one of the highlights of her entire childhood, so it was no surprise that she'd always wanted to visit the Royal Mint.

Gracie thought being excited by coins was a bit nerdy, but she was definitely up for a road trip to Cardiff, as she really enjoyed driving.

At one point she called over her shoulder, 'Get off your phone, Mum! You're missing all the lovely scenery!'

How quickly things had changed.

Laura loved the tour and even Gracie conceded that it was surprisingly interesting. The girls sang unself-consciously all the way home and I filmed them from my seat in the back, hoping for many more days just like this.

Running on Determination

September

Back when she should really have been spending all her energies on A Level revision, Laura had also been studying for her Advanced Drivers certificate, meeting with a public speaking group to practise her skills, and training for her first marathon. It was almost as if she had known that time was short, and that she needed to jam in as much as possible.

Her training had been a bit hit and miss: it had been unseasonably hot, and her longest run had to be abandoned when she accidentally squirted soap into her water bottle while trying to refill it in one of those all-in-one units you find in public toilets. She completed the race in a very respectable 4.5 hours, and cried as she crossed the finish line – and Laura never cried.

'That was the hardest thing I have ever done,' she said, lying on the grass and trying to get her breath back.

This year, I had managed to convince Mark and Gracie that we should enter the Great North Run to raise funds for The Brain Tumour Charity, but Laura had other ideas.

'If you lot are doing it, I'm doing it too,' she stated firmly.

'Laura, it's a long way. Your joints still haven't recovered from the immunotherapy and what if you feel faint? You'd be better volunteering at the recovery centre; they'd love your help at the finish.'

'Nope, one in – all in.'

Mark and I both ran fairly regularly but not very far, Gracie would just wing it and although Laura had managed a few practice runs, I had no idea if she could cope with this level of exertion or the hours out on the course. Even if we walked, it was still a long way, but Laura was determined. She knew that it was likely to garner some media interest and that would only help in raising much-needed funds for the charity.

Sure enough, the BBC came out to record interviews, and filmed Mark, Laura and me as we pretended to run back and forth through the field behind our house.

Fuelling up with bowls of pasta the night before – rule one of long-distance running – we came up with an idea. We would dedicate each mile to people we knew who were fighting a brain tumour or who we'd lost to this awful disease. It didn't take much effort to assemble a long list – their names and heart-breaking stories were burned into my memory, never to be forgotten. We found a suitable book in Spennymore Asda, the only shop open at that late hour, and a pack of felt-tips to write in the names.

Many of the runners on the start line wore black ribbons to mark the death of the Queen three days earlier; there had even been some doubt as to whether the event would take place in the circumstances, and it definitely felt a more sombre occasion than the usual effervescent celebration of humanity in Lycra and trainers.

At every mile marker, we stopped and shared a photo on Twitter of the corresponding page in our book so those support-ing us could follow our progress to South Shields. We were not fast. Mark had initially planned to carry two collection buckets for the charity, but we persuaded him one was enough. What he hadn't realised was that many of the spectators who lined the route brought money for just for this purpose, but it wasn't light, folding money – it was children with coin bags filled with pennies and 2ps saved in a jar for months.

The bucket got heavy very quickly as most people had more sense than to carry big tubs full of shrapnel for thirteen miles: 'Here you go, pet – that man's got a bucket for your bag of change.'

I could hear Mark groan at the prospect, but of course he smiled and thanked them, grateful now it was just the one he had to carry.

We ate the ice pops and sucked on orange segments. Gracie stroked thirty dogs – she counted every one – and we shouted 'Oggy oggy oggy!' as we jogged through tunnels.

Laura soldiered on resolutely but became gradually quieter, her face pale, eyes starey and unfocused as we alternated between walking and jogging. At mile nine Sophie Raworth phoned to give her some encouragement and each time we asked if she wanted to stop, she shook her head determinedly.

Gracie went over on her ankle and limped the last couple of miles; I accused her of being a drama queen and had to apologise the following day, when her foot was a swollen explosion of green and purple.

It was a relief to finally cross the finish line. We collected our medals, then refuelled with crepes and pizza in the hospitality tent. Later that evening, as we watched the BBC footage on catch up, Paula Radcliffe mentioned Laura by name and commented on her perseverance and determination.

Laura was amazed and delighted: 'Oh my God! Paula Radcliffe knows who I am!'

It had been tougher than expected and we were lucky not to have spent time in the back of a St John's ambulance, but it was another medal for her collection and again she'd proved her doubters wrong.

Twenty-three had always been my lucky number. The reason was rubbish: it was the number of my favourite contestant in a Miss World pageant sometime in the 1970s. I can't remember whether she did indeed have a career taking care of animals and children, but number 23 became my favourite number for a whole lifetime.

Laura was born on 23 December and, exactly 273 months later, to the day, we were sitting in the waiting room of the MRI suite again. *Tenable* was playing on the wall-mounted TV, just loud enough to make conversation awkward. Contestants were being asked to name artists with works in the Tate. Turner? Hockney? And chemical elements with two vowels in alphabetical order. Carbon? Neon?

It took two attempts to get the cannula into her tiny, scarred veins, but despite the discomfort, Laura was in a buoyant mood. We were trying to remember the whether Coolio was singing about being twenty-two or twenty-three in the song 'Gangsta's Paradise'.

'Make sure you play it at my funeral, oh, and I've got another one for the cremation – "Girl on Fire" by Alicia Keys,' she said, with a wicked grin.

I laughed uneasily and changed the subject.

After the scan, we waited for a nurse to remove the cannula and send us on our way. Although we'd been told 4 p.m., it was already half past. I caught the eye of a passing nurse and she smiled awkwardly and explained that they were just checking the scans, and someone would come and remove the cannula shortly. This was new.

Then, a little later, a radiologist with bushy brown hair and a white lab coat told me, 'We're just trying to get hold of someone from Laura's team.'

He didn't meet my eye, and I could feel fractures opening up in the ground beneath my feet.

The waiting area was cold. I put Laura's jacket around her shoulders and sent Mark a text message.

'Something v wrong here.'

'Shall I come in?'

'I think you'd better.'

The cannula was removed, and we were asked to go and sit in the café to wait for Dr C, who would be with us in about an hour.

The anticipation of bad news froze my fingers, as all the blood retreated away from my extremities and rushed to support my heart, which was beating unnaturally fast, my breath shallow.

Laura wanted chocolate milk, Mark had sparkling water, I drank tea and messaged our nurse specialist with trembling fingers, then put *The Crown* on my phone to distract Laura from the storm that was just over the horizon.

We met Dr C and Hanna in the Teenage and Young Adult unit. Nothing in her texted reply had provided any reassurance and as we walked into the office, she stroked Laura's arm, so I knew the news was bad.

'I'm afraid the scan shows new growth.'

Dr C turned his screen so we could see the images. It didn't need to be pointed out, there it was, furious and invasive, pushing hard against the midline of the brain to selfishly make space. It was about the size of an apricot or a large conker, like the one she picked up off the ground as we walked back to the car park.

'I don't think it's safe for you to fly to Germany now, it's too risky – the pressure could be dangerous for Laura,' he said. 'I'm prescribing more steroids, start them straight away and hopefully they'll help to reduce the swelling and control the symptoms.'

I was silent, I had no questions, my face hard and set like concrete.

Laura asked if this new tumour was in the same place.

'We don't think so …' he replied, as he moved his mouse and flashed through the wafer-thin slices of Laura's brain, '… but I'll discuss the scans with my colleagues to see if it's operable. If not, we'll have to look at other chemo options.'

Laura was both sad and angry, I was trying not to be sick.

On the way home we listened to a debate on that day's budget, which seemed to only favour the rich, and then to the *News Quiz*. We laughed in all the right places, but nobody had anything to say.

Gracie phoned to ask how it went, and to tell me she was leaving Salford and would be home soon.

I couldn't tell her then, as I was worried she might (deliberately or accidentally) drive into a wall or off a bridge, so I made my voice artificially light and told her I'd see her shortly. She was actually two cars in front as we drove off the motorway and through the village, and my stomach flipped at the thought of knocking her world off its axis once again.

I was crying as I walked towards her. 'I'm so sorry.'

'What?' she said, blindsided.

'It's back. I'm so sorry.'

'You're joking … you're joking,' she repeated, louder. Then she folded down like a concertina, sobbing as she dropped onto the tarmac of the driveway.

I sat beside her, wrapping her tightly in my arms. Ziggy trotted across to us with Tanya following behind; he nuzzled in to make a space between us as we both cried, then flipped onto his back in the hope that now would be a good time for a tummy scratch.

'What am I meant to do now?' Gracie asked, her face striped with tears. 'What am I supposed to do?'

Eventually, Laura walked over and pulled Gracie up off the ground. 'Sorry, Gracie,' she said, ruefully.

Laura didn't sleep that night – hardly surprising given what she had seen on the computer screen and the unmistakable weight of the words spoken.

'I think I need to get my affairs in order,' she told me. 'Do you think I should write people letters?'

'Letters?' I asked.

'There are things I want to say and people I want to apologise to.'

'I don't think you've anything to apologise for, Laura.'

'I wasn't a good sister; I could have been better and I'm thinking of leaving some money to Alice and Alf and giving the rest to

Gracie. Also, what about my help-to-buy ISA and what will happen to the eggs I had frozen?'

Although she'd said very little the day before, there were obviously lots of serious thoughts spinning in her head now the dust had settled.

Gracie interpreted this new pragmatism as Laura giving up and coming to terms with the fact that she was going to die. I found her crying at her dressing table.

'Mum, tell me she's not going to die.'

I hugged her as hard as I could and took the impact of her sobs.

'We're all going to die, Gracie.'

When your specialist nurse, who works forty miles away, suggests popping in for a chat, it's probably not because she's just passing.

When Hanna asked if she could come over and see us, I told her Laura wouldn't be in as she was out with Gracie.

She said that might be for the best.

We made all the usual polite small talk about the house and the dog nuzzling her hand for strokes, then Hanna cut to the chase and suggested we might want to talk to Laura about what she wanted from future treatments. If we were looking down the barrel of radiation and the statistically less effective second line chemo then, with the best will in the world, it was only going to buy her a short extension, and in that time, she would lose her hair again, feel really sick, be prone to infections and potentially need blood and platelet transfusions. So, we needed to discuss with Laura whether she wanted to put herself through that or whether she would prefer her last months to be less painful and more comfortable.

It was the first time I'd seen Mark confronted head-on with the fact that Laura was going to die, and he was too broken to speak.

Hanna had gently put into words the things we knew but couldn't say: Laura wouldn't live to be an old lady; the disease was aggressive and uncontrollable, and it would kill her.

She asked in a roundabout way where we thought Laura would like to die, and the question just sat in the middle of the kitchen table.

In some ways I think Laura knew better than any of us that time was short, but in the same breath she would be talking about trying to get a job with the airport border police. We were now reliant on miracles, there was nothing left in the armoury.

I couldn't have loved her more, but I was going to lose her anyway.

This would probably be her last birthday. And her last Christmas.

The night before Laura had talked about 'getting her affairs in order', but just that morning she had been running alongside Alice, helping her to go as fast as she could on the zip wire in the park.

'Not too fast, Laura!' Alice had yelled.

How could this gorgeous, vibrant girl be so unwell?

Leo suggested the three of us hiked up Pendle Hill, and although it was never said, we both wondered if this was our final chance.

It was a blustery day, and the wind whipped our hair over cheeks flushed with the exertion of the climb. It wasn't just the wind that made my eyes water, this would probably be the last time Laura would be up on the hill she loved, looking down on to the green model villages below. She did so well, just needing a little help with her balance coming down the steps and when we got home, she ate slices of apple and cheese and went for a nap.

We started singing Christmas songs at choir. I had to stand right at the back because they made me cry: my throat closed up too tight to squeeze out a sound, and when I did make a noise, it was tremulous and wobbly. How could I sing, 'Next year all our troubles will be miles away,' when I knew my troubles were coming towards me at a hundred miles an hour. I really did wish that I had a river I could skate away on, although Laura the pragmatist whispered to me, 'She should really specify that the river needs to be frozen. You can't skate on water.'

So here I was again. Woken by a sound in the house or by my own thought bubble popping, lying awake in the dark bedroom then sliding out from beneath a warm duvet, getting dressed as quietly as I could so as not to wake Mark.

The sky was a slash of peach fading out into a sharp clear blue, puddles of mercury on the tarmac from last night's rain and my shadow long and thin on the wet grass. My heart beat, my lungs inflated and deflated, my eyes watered in the wind.

Siobhan was back, but she wasn't cruel anymore. She didn't need to torture me now, there was no sport in it. 'You need to get yourself ready, Nic,' she whispered, and the autumn sun on my shoulders felt like an arm around me.

Mr D looked at the scans and said he would operate, but it was only going to give us another six months.

Radiotherapy might give us a little longer.

Whack a Mole

October

I didn't want to waste days; I wanted each one to count, so I coaxed the girls out of their bedrooms and into the car. We visited Cliffe Castle in Yorkshire, where Laura pored intently over the natural history exhibition, looking at the gold hidden in rocks and phosphorescent stones that promised to glow in the dark as Gracie tried to hurry us to the exit.

We walked through the gardens and sheltered from the rain under a canopy of leaves. I surreptitiously filled my pockets with shiny horse chestnuts and smooth green acorns to plant the forest Laura wanted us to create in her memory.

Gracie cheered up when we stopped off at Salts Mill. There was a food festival on the street outside, and she soon found the artisanal gin stall while Laura ate a Nutella crepe folded into sticky quarters. Inside the mill, we browsed the David Hockney exhibition: luminous turquoise swimming pools and lush sunlit landscapes.

Laura stopped in front of the postcards. 'I think I'll send cards to my friends and family as part of my exit strategy.'

I watched her choosing between designs, then wandered away so I could blow my nose and pull myself together.

I wrote my name with a fountain pen on a small pad of white paper in the stationery section, and then I wrote hers in large cursive orange letters. Laura Mae Nuttall – just as I'd practised twenty-three years ago when I first gave my bump a name. I will write her name in every pen section in every shop for the rest of my life.

Gracie and I cried quietly on the way home.

Mark had found ways to avoid it for months, but we needed to sort out the lasting power of attorney forms. I printed them off and neatly filled the letters of our lives into the requisite spaces: one form for health decisions and one for financial. Leo needed to countersign, and it felt pre-emptive and final.

A parent should not have to do this for their child. These forms were for old people in care homes, not 22-year-old daughters. Laura had to sign too, and her careful signature was beautiful and perfect, her trust in us absolute.

For Christmas, I'd bought the girls a voucher to spend the day throwing pots at a local craft centre. Laura had always wanted to try her hand at a potter's wheel. I watched them, side by side, as they chattered away with bare, tanned arms and matching green aprons, applying gentle pressure to the foot pedals to make the wheel spin, shaping the clay into a circle, and coaxing the sides up to make some kind of vessel. Laura's tongue was peeking out – her concentration face – and Gracie was laughing at the mess she was making. It wasn't dramatic or adventurous, just two sisters absorbed by their creations, remembering things they'd done as children, teasing each other and talking as if they had all the time in the world.

'Why don't we do stuff like this more often?' Gracie asked.

We were still not ready to give up on drama and adventures, though, so I planned a theatre break to London.

On the way through Euston, Laura and I became separated in the chaos of Friday-night commuters. I'd told her we needed the Victoria line but wasn't sure she'd heard me. With no idea where she was, and no phone signal underground I started to panic. I rushed back up the escalator to retrace my steps and as I reached the midpoint, saw Laura heading downwards, on the other side.

We made eye contact and I laughed with relief. 'Stay down there!' I shouted, and made a hairpin turn to take the escalator back down to the platform, just as Laura took the escalator back up to the station concourse.

I don't know why we found it so hilarious, but we couldn't stop laughing all the way to our destination.

First up, we had been gifted tickets to *Cabaret* and enjoyed a fabulous afternoon at the Kit Kat Club, swerving the schnapps but enjoying champagne and strawberries before the show. Afterwards we were invited backstage to meet Callum Howells, who had broken our hearts as Colin in *It's a Sin*, and Madeline Brewer, who'd starred in *Orange is the New Black*, both of which were in Laura's TV top ten. The show was phenomenal, and its stars could not have been kinder or more gracious, chatting happily to Laura even though they had precious few hours before returning to the stage for the evening performance.

We had been lucky enough to stay in some of the very loveliest hotels, thanks to scrambled beg emails. And now here we were, checking into The Savoy – and into a magnificent suite on the Thames.

It was incredible – the biggest bed I've ever seen, with picture-perfect views of the London Eye and down to the Houses of Parliament; a sitting room with chandelier and complimentary fruit bowl; a dressing room; and two bathrooms with the fluffiest of bathrobes. Laura sat on the window seat eating crisps, mesmerised by the view, as I took hundreds of photographs, trying to capture the magic and the sparkle of pure happiness in her eyes. I even have a photo of her in the wardrobe, demonstrating how huge it was.

I could have happily spent day and night just watching the view as it changed, first as the clouds gathered and then as night fell and London sparkled, but we had tickets to watch both parts of *Harry Potter and the Cursed Child*.

The show was fantastic, and we loved every minute, but it was wonderful to return to our suite. I took advantage of the deep roll-top bath and then we sat on the bed in our bathrobes, eating complimentary grapes and watching a Channel 5 documentary about The Savoy.

Laura said that her breakfast of eggs royale was the best she'd eaten in her entire life. The uneaten pastries were boxed up and devoured on the train as we travelled home watching *Everything Everywhere All at Once*. Maybe it was just because it's a film about mothers and daughters, but Laura turned to me and said, 'I struck gold having you as my mum.'

And it meant the entire world to me.

Two days later, we checked into a grubby Airbnb near Salford hospital so that Laura didn't have to get up too early before her operation and so I had somewhere close by to wait for her. The doors banged all night and there was an angry dispute between residents in the early hours, but it meant we were able to walk her to the day surgery unit for 7:30 a.m. without the unpredictable stress of the motorway.

I stayed with her until she was collected by the porters, making myself useful and helping her back and forth to the bathroom, keeping her mind as far from the impending surgery as possible. She was probably fine; the distraction was more for my benefit, really.

The dread you feel when someone you love is in surgery doesn't decline the more you experience it; if anything, it gets worse as the odds of something going wrong increase.

With Covid rules finally relaxed, we were allowed to see her when she returned to the ward later that night. She looked battered and bruised but happy to see us. Gracie fed her cheese strings, and the next day she walked out of Salford hospital full of sass and swinging her hips like a boss.

It felt like the fire in the kitchen had been extinguished, but the curtains in the bedroom were still smouldering.

The next day, Laura checked she could still complete her Rubik's Cube in under three minutes, and we did a loop of the park while she ate a Danish pastry – her ability to bounce back continued to dazzle me. Sometimes I wondered if she was invincible. She was not.

Mr D explained that the tumour had tendrils that had wrapped tightly around the blood vessels controlling Laura's legs, so he'd not been able to touch them. There also looked to be another area of growth deep in the brain which was inoperable. We'd exhausted all surgical options now, and the fact that the tumour had grown back showed that chemo was no longer effective. Radiotherapy was our last-chance saloon. So, Laura was going to lose her hair once again, her bone marrow would take a battering and there was an increased risk of seizures, damage to her vision, and, if it had an impact on the brain stem, even death.

But she still wanted to go ahead. She still wanted to live.

I slunk into the toilets on the way back to the car. Once safely in the cubicle, I wept noisily with my head in my hands. How could we put her through all this again?

I washed my face and rubbed at the tell-tale mascara trails with a paper towel. I was going to have to dig deep for some positivity now. 'Come on, Nic,' I said to my reflection. 'There's no crying in baseball.'

As a result of the surgery, Laura had a fairly large cavity in her head. It was now filled with cerebrospinal fluid and she could hear it sloshing around.

'We're going to have to start calling you the human spirit level,' Mark said, with a smile.

'Very funny,' she replied. 'Hey, wasn't there a Sugababes song, Mum?'

'"Hole in the Head", I believe?'

'Adding that one to my Spotify playlist.'

Four days after the surgery, I took Laura out for some fresh air. If you'd passed us in the park you would never have guessed she was terminally ill. As we walked along the tow path, she told me how much she appreciated the world around her and trees and nature and weather and family.

'Hey Mum, do you remember what I told you I wanted after I've died?'

'Which bit?'

'The bit about the trees – I want you to bury my ashes and plant a tree on top and then all my closest family to plant more trees in a circle around me.'

'I remember,' I replied and thought about the bag of acorns and conkers I'd already collected.

We went home and made Christmas cards, folding paper to make trees. I had no plans to send them yet, I had no idea what I would write inside, so we put them in a box – something to worry about closer to the time.

Gracie drove us up to meet Leo in the Lake District. Laura seemed to need the bathroom more and more frequently, so we stopped at the services, and she nipped in while Gracie parked. We waited ages in the car, but Laura didn't appear. When she finally answered her phone – on silent as always – she had somehow ended up at the services on the opposite carriageway of the M6. It was funny and we laughed about it, but I made a mental note that somebody needed to be with Laura at all times, regardless of her protestations.

It was good to spend a weekend dodging real life with walks and cocktails and films. We passed an amusement arcade and Laura enjoyed furiously smashing little green creatures as they popped up with a big red mallet. 'Whack A Mole – or live footage of my brain tumours?' she asked wryly.

On the walk home, I noticed an Alfred Wainwright quote painted onto a BT cabinet: 'You were made to soar, to crash to earth, then to rise and soar again.'

As we approached the fourth anniversary of her diagnosis, it felt like Laura had a headache most days, she had a dizzy spell in the shower and grasped the curtain to stop her fall, which ripped the shower rail from the wall pulling down clumps of plaster. 'Crash to earth' indeed.

With no better options, we found ourselves back in the radiotherapy suite at The Christie for Laura's new mask to be fitted and an MRI planning scan. I felt a horrible sense of déjà vu; Laura just felt horrible. I covered her with a coat and stroked her hair as she tried to sleep on the hard plastic banquette.

I wondered how much more of this any of us could take.

An Early Christmas

November

I went out for a run and the autumn leaves were the colours of butter, banana and lime, back-lit by the low winter sun. But I could not shake the feeling of cold, hard dread, like stones in my stomach.

I had developed highly tuned bad-news detectors; I could smell it like an electrical charge in the air. I tasted the metallic tang and heard the buzz, like a light bulb not quite screwed in properly.

I heard it before anyone even spoke.

The first question was, 'How are you feeling?' That was never good. Nor was the fact that Hanna was rubbing my arm in a way that was meant to be comforting – it left me in no doubt of what was ahead, foreshadowing the bad news.

The planning scan had shown that the tumour had grown back and progressed into and beyond the cavity. Added to this there was also new growth in a different area. It was everywhere – and just three short weeks since the surgery.

We sat in the small white office, with its examination bed, desk, two chairs and a monitor screen, which Dr C twisted round to show images of the scan that I couldn't bring myself to look at. My dread had been justified: this explained the increasing head-aches, dizziness and exhaustion.

Laura was shell-shocked, her eyes wide and staring. Mark's were swimming with tears.

Dr C was still punctuating his sentences about the importance of having a 'plan' with smiles and awkward half-laughs. Hanna was attempting to skirt the seriousness with light humour and banter about how she needed a plan, too. It fell flat: we were a bad audience.

'Things can change really quite fast when the tumour growth is this aggressive,' he said, and I received the message, designed to float over Laura's head.

We might only have weeks left.

He explained that now would be a good time to sign the paperwork we might need to give to a doctor or paramedic, although we were strongly advised not to take Laura into hospital if she did become unwell, as they would try to keep her alive, which would be brutal for her. I assumed this letter would explain to any future ambulance crew that we were beyond the reach of lifesaving heroics, and they shouldn't waste their time on this girl, this young girl with a whole life ahead of her, because she was dying from the inside out from a brain that was rotten and diseased like a windfall apple.

I let Mark sign. I didn't even want to touch it. He sealed the envelope and slid it into his inside pocket. My nose felt peppery, and I could feel viscous tears slide from the corner of my eyes.

It was an advance directive, a DNR I suppose. There was no longer hope, we were planning for the end of our daughter's life.

Laura was back on high-dose steroids to reduce the swelling from the bastard tumour, which was pushing her brain across the midline like a bully and causing it to squash up against her skull. Radiotherapy was brought forward to Monday, and I needed to cancel the week away we had planned.

Nici and John Robinson set up Thumbs Up For Charlie to offer respite to other families in memory of their son, lost to a brain tumour aged just five. When I called John and sobbed through an explanation of why we couldn't take up his kind offer of a holiday, he knew exactly how broken I was.

I shared the devastating news first with the family, then later on Twitter, which had become a close and supportive community to us over the last four years. I received random, well-meaning advice and suggestions to try the very things that we had already been doing for years. Hard-core investors in a US company recommended we spend 250k on a new vaccine. I explained it was too late but they were zealous and cultish. One man recommended we go to CERN and demand to use the large hadron collider for its cancer-curing properties, and another suggested that Laura should literally give her head a good old rub, like a bang on the funny bone.

She still seemed mostly OK – a bit clumsy and forgetful but relatively normal. We walked to the park, bought sandwiches and had a park-bench picnic, then the girls played Pooh Sticks on the bridge as if they were four and six again.

Balance was becoming increasingly difficult for Laura. She had a tendency to pile her belongings all over the bedroom floor, ready to be sorted and put away. She claimed to know where everything was and didn't want any help, but then tripped and banged her head on the desk, badly bruising her cheek. Despite vociferous protestations, I tidied up so at least there was a clear pathway from the bed to the bathroom. I perched on the toilet while she showered, to make sure she didn't fall again.

Steroids kick-started Laura's appetite, so we took her out for lunch at The White Swan, a local pub with a Michelin star; she didn't have a great deal to look forward to, but at least we could offer her delicious things to eat. Peter Kay came with us, and the press spun the story, so it looked like he was treating his 'cancer pal' to lunch. It didn't matter, of course, as we had a lovely time. Laughter couldn't cure glioblastoma, but it was definitely a good distraction for a couple of hours.

On Bonfire Night, we watched the fireworks from our house on the hill and wrote our names with sparklers in the air. Alice loved it, but it felt as if Laura was watching rather than participating. We took her to YO! Sushi one lunchtime after treatment but she lost her balance and fell off the high stool, crashing to the floor and startling the other diners.

It felt like time was accelerating and we were speeding towards some black hole crisis point. My insides had calcified, and I was full of hardness, like flint or granite; there was nothing soft or yielding about me anymore.

'I know this is going to sound mad, but I think we should bring Christmas forward, Mark.'

'Really? We're only a week into November.'

'I know, but you can see how she is.'

'How's that going to look to Laura, though? Is it going to make her think she's only got a few weeks left? I don't want anything to take away her positivity.'

'Well, the radiotherapy's going to make her sick, she's going to lose her hair again and even in a best-case scenario, she's not going to be as well as she is right now.'

'You need to be really careful about how you explain this to her.'

'I will, I'm not an idiot! But surely it's better we do it now while she can still enjoy it? Who knows where we'll be in seven weeks' time?'

So, we dragged the Christmas tree down from the attic and decorated it while watching *Elf* and trying to pretend that everything was normal. Our quiet early Christmas developed a momentum all of its own – my fault for sharing it on Twitter – and we were inundated by people asking if they could send us cards and presents so that our fake Christmas could feel as real as possible.

At first, I blithely shared our address with anyone who asked, barely giving it a thought.

'What on earth are you thinking, Mum!'

Gracie gave me a stern lecture regarding online safety and instead we arranged for our local post office to hold any correspondence for us. We were contacted by both the local broadcasters and BBC *Breakfast* to talk about why we were bringing our celebrations forward. Those interviews were so much harder – I had little jolly positivity left to share, and every question nudged me closer to the edge of tears, like one of those coin-pushing arcade machines.

I bought a pack of Christmas cards and some crackers from the small Marks & Spencer's in The Christie.

'Ooh, you're nice and organised, aren't you, love!'

'No, not really. We're just bringing Christmas forward because my daughter is dying.'

I'm not sure why I couldn't just smile and nod, but I wasn't really sure who I was anymore.

We came home to stacks of Christmas cards held together with rubber bands, and boxes containing gifts of decorations, crackers, games, photograph frames and even luxury food hampers. We were interviewed by the *Telegraph* and received messages from all around the world, wishing us happiness and seasonal joy and as much time as possible together. A London choir even recorded a Christmas song for us.

I could never have anticipated the reaction; we were astounded, and Laura was completely bemused.

One night, I gave her a mini facial in the bathroom. The aggressive radiotherapy was irritating her sensitive skin and I massaged in soothing oils to help it heal.

As I tucked her into bed and turned off the light she said, 'Thanks for everything you do for me, Mum.'

And I cried as I walked down the stairs, because I wished I could do more; I wished I could save her.

I was ironing in my pyjamas the next morning when a car pulled up outside and two people got out.

Shit, I thought, *I've forgotten an interview or something, and I'm not even dressed.*

With no time to change, I opened the door sheepishly as they stood and stretched, suggesting that they'd had a long drive.

'Hello!' I called apologetically. 'Sorry about the pyjamas. Please come in. Can I get you a drink?'

It was only halfway through a conversation round the kitchen table with cups of tea that they realised I had no idea who they were.

'Did nobody tell you we were coming?'

I shook my head.

It wasn't an interview: these lovely people had driven down from Carlisle on behalf of Marks & Spencer to deliver all we could possibly need for our fake Christmas dinner. There was an entire carful of food: six large zip-up cool bags with everything from smoked salmon and prawn cocktail starters, to two turkey crowns, every possible vegetable accompaniment, gravy, cranberry sauce, Christmas puddings and cakes, and boxes of crackers.

We were completely and utterly overwhelmed by their astonishing generosity.

The presents and cards continued to flood in: a box of wine, then a box of donuts and cards from Australia and the US. I don't think I'd really appreciated how far and wide Laura's story had spread. It was humbling and heart-warming to read all the kind and supportive words.

Fake Christmas Day was brilliant. We didn't have too much work to do as the prepared vegetables made everything considerably easier. We needed all the spare chairs and dressing-table stools to fit twelve of us snugly around the table, and it was the most fabulous Christmas feast, rounded off by an extraordinary cheese board dropped off by Gareth from The White Swan.

The day before, my friend Lorraine had arranged for two ladies to come to the house and assemble a balloon arch in the hall. It was a ridiculously huge structure in festive shades of red and green and although it was a major trip hazard, it did look brilliant: like Elf himself had been in charge of the decorations.

Tanya and Yeva had their first British Christmas, we played the Guess Who? game from the crackers and the only thing that felt strange was that this was just a normal working day, and the rest of the world was still going about its daily business.

There hadn't been time to buy proper presents, so we'd hurriedly arranged a mini secret Santa with a £10 price cap. Everyone seemed delighted with their gifts. The evening finished with more sparklers in the garden. It was perfect.

'Today has been really great, Mum. Thank you.'

The next day wasn't fake Boxing Day, though, as it was back to radiotherapy. Laura came downstairs wearing her Oodie back to front and wondering what had happened to the pocket. She saw an article written about us in *The Sun* and instead of recognising the photo, she just said, 'Hey, I've got that top.'

In the interview she'd described the early Christmas as her insurance policy. 'I get angry sometimes,' she went on to say. 'But I don't feel sorry for myself. I'm not afraid.'

Her speech was beginning to slow and sometimes it sounded like she was slurring her words. Getting to the bathroom in time was becoming a major issue, and I didn't want to think about my proud, independent girl struggling with something so simple because it hurt my heart.

Months before, I'd been contacted by the LADbible production team. They'd followed Laura's story and wondered if she'd consider being interviewed for their *Minutes With* series. It took a while to arrange, but they called regularly to check she was still happy and offered her counselling and support both before and after the interview, which was kind, but Laura just rolled her eyes at the thought.

The interview would be titled 'I Could Have Weeks to Live'.

Gracie and I went along for moral support but when the time came to record the interview, Laura was all on her own, small, and vulnerable, circled by studio lights and cameras.

'I just felt like a rug's been pulled from under me. I had this whole life plan about what I was going to do and where I was going to do it and how it was going to happen and then this one bit of news – and my life changed, and my plans are out the window. It's like the hardest thing you can possibly hear, when your sister, or your daughter's got a terminal diagnosis.

'It broke them, in many ways, but I feel like we've managed to forge together and we're stronger as well – definitely.'

I found it so hard not to help her with the answers. I'd grown used to talking on Laura's behalf, it had become second nature to me, but these days I jumped to help when I saw an unfamiliar blankness in her expression. Here she was on her own and although she sometimes lost her thread, she was truthful and frank and made me cry more than once.

'I've had some good times despite having a brain tumour and that's what I'm going to carry on doing – living live to the fullest, because when it feels like it's getting taken away from you, you realise how much you've not actually lived.

'Sure, everyone's got a life, but are they actually living it or are they just waiting for tomorrow?'

It was hard enough to listen to; I can't imagine how painful it must have been to talk with such unflinching honesty.

'It's terminal, I should make my peace with that, but it's difficult. All my peers have hair and plans for the future. I'm just hoping that I don't lose my hair again this time or my eyebrows and eyelashes 'cause that can really knock you out of place a little bit – when you go into a room and everyone's just staring at the baldy.

'I'm living for today, as much as I can.'

As the interview drew to a close, Laura was asked about her experience at the Women's Euros. 'It was probably one of the best days of my life, I loved it.' As she rhapsodised about the Lionesses, a tablet was passed to her, and on it was a video message from the England goalkeeper, Mary Earps.

'We're all going to sign a shirt for you, Laura,' she said.

Then from the back of the studio, in walked winning-goal scorer Chloe Kelly with the very shirt. To Laura's delight and amazement, she pulled up a stool and sat beside her for the last few questions of the interview.

Chloe was lovely and spent ages chatting to us afterwards in the bar downstairs. Laura was understandably drained by the interview, so she let Gracie do most of the talking but her face still wore the widest of smiles.

Inevitably, Laura's hair came out in handfuls. She was going to be bald for the second time in four years, and now her head was criss-crossed with scars.

'This is disappointing. Not unexpected, but still disappointing,' she said ruefully, but I could see how sad it made her.

We were trying our best to keep her mood buoyant so I suggested a trip to the gym. Maybe we could try a short, low-impact workout.

She was enthusiastic: 'If I make myself healthy and strong then surely that's going to give me the best chance, isn't it?'

I roped in one of the trainers to make sure we were using the equipment properly, just a few minutes on the bike and a little bit of strength work so she felt she'd been productive. We came up with a plan and Laura was optimistic about getting her fitness back.

When she rang the bell a second time to signal the end of radiotherapy treatment, it made a hollow sound. We had little to celebrate.

'I Need You to Prepare...'

December

With things a little more settled, we were able to take John up on the offer of a family break in two lovely cottages in north Lancashire. Neil, Georgina, Alice and Alfred shared one with my mum and dad and we had the cottage next door.

It was far enough from home that we could feel like we were on holiday, but close enough that we could get back if something went wrong. Laura wasn't well enough to do a great deal – she seemed fragile and needed lots of rest in darkened rooms – but despite the headaches and the nausea she was determined to have fun.

We spent gentle, ordinary time eating together and watching the World Cup on TV, and I arranged a visit to a wildlife park where the girls fed tigers, wolves and giant otters, with Alice joining in for the less carnivorous capybaras, giraffes and penguins.

I persuaded Laura to have a relaxing bath one evening, but she got stuck and needed help getting out, all power having melted from her previously strong and capable arms. We both laughed at the ridiculousness of the situation, but it was the kind of laughter that can so easily turn to tears.

Gracie became really upset late one night, there was only so much time and so much of me, and I struggled to give her what she needed. We still clashed like this fairly regularly, but it didn't tend to last. Her head understood, even if her heart was bruised. She and I arranged to get up extra early the next morning and drive out to the coast with Ziggy to watch the sun emerge from the Irish Sea. It was a crystal-cold blue morning, and we took deep breaths of salty ozone and ate floury sausage baps on a bench. Just a temporary fix, but we both appreciated the recharge of our emotional batteries.

When we packed up to leave, I stripped Laura's bed and then hoovered it – so much of her hair was stuck to the pillow and the mattress.

'Mum, I know this is going to sound mad, but last night, when I was asleep, I was visited by a spirit, and it traced a cold finger down my back. It's happened a few times before,' Laura said. 'But I'm not frightened of it.'

I was, though.

Back in her own bed, Laura rang the bell at 5 a.m. She had a horrible headache and started to be sick. She couldn't keep the anti-nausea medication down, even when I crushed it with a tiny bit of honey.

At one point between vomiting, she looked up at me and said, 'Mum, when can I give up?'

And I said the only thing I could possibly say: 'Any time you want to, my darling.'

I slept at the side of her bed but she was sick every ten minutes so we called the district nurse, who came out to administer an anti-sickness injection and morphine from her emergency drug bag – but that only seemed to make things worse.

I phoned Hanna and she told us to pack a bag and bring Laura into The Christie.

They stabilised her with a drip and then a succession of juicy bags of saline to replenish the lost fluids. She woke up every hour or so and I took her to the bathroom, still attached to the drip stand, like a tall and uncooperative dance partner who bleated when his bag of fluids ran dry.

I thought back to those patients being wheeled into the scanning suite at Homerton, the skeletal geriatrics in the last throes of life. That was us now: it was Laura on the bed being pushed to the front of the queue because it was patently clear she was the one dying. Everyone there had cancer, but only the sickest arrived on a big white chariot escorted by kindly porters dressed in black and white stripes, like referees on a TV darts tournament.

And while we waited, purple tubs of Quality Street were passed between nurses and given a shake in the hope that there was still a green triangle left and Noddy Holder yelled 'It's Christmas!!!'

Later, I picked strands of hair from Laura's pillow while she stared into space. The room was dark, the only light from an angle-poise lamp casting shadows on the wall.

The radiotherapy hadn't worked. The scan showed further progression, and we didn't have much time left.

'Once she's stable you should take her home and we will help you manage her pain. We should think about moving her bed downstairs or requesting one from the hospice-at-home team,' Hanna told us quietly in the bad news room.

And then the words I will never forget.

'I need you to prepare for the hardest two weeks of your life.'

I was livid. Mark was in tears. I asked Hanna if she'd speak to Gracie because I knew how angry she was going to be. If I told her, she'd direct the fury at me, firing questions like bullets.

I went to fetch coffee and snacks from the shop downstairs. There was a long queue behind me, but I couldn't seem to pay on my phone and the more I fumbled, the more frustrated I became until I couldn't see the screen for the hot tears that filled my eyes and rolled down my cheeks.

Back in the room with Laura, who seemed unaware of what was happening, we pretended that everything was fine, and laughed at the TV as we passed around the posh Jaffa Cakes.

I walked Gracie back to her car and we cried and cried. She listed the things Laura would never get to do: the Christmas trip she was planning to the Sovereign Light Café in Sussex, because it was the title of Laura's favourite song, the holiday to Canada we talked about, the chance to be an aunty.

'I don't want to be an only child,' she wept, and we held tight to each other under the sodium halo of a streetlight.

After breakfast, Laura was assessed by the hospital physio, a wheelchair was found, and we were discharged. She was much brighter when we got home, well enough to handle a short walk for hot chocolate. The next day we even managed to take up Chloe Kelly's offer of tickets to the WSL Manchester derby, and without Laura needing to use the wheelchair. Our seats were up in the directors' box, and we were grateful for the fleece blankets on the cold December afternoon.

As we stood up to leave, we spotted some friends in the next bank of seats. 'I bet you were glad of those heated seats today!'

'Heated seats?'

Somewhere in the background, Tanya and Yeva were going to work and school, doing their best to help out and trying not to get in the way of the weeping and misery that took up so much space in our house. It hardly seemed fair: they'd escaped from one war zone only to find themselves in another. Fortunately, Lorraine found them a house in the village and assembled a crack team of volunteers to requisition unwanted furniture, surplus kitchen equipment and soft furnishings from friends and family. Within a few days, Tanya and Yeva were happily settled in their own little cottage where they no longer had to share a bathroom with a vomiting girl, or the kitchen with our family of sad ghouls.

We took Gracie to a spa for her birthday and tried to make it as special as we could. It wasn't the perfect twenty-first, but Leo arranged for us to be collected in a friend's Rolls-Royce and the family came over with presents and cake. For the past five birthdays, Gracie had wondered if this was the last one she'd get to spend with her sister: we were all painfully aware that this one probably was. Meanwhile, the girls sat shoulder to shoulder playing Mario Kart and screaming with delight as they raced each other to the finish line.

I was eating everything in sight: I stuffed my face whenever food was presented and loathed myself at bedtime for my weakness. I think my body was hoarding in preparation for what was to come. Gracie and I were both planning funerals in our heads, wondering about dress codes and venues, and although I told her that we needed to just live in the moment, I knew how hard that was to do.

We returned to the craft centre so the girls could paint their freshly fired pots. As they loaded up paintbrushes with coloured glaze, Laura talked about the MA in Security and Terrorism she'd applied for, and where she planned to live. I almost believed it could be possible until I had to take her to the toilet like a toddler.

Laura spent hours at her desk, making spreadsheets and flow charts, trying to wrangle control of a life that was spiralling away from her. She'd signed up for a course in coding and another to improve her German. She wanted to get a proper job but was considering bar work as a stop-gap to earn some money. I was humouring her but there was no way she could stand up for long enough. I loved that she was still fighting to remain positive, and we were all going along with it, but it felt disingenuous.

When I came downstairs the next morning, Laura was eating scrambled eggs and kale. She'd already walked the dog and been shopping for fruit and vegetables to improve her diet. I knew it was probably just the steroids, but I marvelled at the determination and the guts and grit of this girl. She would not make it easy for cancer.

For Christmas I'd bought Laura a necklace from jeweller Bryan Anthonys: a little pearl with a silver tag that said *Grit* on it. I'd always believed it was grit that made her so determined and resilient, and the card in the box seemed almost written for her.

'She is unshakeable, not because she doesn't know pain or failure but because she always pushes through. Because she always shows up and never gives up.

'She is a pearl – made from grit, but full of grace.

'She is unstoppable – she knows it's not what happens, but how she chooses to respond, with perseverance in her mind and passion in her heart.'

Anyone with sense would have kept things local and low-key in the circumstances, but we've never claimed to have sense.

We arranged a tour of Everton's new stadium – essentially still a building site, so we borrowed steel-capped boots, hard hats and high-vis jackets and clambered around the structure. Then Laura was invited to join White Watch at Oldham fire station. Clad in helmet and uniform, she grasped the hose to put out a car fire and then was lifted high up on a precarious platform 26 metres into the sky

'What if the change in pressure makes her sick,' I whispered furiously to Mark, but I could hear her laughter from high above me.

For Laura's birthday, the girls had a trip to a smash room. They dressed in overalls, boots and safety glasses and, armed with mallets and baseball bats, smashed up bottles and crockery and printers to their heart's content.

Having thought it impossible two weeks ago, I sang at the Christmas carol concert in a small barn decorated with fairy lights. I even managed the songs that made me cry in rehearsals. The girls came down to watch and we stopped for a drink in the pub on the way back up the hill.

Laura was philosophical and grateful to be here, appreciating every moment. As we walked, she photographed trees and the reflections in the canal and clouds and icicles. She breathed deeply and soaked it all in.

Laura had always seen the beauty in the ordinary and the mundane. When on family walks, as we marched along, she would dawdle behind to pick up a stranded bee on a leaf and place it on a flower, or to shake open her phone – a sturdy Motorola with a battery that lasted for weeks – to take photos of a sheep, or a view. She had saved up memories on her phone and used them to sustain her when she was sick, confined to bed or waiting in a hospital for her name to be called.

When we were together as a family, she would look from face to face with a half-smile, drinking it all in, savouring each moment and storing every laugh. On her phone she saved lists of the stupid things we said so she could squeeze a second round of joy from how daft her family were.

We knew this time was a blessing, and we had no idea how long it might last.

On Christmas morning, Laura cleaned the bathroom, walked the dog, and made pancake batter before anyone else woke up. She'd blown the budget on Gracie's present: an album of signed photos of all her musical heroes. It had taken months and hundreds of pounds to put together, but Gracie's astonished reaction made it all worthwhile.

'You'll be able to sell those if you're ever short of money,' Laura told her sagely.

We had enough food left in the freezer from fake Christmas to run a repeat performance on the 25th. It was a smaller, sadder affair, though, as my gran had been taken into hospital on Christmas morning; she died in the early hours of the 26th.

This year's Giddy Kippers Boxing Day party offered a choir rather than a brass band and the number of Syrian refugees was matched by those escaping Ukraine, but it was a wonderful day and it felt good to share in the simple, uncomplicated joy of small children receiving presents from Santa and his elves.

The year ended with a scheduled scan nobody really wanted. We had hoped and prayed for a Christmas miracle, but the steroids had only reduced the swelling, not the size of the tumour.

My mum was organising her own mum's funeral and although I should probably have helped, it was the last thing I wanted to do – my heart could not stretch to coffins or hymns or the order of service. Grief had made me cold and cruel, and I struggled to find tears for a life that had lasted ninety-six years. I zipped my mouth for fear of further upsetting my mum, who was already sad enough.

I had my first panic attack in the Marks & Spencer food hall. Very suddenly, everything crowded in on me and the reality of the months ahead hit me like a slap. I abandoned my shopping basket and ran out, gasping in the frigid air.

On New Year's Eve we watched *West Side Story* and ate melted raclette cheese with potatoes and pickles, Laura's favourite. I remembered the personalised crackers we'd been sent, which were still wedged between the branches of the Christmas tree.

Inside mine was a little key ring with three shiny buttons and on the back of the largest it said: 'Mums are like buttons; they hold everything together.'

It felt more like an instruction than a description.

2023

Forest, Beaches and Stars

January–February

We tried to find moments of joy in every day; not big things, but small delights like my dads's roast potatoes and my mum's white chocolate cheesecake, playing hide and seek with Alice – her hiding behind a cushion with her legs stuck out – and cuddling baby Alf. We were clinging to our family like a lifeboat and although it looked like smiling and waving, we were really just fighting to keep our heads above water.

I didn't know it was bad luck to do washing on New Year's Day. I doomed 2023 from day one.

'If I'm going to be stuck living at home aged twenty-three – no offence – I want to decorate my room and make it all calm and serene, like a woodland.'

'A woodland?' Mark asked.

'Lots of plants, and maybe wallpaper that looks like trees—?'

'Sounds like a bloody doctor's waiting room to me.'

I found a wallpaper. It was called 'Tranquil forest' and pictured shafts of light falling between tall green trees. Laura loved it and I would do pretty much anything to make her happy – including going to IKEA to buy bookcases and fake plants to trail from the shelves. I took her shopping in TK Maxx to buy a globe, too, but she lost her balance and knocked over a display of glass bottles. No harm done, but she was veering to one side now like a trolley with a dodgy wheel.

There was no good news from the Multi Disciplinary Team meeting, although one tiny sliver of light was that they'd agreed to support the use of a fortnightly Avastin infusion. It was unlikely to shrink the tumour but would temporarily starve it of a blood supply, reducing the symptoms and the dependence on steroids, which Laura hated taking because of their side effects. It wasn't available on the NHS, but if the insurance company wouldn't cover it, we could fund it ourselves – anything to give Laura some quality of life.

My friend Steph offered us a few days in her rental house up in Seahouses on the Northumberland coast, and we walked on the beach collecting shells till we couldn't feel our fingers, with Zig running in and out of the waves, his coat wet and salty. The endless blue sky was reflected in the pools left by the retreating sea, a mirror image, an infinity. The air was so fresh and sharp that it burned cheeks and chapped lips.

Later that evening, Laura and I wrapped up warmly and walked back to a bench overlooking the sea to stare up at a million stars in the velvet sky, untroubled by light pollution.

'When we're dead and buried, the stars will still be there, and the tide will come in and go back out; we're really hardly anything at all, are we?' she said softly.

Her words were humbling, perfect and profound, and I found myself too choked with emotion to reply coherently. We stumbled back to the house on unfamiliar footpaths, our breath condensing before us like dragons.

The next morning, we found the beach covered in a dredging of snow, Gracie cartwheeled on the compacted sand, and Laura (with a carrot in her pocket) found herself cornered by wild ponies with an excellent sense of smell.

We were grateful for the option of Avastin, and that the insurance company grudgingly agreed to foot the bill, but it was always difficult to find a suitable vein, so hot packs were placed on the pale skin of Laura's inner arm to tempt one to the surface.

In the end the needle had to be inserted between the fingers, and her flinch told me how much it hurt. She clenched her blanket tightly with white knuckles. I'd had it made from all her favourite T-shirts sewn together, each square a memory of a happier time: a concert in Chicago, a race in Boston, and her favourite childhood T-shirt – a skull design made up of butterflies, bees and flowers. A blanket that told the story of her life so far, like a fleece-backed equivalent of the Bayeux Tapestry.

Laura asked Mark to shave her head again in February. It was neater, but my heart ached to see her bald head and the patchwork of war wounds. She'd been having some telephone counselling.

'Has it helped, do you think, Laura?'

She made a non-committal noise.

'Have you got anything from it at all?'

'Well, basically, I'm jealous of Gracie and she's jealous of me.'

Gracie had sent me a message with a link attached to a TED Talk on YouTube. 'Watch this,' she'd said. 'But you probably won't have time because you're so busy.'

She was right, and despite my best intentions, the message was soon buried beneath notifications from the pharmacy and updates from delivery companies regarding missing Christmas presents, but late one night I watched with subtitles as Mark slept beside me.

'The glass child ...' the presenter began, with a warm and slightly nervous smile.

When a child grows up in the shadow of a sibling who needs more care and attention, their own needs can sometimes be forgotten. It's not that they aren't loved but, unfortunately, it's a matter of time and priorities.

My daughter had become a classic glass child: people saw through her as they made a beeline for her sister. Even the most well-meaning family members asked Gracie, 'How's Laura?' then, 'How are your mum and dad?' and sometimes forgot her completely. She was treated as a conduit.

Apparently, they didn't want to ask me, because I was too busy and they were reluctant to disturb; but in reality, it was probably because I was spiky, combative and defensive ... I recognised our family in the TED Talk, our vulnerabilities exposed, and Gracie vindicated.

One Last Shot
March

It felt almost like spring, although snow was forecast for the following week. Maybe it was the daffodils or the days stealing minutes back from the night, but we had our positivity pants pulled up high.

Laura spent a day clay-pigeon shooting; we visited a brewery that had named one of their beers – a tasty blonde – *Doing It For Laura*; and we managed another walk to the summit of Pendle Hill – 1,300 feet in tricky weather conditions – making sure that Laura always had an arm to link in order to keep her upright. Her balance was becoming gradually worse: she slipped over walking down to choir, and I fell on top and squashed her; then it happened again as we walked through the snow. It was hard to tell whether it was weakness or balance – we just laughed it off, but it really wasn't that funny.

Professor VG told us that sadly his clinic had no suitable treatment for such advanced disease but referred us to a colleague who was getting good results using the Newcastle disease virus administered intracranially – injected via a catheter directly into the tumour site.

Just the thought made me queasy.

The first step would be a state of the art nuclear FET-PET scan, at a hospital in Munich, and then we'd need to travel 500 miles north to a clinic in Dusseldorf. It sounded risky and complicated but realistically it was probably our last shot.

Laura wasn't as physically strong as she once was, and the situation felt unpredictable and volatile, so Mark and I decided we should both travel with her.

During our time in Munich, all three of us managed to pick up a stomach bug; Mark and Laura were sick first, I waited until we were on the five-hour train journey to Dusseldorf.

It seemed that some specifics had been lost in translation: this wasn't a clinic we could pop into for an hour each day, Laura would be an inpatient for at least a week. Thankfully, I was encouraged to stay with her, so while Mark got her settled, I went to buy appropriate pyjamas for us both as the saggy T-shirts and shorts I'd packed weren't going to cut it.

We met Dr S in his airy corner office, a small man with a moustache who seemed unable to sit still. He wore white trousers and a white fleece which give him the appearance of a small, furtive mammal.

I could see the images of Laura's PET scan on his computer screen, and I didn't need to translate the words to recognise that it was grim: there was significant growth around the second tumour site and on the periphery of the primary cavity.

To get the virus into the brain, Laura would need surgery to fit two Ommaya reservoirs on the top of her skull with thin catheters directly into the tumour sites. I felt a rising panic: how had I missed the seriousness of this procedure? But even if I'd known, what alternatives did we really have? Standing still was not an option.

The night before surgery was spent on my phone, pacing the apartment while trying to process payment for the clinic. Despite speaking to a multitude of advisors, in both the international payments team and then the fraud department (as the transaction had triggered a 'red flag'), nobody could help, and then the phone lines closed, leaving me in angry, frustrated tears.

I was still trying to make the payment in the waiting room the following morning, when a nurse came to collect Laura. She didn't speak much English, and we assumed this was the standard pre-op checks; it wasn't – Laura had gone for surgery, and we hadn't even said a proper goodbye.

Mark and I watched stupid pointless videos on my phone: a man making a giant pencil from cobs of corn for no discernible reason. Then the algorithm thought we'd also be interested in a man making a sword from a salt lamp. We really weren't.

Hours later we saw Laura, just briefly, as she was wheeled from theatre to the CT scanner and back again for the precise location of the catheter to be adjusted. Eventually she came out of surgery and we were escorted to a private room with two beds and a bathroom.

She was heavily medicated and sleepy, but the site of the incision in her scalp was painful. During the night she woke four times, for the bathroom or pain relief or because the drip has stopped.

She only had to whisper 'Mum' as quiet as a breath and I was by her side before I knew where I was.

I slept with my ears open, tyres on the wet roads below sounded like waves and I wished we could wake up to the murmuring of the ocean.

The electro-hyperthermia clinic was on the first floor of the hospital. More homely and less clinical than Cologne, although the treatment was the same. The pillow had a cheerful yellow coverlet with a positive affirmation printed on it, while the blanket was white and fluffy like Dr S. He darted between rooms like a quicksilver fish; his wife – who ran the office – moved slowly: I would hear the static swish of polyester skirt against nylon tights as she moved down the corridor to adjust the machine. They spoke Turkish and German, we spoke English, so communication was tricky.

The waiting area had an ostentatious samovar, the gentle background music was beauty spa 101, but it wasn't easy to create a relaxing environment when the stakes were this high.

Laura selected a German children's book from the shelf, and we experimented with the unfamiliar words for familiar animals, in a jungle, on a mountain, at a farm – '*Der Gepard, Das Wildschwein, Der Truthahn*' – while we waited for her waterbed to be prepared.

Laura's head had been shaved again for surgery, but it was already raspy with stubble. The Ommaya reservoirs were secured with thick flesh-toned plasters, that were now starting to unpeel and catch on her woollen beanie. In the crook of her arm there was a cannula with a red cap and a criss-cross of white tapes to hold it in place.

After treatment, we headed out for fresh air. Laura wasn't too steady on her feet and needed my support as we walked, but I accidentally linked the wrong arm and she winced as I caught the cannula, the physical sympathy of it making me cringe. The last thing I ever wanted to do was cause her pain.

That night we sat shoulder to shoulder on my bed, wearing our new pyjamas and watching *Daisy Jones & the Six* on my laptop. How lucky I felt to have this time with her, and I wondered, as I did every day, how on earth I could keep living when she was no longer here.

The treatment wasn't exactly painful, but the cannula had been in for a week now and the sticky tapes flapped around, becoming less sticky every day. During one IV infusion, the needle missed the vein, and her upper arm became hot and engorged as the misinjected fluid filled the tissue instead. It really hurt and required the application of cooling gel and an ice pack.

But then Laura spotted something under the bed that put everything into perspective.

'Look at that,' she said quietly. 'A little plastic step, to help a child get up onto the bed. Imagine having to put a kid through this. It's hard enough for me, but that would be unthinkable. Cancer is so utterly shit.'

On the day Laura had the virus injected she came back to the room, shivering violently: 'S-s-s-something's gone wrong. I'm freezing.' Her teeth were chattering so hard she could hardly squeeze out words from between her blue lips.

I rang the buzzer for a nurse, who arrived with extra duvets.

'Go and t-t-t-tell the doctor, quick. Something's wrong.'

I ran up the stairs to the clinic. 'Laura's had a reaction to the injection – she must be allergic to it or something. She's freezing cold and panicking,' I explained breathlessly.

'She is very cold?'

I nodded.

'Ah, this is good, this is her immune system reacting to the virus. We are happy to know this, all is well.'

I ran back downstairs. 'Apparently it's all fine, Laura. This is what the doctors wanted – the virus is making your immune system react, this is all good.'

'Would have been n-n-nice if someone had thought to b-bloody warn me!' she replied, shivering beneath five duvets as a fan heater blew hot air down a wide tube into her bed.

A few hours later she returned to normal colour and temperature, and my frantic heart rate finally slowed back to human levels.

As Laura became stronger, we wandered a bit further from the clinic, had lunch in a shopping centre where she bought a Lego graduation figure for Gracie and took a lift up to the top of the Rheinturm, where we drank milkshakes and took photos of the winding river and the Dusseldorf skyline.

We walked the long avenues of Little Tokyo, where Laura bought bubble tea – apple with lychee – and, as it was pouring with rain, we ended up in the cinema, watching *Everything Everywhere All at Once* for a second time, now with German subtitles. Something about the film had become really special to us: Laura squeezed my hand in the emotional scenes between mother and daughter and my eyes brimmed with tears. I don't think we had ever been so close.

It rained again the following day, so I suggested we visit the Turkish hammam opposite. What looked like an ordinary shopfront on a city street disguised a beautiful, ornate bath house with mosaic tiles and tinkling water fountains. We sat in the fragrant steam room and rubbed our skin with olive oil soap and a wiry mitt, then lay on marble slabs to be thoroughly scrubbed and massaged with foam and oil. I kept shouting over to check that Laura was OK, wondering why on earth I had thought this was a good idea, but without needing any explanation, the masseurs had instinctively understood that she was fragile and treated her as though she was made of the most delicate porcelain.

Later, we sat in the relaxation room sleepily drinking sweet mint tea.

'I love it when we do new things – this has been brilliant. Can we come again next time we're here?'

'Absolutely,' I replied, just hoping that we would get the chance.

The stitches on Laura's head needed careful removal, as the skin on her scalp had been rendered paper-thin by repeated radiotherapy and the surgeon was concerned about how they might heal. I'd understood that the Ommaya would be almost invisible, just a tiny bump under the skin, but the two on Laura's head couldn't be missed. Perhaps they wouldn't be so obvious once the swelling went down – and if it saved her life, then did it really matter anyway?

'You Were Just Unlucky'
April

Back in September we'd been invited to The Brain Tumour Charity's 'Celebrating You' event, and Laura was modestly delighted to find out she'd been shortlisted for an award. When it hadn't looked like she'd make it, her Special Recognition trophy arrived in the post, and we took photos of her proudly holding the red Perspex star with her name printed on it.

But she had made it to April, and travelling down to London seemed tentatively feasible. Laura bought a funky purple wig to wear for the occasion and was excited at the thought of meeting up with her friends and supporters from the charity.

As you might imagine, I looked for a lovely hotel to make the event really memorable, and Nobu in Shoreditch had been happy to offer us a room for the night. I'd been emailing back and forth with the guest experience manager Cristina for a few weeks, and she greeted us in the sleek foyer before taking us up to our rooms.

Laura and Gracie had the most incredible suite, complete with kitchen and two balconies, while Mark and I were in an adjoining room, which connected to make a space bigger than most London apartments. On the table in the dining area there was a bouquet of tightly furled pink roses, champagne on ice and, in a silver picture frame, a photograph of the four of us, all smiles at the start line of the Great North Run. Cristina had gone to such a lot of effort to make the experience as special as possible for us.

When we left the hotel for the awards ceremony, she joined us on the pavement as we waited for the taxi.

'I like your necklace,' Laura said to her.

Cristina lifted the long silver chain to show us the black stone in its filagree setting. 'This is onyx,' she said. 'It is from Sardinia, where I come from. You cannot buy these for yourself, they have to be given to you as a gift. Then, the stone needs to be left outside in the sun until it is charged with energy, after that it will give you protection.'

We all agreed that it was really quite beautiful.

It was lovely to catch up with friends from the charity and the supporters and trustees we'd got to know over the past four years. Laura walked up on stage to receive her award in person with Gracie keeping her upright. She looked fabulous in the purple wig: it made her eyes look greener than ever. But after an hour it irritated her sore scalp and ended up stuffed into my handbag.

Everyone in the room seemed to know Laura's story, and her tireless efforts to increase awareness of brain tumours. She received a huge round of applause and lots of congratulations; it really felt like we were among friends.

After the awards ceremony, we took a taxi back to the hotel where we'd been invited to enjoy dinner in the elegant Japanese restaurant. We were brought a succession of platters decorated with delicately sliced fish and meat, plates that were as artistic as they were delicious. It was a wonderful meal of exquisite mouthfuls; but I think Mark might have fared better with a meat and potato pie.

We returned to our room and on Laura's pillow there was a silver Nobu box.

Inside it was Cristina's necklace with a note.

Dear Laura

What a pleasure to meet you and your family, I will never forget!

I hope you enjoyed your Nobu experience. This necklace is just a little gift from me, so that the traditional Sardinian protection will be with you from now on.

Cristina x

Mark was mortified. 'Oh, no, I hope she didn't think you were after it! This is too much.'

We did try to give it back, but Cristina was quite adamant. It never failed to amaze and astonish me just how kind and selfless people could be. We would never forget her kindness.

In the days that followed, Laura fell over again – we went for a walk through the fields and she was chased by a large horse who wanted to eat her hood. I also noticed that she was dragging one foot on the ground: it rasped on the gravel, and she didn't seem able to lift it, even when she made a conscious effort. And when I momentarily let go of her arm to open a gate she slipped over into a clump of brambles and nettles – stung and humiliated, but not hurt. I phoned Mark, and he collected us in the car.

'Sorry about falling over again, Mum,' she said later.

'What on earth do you have to apologise for? It's just this balance issue. It's not your fault, you daft thing.'

'It's so frustrating – my legs just seem really uncooperative at the moment. I feel bad for cutting the walk short.'

'I know, it must be so annoying for you,' I said lightly, as if it was nothing at all. But it felt like a black cloud on a sunny day or the obvious foreshadowing in a horror film.

She reached up for a hug, which was wholly untypical of Laura.

I loved that she was more affectionate, but equally terrified of any change in her personality.

The next day she managed to fall off the toilet, she was struggling to swallow tablets and tired all the time. With no strength at all in her arms, she was no longer able to get herself up out of bed, and had to ring the bell for assistance.

I had a horrible jittery feeling, like a cold fluttery bird in my chest.

We had a lovely family Easter and Laura helped Alice hunt for eggs in the garden. She'd dressed up in new dungarees bought in Germany and was proudly wearing Cristina's onyx necklace.

'Can you do my makeup, Mum?' she asked. 'I want to make a proper effort today.'

But as we enjoyed my dad's fabulous Sunday roast, I noticed that the Ommaya was leaking fluid. Just a tiny drop, like a drip of amber sap on a tree trunk, but when I touched the site gently with my fingertip, I could hear a clicking noise. I hoped to God it wasn't an infection of some kind and tried not to panic.

Mark took photos and we emailed them through to the clinic in Dusseldorf, but as it was a weekend of national holidays, we had no reply. Laura seemed OK, though, thankfully she had no pain or signs of a fever.

When the medical team finally replied to Mark, however, it was clear that this was a serious problem: 'They're saying that the Ommaya needs to be removed immediately and we should get back to the clinic as soon as we can.'

'I'm not happy with this, Mark. I think we need to see if there's any way we can do this in the UK. I don't want her to have to fly or spend ages travelling, and I don't want her to get stranded in Germany either. I think we should speak to Hanna.'

Hanna's advice was to take Laura to Salford A&E and hope that one of the neurosurgical team could take a look.

The middle of a junior doctors' strike was not the best time to rock up to an emergency department, so we took two boxes of donuts by way of an apology.

Laura lay with her eyes closed and her head on Mark's lap; we fashioned a coat into a pillow and covered her with my tartan wrap as a makeshift blanket, but before too long she was taken into a bay, then admitted to a neuro ward to wait for a surgeon.

Later that evening, Mr D arrived to see Laura. I felt uncomfortable and slightly embarrassed that we were taking up his time and he was having to fix something that a surgeon in another country had done, as if Laura had travelled abroad for some cut-price plastic surgery and was now relying on the NHS to patch up a botched tummy tuck.

'Don't worry,' he said reassuringly. 'It's no problem – I follow you on Twitter, so I know what Laura has had done and I have no problem with it. You were just unlucky.'

I really hoped that he hadn't come all the way out just to see her but suspected that was probably the case. I stayed over in a budget hotel that was providing housing for refugees – it was close and meant I could be back at her bedside early the next morning.

After a scan she was taken down for surgery: her fifth brain operation in this hospital.

This time they needed a team from plastics on stand-by as there was a chance that skin would need to be grafted from her thigh to her head. My heart plummeted at the thought, but when Laura was returned to the ward, Mr D had managed to avoid the need for plastics, for now at least.

'I'm afraid it was really quite bad,' he told us, gravely. 'The skin had not healed and there was an open hole underneath the scab. I have put in a plate, but we may still need a graft if it does not heal as well as we would like.' Then he added, 'But the scan and the tumour – it looks remarkable.'

And there was the great irony. It seemed as though the virus had done as we'd hoped and shrunk the tumour in at least one place, but now we had a more urgent problem to deal with.

I'd imagined that we would be bringing Laura home after a day or two.

'Oh, no, love,' said the ward sister. 'There's a serious risk of infection now, she's going to have to stay in for at least two weeks of IV antibiotics, it might even be months. We're sending swabs off to pathology now, but we'll be starting her on the drip today.'

'Well,' I said weakly to Laura. 'You need an infection like you need a hole in the head.'

'Got one of those too,' she replied.

Once again, she had a cannula inserted and a succession of fluid bags were hooked up, emptied, and replaced. She shared the ward with three older ladies, none of whom seemed really able to speak. Every day they would be visited by a family member, usually a daughter or a husband, who would cut up food, maintain a one-sided conversation, gently brush hair, replace dirty laundry with clean and provide snacks and endless patience. The kindness and extraordinary love I witnessed was truly humbling.

Laura shuffled between bed and bathroom, and I tried my hardest not to get frustrated by her inability to set off in time. We were both humiliated by the pull-up hygiene pads, but I maintained a mask of bright positivity so that I didn't hurt her feelings. She must have hated the loss of her precious independence.

I helped her to get showered, moisturised her limbs, gave her a foot massage and wrestled her back into the skinny surgical stockings, designed to prevent blood clots. I sprayed her pillow with scented sleep mist and racked my brain for ways to make her stay more bearable while she nibbled listlessly on her third meal of cheese sandwiches in a row.

When the visitors were asked to leave, I returned to my budget hotel room and tried to eat instant noodles with two wooden coffee stirrers.

The days were long, and Laura became bored and monosyllabic. When family came at visiting time, she would smile, but now it seemed the tumour would only let her do so with half her face. Sometimes we ate takeaway pizza squashed into the small visitors' room. I bought a fancy lunchbox system and filled the compartments with fresh fruit and carrot sticks, olives and cubes of cheese and we walked laps of the hospital to keep her active.

I was terrified that I'd never get my Laura back again, but when I changed her pants and pyjamas for the third time in one day, she reached up for a hug and told me that she loved me.

Things changed. As the world outside moved into the light and lengthening days of spring, we were chilled by an approaching winter. We were losing Laura by degree; she stared with wide eyes but answered questions with a single word, or didn't answer at all, or made a small mime to save her from speaking. She watched as others talked, no longer able to contribute, and when she did, it was a random non sequitur but we humoured her, just happy to hear her voice.

She was washing her hands one afternoon and our eyes met in the bathroom mirror.

I whispered into her fluffy new hair, 'Things will get better, my darling. It won't always be like this.'

But, honestly, I didn't know if this was true; or if it was, would that mean it was all over?

Who were we even fighting for now?

Leo came to visit, and I could tell from the look of shock that flashed across her face how much Laura had declined. She'd developed a tic – or maybe they were mini seizures. I hoped it was just temporary, but it felt as if her brain had been irreversibly damaged.

Laura had a meeting with a neuropsychologist. The curtain was drawn behind me and I wandered around the hospital to give them time to talk. When I popped back to check if they were finished, I heard Laura say, 'I haven't always been a good sister.'

It was the longest sentence I'd heard her speak in ages and it broke me.

Microbiology confirmed that there was no infection and the newly installed PICC line could be removed, as oral antibiotics would be sufficient from that point. The only problem was that Laura now seemed unable to swallow tablets.

We were allowed to bring her home and Mark was full of optimism.

'Once she's sleeping in her own bed with her own food and the family around her, she'll be so much better. She was getting institutionalised in there.'

The day after Laura was discharged from hospital, she chewed on a bagel as we chatted to Hanna at the kitchen table. I offered to buy her whatever she fancied, and she asked for a chicken sandwich, tonic water, and Turkish Delight. By the next day she couldn't swallow the sandwich, so I made her soft food, mashed ripe avocado with cream cheese, which she used to love.

We tried crushing the antibiotics into food, but she just spat them out. We couldn't tell if this was a deliberate act of refusal or a physical inability, and Laura was no longer able to tell us. It was hard not to lose patience, and everything felt horribly stressful and tense. At one point I had to leave the kitchen to scream outside in frustration. Things were really grim.

It was becoming clear that Laura wasn't the same girl we had taken to A&E two weeks ago.

Friends and family came round with the intention of helping. In reality, I made them tea and they sat expectantly, waiting for me to say something, to start a conversation, maybe even make them feel better.

But I made myself hard to help: I lined the paths with barbed wire and minefields, I was brittle and spiky and I didn't welcome the concern or the sympathy. I was a hostile environment for kindness, too tired to worry about anyone who wasn't living in this house and going through this hell.

When did I lose my girl? I couldn't put my finger on the moment that she slipped away; it was only minutes ago that we walked down the wide avenues of Dusseldorf – it was just the blink of an eye. She had applied for a Masters but in the weeks between the application and the acceptance she had disappeared; now she could no more complete an MA than walk on the moon.

She needed help to get a spoon of soggy cornflakes from bowl to mouth: it wavered in her hand and failed to make it, dropping clumps of cereal like wet stripped wallpaper on the front of her hoodie. Her words were scrambled and confused, they slid half formed from her chapped lips and we puzzled over them like cryptic clues.

Some mornings I would stand in her bedroom and watch her sleep. She looked just the same as before and, despite everything, I still had the ridiculous hope that when she woke up, she would be a bit better than yesterday, that this wasn't actually the end, and we weren't really barrelling towards a finality.

Hope is the hardest thing to kill.

Hanna came round to see how we were doing. She said in her calm, measured voice,

'It will be weeks now.'

And Mark replied, 'Till what?'

I stared at him with barely contained incredulity. He still wasn't on the same page yet; his fierce positivity has blurred the edges of reality.

Hanna advised us again to keep Laura out of hospital. 'She'll be better at home where you can care for her, and when swallowing becomes more of an issue, don't push it, because if food goes into her lungs, she may well get a chest infection or pneumonia and we really don't want that. I'll make sure the GP comes round to see her soon.'

I knew that was so that they'd be able to sign the death certificate when the time came.

Laura was still managing to feed herself soft food with a baby spoon, but she would always overfill it, scooping ridiculous quantities onto the orange plastic spoon. Gracie would sit beside her and knock some off, so Laura had a chance of fitting it in her half-mouth. One time this turned into a play fight with plastic spoons, which made Laura laugh. She was so much brighter when her sister was home, but I knew how that increased the pressure on Gracie to be there every day when she had such a lot of work to do and so many filming days coming up.

A nurse from Hospice at Home came to see us. She flicked through a bundle of leaflets, drawing our attention to the hospice lottery and a choir concert where lost loved ones would be remembered. She talked about palliative care and Mark bristled at the casual references to 'end of life', as it was the last thing he wanted Laura to hear. The nurse was just doing her job, but I'm quite sure that, although her face remained impassive, Laura understood every word.

Each day was a little bit harder. When we thought things had bottomed out, there was always a further step down. Laura developed a compulsion to rub her fingers over surfaces as if she was trying to remove a dirty mark and would wash her hands compulsively. If I asked her a question, she'd just repeat my own words back to me.

We tried to get her in the shower. Uncle Phil would pop round to help with the stairs, as it was a three-man job, but it was now becoming unsafe. Laura could still walk but she was like one of those inflatables you see outside used car showrooms – arms in the air and waving in the wind: her legs would slip from under her without notice.

A hospital bed was delivered, with an air mattress to prevent bed sores, and it hit me like a punch to the stomach that Laura would never again sleep in her own bed.

I massaged her hands and feet with scented oils, just trying to manufacture moments of quiet pleasure to break up these miserable days. We danced in our chairs to 'Jump Around', and it was clear from her face that she loved to be in the company of her little cousins.

I had no idea how Alice was reconciling this in her three-year-old head; it was hard enough to cope with as a grown adult.

We took Laura in the car to my mum and dad's for Sunday lunch. Mark fed her like a baby and then she napped on the sofa. Later, he was helping Laura downstairs and lost his balance, very nearly falling. Her eyes filled with tears, and I could see how frightened this made her feel. Her emotions were primal and uncomplicated.

Mark cried too once she'd gone to bed. We had both maintained stupid hope and now reality was biting down hard.

'I miss her,' he said, through tears.

Whenever You're Ready, My Love
May

We were trying to fire darts at a moving target that became smaller every day.

Laura could talk, then just odd words, then yes or no. We used a pen and paper, then a child's pink plastic Magna Doodle, and then it was thumbs up or thumbs down, then nothing more than a long blink in place of communication.

We helped her up the stairs to the bathroom; then, when her legs became cooked spaghetti, we carried her upstairs in a fireman's lift; then we used the spidery toilet in the garage; then the commode; and then we just used the kind of pants used by people with bladder issues and I changed her like a baby, but one with impossibly long smooth legs. I was astonished that she needed to be changed at all, as I expected the physics of 'what goes in needs to come out' but in fact, her organs were ridding themselves of liquid as her body prepared to shut down.

Without the structure of mealtimes, the days stretched and lengthened. We pushed the sofa flush against her bed, and I would play the music she liked, or read from *The Magic Faraway Tree* while she stroked my arm or plucked at her clothes. We moved the television so Laura could watch her favourite films from bed, *The Net*, *Ocean's 8*, the *Ghostbusters* re-boot, and her favourite, *Miss Congeniality*. Mark often forgot to put her glasses on and would jump anxiously to his feet when I reminded him that she couldn't see – Laura no longer able to alert him to the blurriness of her world.

Before the hospital bed had been installed downstairs, Mark slept on a camping mat on Laura's bedroom floor to prevent her from falling out or becoming confused in the night – she had already managed to pull a heavy desk lamp onto her head, leaving a sizeable bruise above her left eyebrow. When the hospital bed arrived, he slept downstairs next to her on the sofa, and she still managed to fall out.

We asked the district nurses if sides could be added to the bed.

'They don't come with sides anymore.'

'The beds don't have sides?'

'I think it's something to do with the air mattress.'

'Is there someone you could ask for us? She keeps falling out of bed.'

'I can ask for you, but I don't think we do sides. Maybe you could get a couple of mattresses from somewhere and put them on either side of the bed?'

'She'd still be falling out, though, wouldn't she? The landing would just be softer.'

'Yeah …'

'She's got a brain tumour, so surely falling out of bed isn't ideal.'

'No. I suppose I can ask for you.'

I asked another nurse the following day.

'We don't do sides because there's a risk of entrapment.'

'Entrapment?'

'Yes, she could get tangled up in the sides.'

'Really?'

'I tell you what,' Mark said, losing patience, 'I'll go out and get some three by two and make some sides myself. This is bloody ridiculous.'

The sides arrived and were fitted the following day.

We tried to get Laura out for fresh air every evening in the borrowed wheelchair. I avoided times when we were likely to bump into people we knew, as I didn't want them to see her with her head lolled onto her chest, unable to speak, saliva pooling on her coat. It was too painful to see the pity and sympathy in their eyes.

The first time we went to the park, we were halfway down the hill when Mark realised the chair had no brakes, so Laura had the white-knuckle ride of her life, it was wonderful to see something that resembled a smile on her face and a little sparkle in her eyes. Pushing the chair back up the hill was the most exercise Mark had had in months.

Mark had been brilliant, spending as much time as possible with Laura and trying to pre-empt her every need; he'd dedicated an entire afternoon to cutting and filing her nails, nothing was too much trouble. I don't know how we could have coped without his patience and cheerful disposition.

Laura still had occasional moments of lucidity. As we wheeled her round Towneley Park one evening I reminisced about her high school cross-country team and she chipped in with both the name of her PE teacher and the big private school she'd raced around.

That excursion ended with Mark spinning Laura on a roundabout designed specifically for wheelchairs; I hadn't known such a thing even existed.

We bumped into my friend Dany on the way back to the car. 'What about trying a McDonald's milkshake as a way of getting some easy calories in?' she suggested.

'Brilliant idea!' I enthused, as if it was the cure for cancer itself.

Laura nodded in agreement. 'Chocolate,' she rasped.

We drove to three restaurants until we found one with a working milkshake machine. By the time we got home, Laura wasn't able to draw the milkshake up through the paper straw, so I fed her tiny mouthfuls on a teaspoon and tried not to let the wave of despondency overwhelm me.

Later she reprimanded me for putting her deodorant back on the wrong bathroom shelf, reminding me that she was still in there somewhere. It only made it harder, though, the thought of her trapped inside. Watching someone you love lose every aspect of themselves is torture. My beautiful, kind, clever girl was in there somewhere and I missed her with all my heart.

One morning I tried to move Laura from her wheelchair to the sofa so she could take a nap. She wasn't able to help much and I messed up the manoeuvre, ending up trapped underneath her, neither of us able to move. 'Worst game of Twister ever.' I laughed.

She found this funny and we lay there giggling until Gracie eventually came to untangle us.

It was the little things that broke me: the half-drunk bottle of flat Coke in the fridge that Laura saved one ordinary lunchtime with every intention of finishing; the Timberland boots by the back door that she'd never wear again; the handwritten 'To do' list on her desk; books bought and never read; the white summer top she'd bought in Dusseldorf with the swing tag still attached, never to be worn.

All the hopes and dreams never to be realised.

She began to have seizures. Not the huge dramatic kind she'd had before surgery or the little shivers that started in hospital: these made her body rigid and stretched out her limbs, they were persistent and frightening. We used Buccolam syringes directly into her cheek as instructed, but the taste and the fact she couldn't swallow distressed her even more.

Leo suggested that it might be time for a syringe driver to be fitted to send small amounts of muscle relaxant into Laura's bloodstream to keep her calm and comfortable.

Duets of district nurses would arrive twice a day in their navy dresses, flushed and hot from walking up the hill. They would review the paperwork in the ominous black folder then check the driver and refill its reservoirs with the drug that subdued the sparks and flares of the electrical storm in Laura's brain.

On the first visit, one nurse explained that she needed to go through a list of questions with me. 'Does Laura have any wishes or hopes?'

'Yes, to say alive,' I snapped, tears brimming dangerously.

The girls had talked for years about getting matching tattoos, but some of Laura's medication came with risks of excessive bleeding so it was strongly advised against, and no reputable tattoo artist would take a needle to a someone undergoing active cancer treatment, so it hadn't been possible and now it was too late. Gracie took her friend, Erin, for support and came back with a delicate apple and a strawberry on the inside of her wrist.

When they were small, the girls used to say that those would be their last words: 'apple' for Laura and 'strawberry' for Gracie. One previous Christmas, Laura had commissioned a local jeweller to create matching necklaces.

'Do you like it?' Gracie asked, as Laura traced the design with her finger. 'I got one for you too,' she added, and produced the stencil that the tattoo had been traced from. She gently applied the design to Laura's wrist with a damp cloth, and they finally had their matching tattoos. I watched as they pushed their wrists together, as if some power was being passed between them, or maybe it was just love.

More and more, Laura's eyes would search the room for Gracie's, then lock on with a laser focus. It was impossible to know what she might be trying to communicate and left us all feeling more helpless than ever; especially Gracie, who until now had always been able to second-guess what her sister might need.

We bathed her every other day. Leo was an expert and taught me how to roll Laura's passive body from side to side to clean her with a warm, soapy flannel and her favourite shower gel. I shaved her legs and armpits and lashed her limbs with body lotion. We talked throughout, explaining what we were doing, reminding her of funny stories and things we'd done together. To begin with, she found it dryly amusing, but slowly her hands and feet turned a shade of purple as the blood concentrated in her essential organs, prioritising the brain and the heart, I suppose.

I'd been told that hearing is the last sense to go, so I played her long rambling voicemails from her friends and the girlfriend who had become an ex but stayed in touch. I hope that Laura heard and knew how loved she was. Then I tried to get messages from people Laura liked to watch: the lovely actress Diane Morgan; then a friend in Ireland sent one from Tina Fey; followed by an incredible three-minute-long message from Sandra Bullock which began, 'I've just spent the past day and a half looking at the extraordinary life that you have lived so far.'

She was humble and kind and Laura watched intently on my phone, her eyes moving but no longer able to respond.

Late at night I walked around the village raging at the fucking shitness of it all. My howls of misery echoed back from the walls of sleepy terraced houses. It was the thought of future Christmases, and summers, and all that lost time together. Laura had worked so hard for good grades and straight teeth and personal statements, all those small investments in a future she didn't get. She lay silently in a bed, skeletal, all cheekbones, eye sockets and teeth, waiting for death to put a cold hand on her chest and stop its determined rise and fall.

I didn't ask for her to be special, I just wanted her to be here, ordinary, and alive, like other people's daughters.

I had never thought about how long a person could go without food or water; Laura had managed only ice chips for days. I'd always known how tough and determined she was but hated the idea that she was holding on for our sake.

'Laura, my darling girl, it's OK. You don't need to fight anymore or stay for us. I know you're tired. Whenever you're ready, you can rest, my love.'

The curtain covered three-quarters of the window, diffusing the bright spring afternoon light. The window was open and the breeze surprisingly fresh despite a heatwave, but it was the birdsong we heard most clearly; pure and sharp over the baseline notes of motorway traffic, the occasional aeroplane on its way to or from Manchester airport, a siren and the sudden, intermittent growl of the compressor powering the air mattress on which Laura slept.

She was turned towards the open window, an oyster-silk eye mask on to block the light. Her hair was growing back dark and fluffy, like the feathers of a baby bird, against the cream pillowcase. A line of stitches and hard red scabs dissected the front of her scalp – no point in removing them now, they no longer mattered in the grand scheme of things. The TV was playing on mute and Chelsea had just beaten Manchester United in the women's FA Cup Final. A bee fought angrily against the glass, looking for a means of escape. Laura was always rescuing bees with a cup and a piece of paper, resettling them on flowers or feeding them sugar water. What would they do without her?

What would I?

Her hand was hot. It squeezed mine rhythmically and sometimes stroked the webbing between thumb and finger. This hand was pretty much the only part she could move by herself, and I clung to this fragile connection. When her grip released a fraction, she seemed to lift slightly on the bed and I checked, but the white duvet cover still rose and fell, almost imperceptibly.

Her breathing was shallow and soft, but it was still there.

It was a liminal, twilight world, watching and waiting for something to happen. We all slept downstairs now on sofas with cushions and spare duvets, like some strange indoor camping adventure. At night Laura was fidgety, reaching her arms out to stroke my hair. We woke at every whimper, not knowing if she would still be with us in the morning.

I worried that this would be all I remembered; that all the years of happiness would be overwritten by the trauma of the last few weeks.

On the eleventh day without food, Laura's breathing changed to a watery rasp. The district nurses administered an injection to subdue the rattle, her pupils widening momentarily with the scratch of the needle.

I told her that being her mum had been the privilege of my whole life and she squeezed my hand.

We opened the window to let in the soft May air and the song of an evening blackbird. We lit candles that smelt of 'calm' and switched on the fairy lights that lay across the mantelpiece. I read to her of Moon-Face and Silky and Dame Wash-a-lot, then played her favourite music from Spotify. We drifted in and out of sleep while Mark kept watch and woke us when the time came.

We held her hands and told her how much we loved her, and then she left us.

I opened the window so her soul could leave.

I cleared the room of medical kit, washed her and changed her into fresh pyjamas. A few hours later a private ambulance came to collect her. She had on the compass necklace that I'd bought for the three of us, hoping it might help her find a way back to us one day.

Without Laura to care for, we had no idea what to do with ourselves. The family rallied round, and we took Ziggy for a walk down to the river, but everything felt surreal, like we were playing characters in some badly written film. I wasn't sure what I was meant to say or how I was supposed to feel; I was sickly and shaky from the lack of sleep, but inside I was numb.

A few hours later I went to give blood. The donor nurse prepared me for the sharp scratch I barely felt.

'Do you feel OK?' she asked.

'Yes, I'm just tired.'

'Late night?'

'No, my daughter died this morning,' I replied.

She stopped attaching labels to the empty blood vials and stared at me. 'What on earth are you doing here?'

'Laura wouldn't want me to let anyone down, and also, I have no idea what I'm supposed be doing.'

Sometimes I walk from room to room asking, 'Where is she?'

I miss her so much.

I dreamt we were waiting to travel by plane. Laura had boarded first, probably due to her mobility issues, but Mark and I had to wait at the gate. Then it was announced that the flight was full. I complained vociferously but was told by the airline staff that it was fine.

'She doesn't need you now.'

I miss her terribly, the child she was, the teenager we knew and the adult she was becoming. I miss seeing her walk into the room chewing on a carrot, I miss seeing her sitting at her desk with headphones on and a tube of Pringles, watching *The Office*. Her shoes are by the back door and will never be laced up again, her Turkish Delight still in the fridge. I cannot believe that I will never see her face again; I probably haven't even begun to process the fact, kidding myself that she's still away at university.

'I'm heartbroken to share the news that we lost our beautiful Laura in the early hours of this morning. She was fierce and tenacious to the end, and it was truly the honour of my life to be her mum. We are devastated at the thought of a life without our girl. She was a force of nature. Her flame burned brightly but not nearly for long enough.'

This tweet announcing Laura's death was seen by almost ten million people and messages of condolence flooded in from around the world. But I know that the worst of grief is still to come. I tell myself that her life contained more joy, excitement and adventure than some that last for seventy years. It was a life full of love and experiences that made us look at each other and ask, 'Can you believe this?' It was a shorter life than it should have been, but in many ways, it was still a full one. If she'd been given longer, she might have changed the world, but if she touched some lives and made a difference to a few others, that will have to be enough.

'Will she be back in three weeks?' Alice asked.

Laura was passionate about the search for a cure and, as she had instructed, her brain was donated for research. If a legacy is 'planting seeds in a garden that you never get to see', then who knows what hers might be.

The Stars Will Still Be There

The question that keeps me up at night is *Could we have done more?* It felt at the time that we'd exhausted all options, but was there something we missed that could have cured her? I suppose that's the question I'll ask for the rest of my life, but I don't regret any of the things we did. We had four-and-a-half years with Laura when we expected twelve months and, for the majority of that time, things were good, sometimes even wonderful.

The most important thing I've learned from Laura is that really *knowing* your life is finite is a blessing – no, really. Laura told me that it was only when she realised she was going to die that she truly began to live. Her life until that point had been entirely focused on making deposits for the future, passing exams to get a job, securing work experience to look impressive on a CV. Paying in time and effort to see her investment mature and grow. Thinking about how perfect and complete life would be when she'd finished her A Levels, got a degree, passed her driving test, and become fluent in Persian.

Laura's diagnosis taught all of us that's not really how life works. This bit, today, reading these words on a page, this is it. These are the moments we should relish, breathing in the sweet smell of the mown field where we walk the dog, taking photos of a beautiful sky or a funny shaped cloud, playing Mario Kart with your sister, laughing, and sucking the sauce from your fingers.

If life was an endless, all-inclusive sun-drenched holiday, you might find yourself spending the afternoon watching TV on your bed, playing solitaire with the curtains drawn and bemoaning the lack of choice in the all-you-can-eat buffet. It's knowing that you only have days left before the flight home that pushes you to get to breakfast early, book an excursion or stay on the beach till the sun sets and the kids are shivering. It's knowing that your holiday will end that makes you use your time and really appreciate it.

Why don't we adopt the same approach with our actual lives? Is it because we imagine those decades stretching out to infinity, convincing ourselves that we have all the time in the world? Or is it perhaps because we don't really think we'll die? How can we imagine a world without ourselves in it, after all?

But imagining your own death is actually quite liberating as well as sobering.

What will people say about you?

Whose lives have you touched, what was it all worth?

And if, on reflection, you can't think of all that much, the good news is that you still have time to change that. It's a gift, you know, which is why they call it the present.

Epilogue

September 2023

Hey Laura,

I got a tattoo. Gracie talked me into it, you know what she's like, you could call it persuasive if you were feeling kind! I have a compass – like our matching necklaces – on the inside of my wrist with L as my north and G as my south. You always were 'my north, my south, my east, my west. My working week and my Sunday rest'.

Gracie has the same, and she also had: 'I've got you dude' tattooed on her upper arm. You wrote it for her when you were poorly and it's so clearly your handwriting. She likes to think that you've still got her back. I know I'm a massive cliché with a tattoo at fifty-three, but I hope it helps us to find each other one day. I needed to have some way of wearing my loss, like a cattle brand to show the world that you lived, and I miss you every moment of every day.

Talking of cattle, you would have loved the celebration of your life. We held it at Thornton Hall Farm – there were chickens under the tables, and to get to the toilets you needed to go through the llamas and the goats; loads of children came and played on the go karts and jumped up and down on the bouncy cushions. Some of the adults did too.

Steph acted as our celebrant – she'd only just completed her training, so she was understandably nervous, but honestly, she was fantastic. Gracie did the most incredible speech; she was terrified and said it was much scarier than introducing Peter Kay, but she was so brave, you'd have been really proud of her, Laura.

She told everyone that you charged her 20p an hour to play dolls, but the rest of it you'd have loved:

'There were certain things in life I never learned, like Excel spreadsheets, because Laura could conjure one out of thin air and I never had the patience, and child locks, and knowing which banks had good interest rates, or even what interest rates actually were, because Laura would always tell me what to do.

'My sister was the kindest human, but only on the sly. She didn't want anyone to know how big her heart was, but the kids she sponsored in Africa for years and the people whose lives she changed will testify to what a heart of gold my sister had.

'I miss her every single day, but she will never be gone until the ripples she made in the world disappear. Now I'll have to spend longer remembering my sister than I did knowing her, but I'll forever be grateful for the privilege of being Laura's little sister.'

Gracie's housemate Ben made a film using clips from our phones and Dad made the most wonderful montage of old home movies; he even included the guinea pig video diaries which everyone thought hilarious – you all serious and shouting, 'Cut!' while

Gracie tried to upstage you by cartwheeling into shot. It was streamed all around the world, Laura – it's incredible how many people felt like they knew you and wanted to be a part of it.

We had a brass band to start with, then the choir sang 'Together in Electric Dreams', 'Golden Slumbers' and 'Bridge over Troubled Water' and we finished with a brilliant ska band; all your old primary school teachers had a proper good dance and although everyone cried buckets, it was really joyful too. I just wish you'd been there to enjoy it.

I found that thing you'd stuck to the inside of your wardrobe, and I hope you don't mind, but we included it in the order of service.

Everyone dies alone

But if you mean something to someone, if you helped someone, if you loved someone, if even a single person remembers you, then maybe you never really die at all.

I just thought it was perfect. You touched so many lives, Laura, some you have absolutely no idea about, so this must mean you'll live for ever. We were sent cards and messages from all around the world; it was incredible, and I know you'd have found it really quite bizarre. I also had an email from someone who'd been bullied at your school. Apparently, you'd been kind, going out of your way to include her and encourage her passion for poetry.

'Her acts of kindness really kept me going through that very dark period,' she wrote. 'I never, ever felt judged.'

I cried when I read it, you always made me so proud.

We miss you such a lot.

Dad sits in your tranquil forest bedroom every day and has a one-sided conversation with you; he's finding it so hard. You know how adamant he was that everything was going to be fine, he was so determined that you'd live, and he feels that he let you down because despite all his promises, you died.

I told him that he has nothing to feel guilty about, that you always knew. You went along with his passionate positivity, but you knew how this would end and you were always more worried about how he'd cope when it did.

We talk about you all the time. I've convinced myself that you're off on an adventure somewhere, that maybe you did become a spy after all and this is just some elaborate cover story.

The Lionesses made it to the World Cup Final, beaten by Spain, unfortunately. Not long after the match finished, Gracie said she saw you go into your room and slam the door, which is exactly what you would have done.

Where are you?

Gracie had her graduation day, we were so proud and it was lovely, but we really missed you. I gave her the Playmobil figure you bought for her in Dusseldorf, and she cried. She was so touched that you'd thought of her back then. We went for afternoon tea, and I missed having the debate with you about the order of jam and cream on scones. Neil and Georgina bought Gracie a big fancy personalised balloon with smaller rose-gold balloons inside it, but as we left the hotel Alice managed to loosen it from the ribbon and it floated away. Gracie was gutted until Alice said, 'Laura's really going to love that.'

Epilogue

Alice said you'd gone to Bethlehem initially, but now she seems to think you're in the sky. If I push her on the swing, she shouts, 'Hello, Laura!' when she's at the very highest point of the arc.

We're going to France again soon, and she asked if we might see you from the plane.

I have those figures you bought for her birthday, the one with the bald head that you planned to use to explain why you didn't have hair. She talks about you all the time. Gracie and I took her to the theatre and in the car, she said, with all the wisdom of her three years and eleven months, 'We're all just a little bit sad about Laura, aren't we?'

When she's a bit older we'll read her *My Naughty Little Sister* and *The Magic Faraway Tree*. That's where I imagine you, in some magical land at the top of the tree with Silky, eating pop biscuits and having magical adventures.

On the day you died, I turned on the radio to hear your voice on the news and immediately burst into tears. You were everywhere for days, and it was nice that people cared, but heartbreaking too.

We're struggling with the kitchen table – it's hard to sit down for a meal when there are just three of us and an empty chair. We miss seeing you with your four drinks on the go, taking hours to finish your dinner and scrolling through your phone to find that interesting thing you wanted to show us. We've tried swapping places a few times and Erin is here a lot, which is lovely and distracts us from the obvious fact that you're not opposite Gracie, arguing about who kicked who first under the table.

She's doing OK – mostly. I'm keeping a close eye on her and we're holding each other together as best we can, but there's just this giant Laura-shaped hole in the middle of the family. Ziggy is still looking for you – his ears prick up when he hears your name and he wanders around your room, sniffing your slippers, wondering when you'll be back.

Gracie's making a podcast called 'The Dead Sibling Club'; she chose the name because she knew you'd love it. Olivia has become a really good friend to her, they talk all the time and there are rumours of matching carrot tattoos!

Your dad floated the idea of moving house and I just burst into tears at the thought of it and not only because it's full of junk. How could we leave the house when it's bursting with memories, especially if you've got any plans to stick around for a bit and haunt us.

Gracie's booked in to visit the medium again, but she can't get an appointment until next year. I'd like to go too but I'm scared that we won't make contact and I honestly don't think I could handle the disappointment. Do you remember when I went, before you were diagnosed, and she gave me my money back? I often wonder if she could see what was coming for us. I wouldn't have wanted to know – would you?

When I go to the supermarket, I struggle not to automatically reach for the things you liked: the cheese strings, Pink Lady apples and green Pringles. Stupid, inanimate objects sometimes knock the breath out of me – I cried in Sainsbury's at the sight of a punnet of lychees: they were always your favourite, and I'd buy them for breakfast on your birthday, sometimes racing to the shops late at night if I'd forgotten.

I'm still buying healthy stuff, but the carrots tend to shrivel to witchy fingers in the salad drawer and the broccoli trees just fade to autumnal yellow. Chicken Kyivs come in packs of four and the one left over, covered with cling film in the fridge, just reminds me that you're not here.

On good days, we are unbalanced, a wonky table with a folded beer mat under one leg; on the bad days, it feels like the skin has been ripped from my body.

I hoped that I might get the skinny grief, but it feels like a great hole has opened up inside me and I'm stuffing the void with crisps.

Epilogue

To be honest, I can't look directly at the grief, it's too painfully sharp and nuclear bright, like direct sunlight or a solar eclipse, so I keep my eyes down and focus instead on the shadows it casts.

I'm trying my best to make you proud, Laura.

We did the Pride parade again this year for the Brain Tumour Charity, and there were more of us than ever. I had your picture printed on some A2 boards and I carried you high above my head, tears rolling down my cheeks. Grandma and Gracie rattled the collection buckets as usual and told everyone all about you. Gramps carried your picture, but he found it a struggle, he was just so sad. I gave him the personalised *MasterChef* apron that you'd bought for his birthday, and he cried and said, 'I just miss her so much.'

The University of Manchester are considering awarding a scholarship in your name. How good would that be? Imagine someone who's having a tough time being able to study for a degree because of the Laura Nuttall Scholarship. I hope they search your name and read about all the incredible things you managed to squeeze into your twenty-three years. We've installed a bench with your name on in the park where you used to get drunk with your friends and there's even a road in the village that's been renamed Laura Nuttall Way, it's on Google maps – how brilliant is that?

In July I was a delegate at the annual conference of the British Neuro-Oncology Society at your uni. I had to register in the room where we collected your graduation gown, which hurt. I can't honestly say that I understood every presentation, but more than you might think, and I've even told them that I'd like to speak at next year's conference in Cambridge. I just want them to know what it feels like to be in our shoes, to be told that there is nothing that can be done to save the person you love. Neil says I'm having my Erin Brockovich moment. Dad and I also went down to the House of Commons to an All-Party Parliamentary Group meeting on brain tumours, which brought back memories of our day there and trying to console Gracie on failing her driving test in the toilets while the female MPs nipped to the loo between debates.

I miss you in so many ways: some so big that they swallow me whole; and little things too, like the way that you'd always rub the foundation into my jawline when I'd applied it in my usual slap-dash manner; how good you were at untangling knots on the finest of necklace chains; how you couldn't sit without jiggling one knee; how you'd rush into the kitchen to inhale the smell of melting butter; and how kind and thoughtful you were when one of us was ill. Sometimes I think that you were just the best of us, Laura.

Remember that letter you wrote for Barrowford School? Well, your very talented sister made the last part into a rainbow-coloured logo that we had printed onto T-shirts and tote bags.

Be Kind
Be Brave
Be Silly
Be Honest
#BeMoreLaura

We've sold thousands, it's been insane, but really wonderful that people want to remember you and support your legacy. Some have even told me that they behave differently when they wear them, and your words are on the walls of classrooms all over the world. We've set up the Be More Laura Foundation to fund research into glioblastoma and already made the first grant to support a medical cannabis trial. I know how important it was to you that we continue to fight for a cure.

You know that post you saw on Facebook? It popped up on my timeline again today, and it had a poem alongside the image of a queue of people in a field.

Epilogue

'Every minute someone leaves this world behind. Age has nothing to do with it. We are all in "the line" without knowing it. We never know how many people are before us. We cannot move to the back of the line. We cannot step out of the line. We cannot avoid the line.

'So, while we wait in line:

'Make moments count.
Make a difference.
Make the call.
Make priorities.
Make the time.
Make your gifts known.
Make a nobody feel like a somebody.
Make your voice heard.
Make the small things big.
Make someone smile.
Make the change.
Make yourself a priority.
Make love.
Make up.
Make peace.
Make sure to tell your people they are loved.
Make waves.
Make sure to have no regrets.
Make sure you are ready …'

Loads of people take credit for it but I think it was written by Marianne Baum. Sound advice, though, isn't it?

So, I'm going to do my best to 'be kind, be brave, be silly, be honest'.

But all I truly want is to be your mum again.

Until we meet again, my darling x

Acknowledgements

Thank you to the fabulous Charlotte Robertson at Robertson Murray for her encouragement and support, Kelly Ellis for having faith in the story, and the fantastic team at HarperCollins for making it a reality: Ajda Vucicevic, Imogen Gordon Clark, Belinda Jones, Isabel Prodger, Alex Layt, Lexi Bickell and Ameena Ghori-Khan.

A huge thank you to

The Ansons, the Nuttalls and the extended family who did so much to help us at every stage. We could not have got through this without your love and kindness.

All our wonderful friends for the constant support, especially Leo, Lorraine and Steph for always being there for us, and the friends on Twitter we have never even met.

Every single person who raised funds or generously donated to our fundraisers and every big-hearted person who responded to one of my scrambled beg emails.

Laura's friends who stayed the course: Iona, Thomas, Ilona, Lisa, Kirstie, Hannah, Emily, Caitlin, Patrick, Herbie and the 2019 Young Ambassadors. Olivia – Laura loved you very much – you're an honorary Nuttall now, remember?

The incredible staff at Salford Royal, especially Mr D'Urso and Mr Leach, and the wonderful team at The Christie, with special thanks to Dr Colaco and Hanna Simpson. The district nursing team, Amber at Homerton Hospital, Matt Williams, the staff of IOZK and the indefatigable Professor Van Gool.

Peter Kay for making us laugh when things were grim, and making treatment possible.

Sophie Raworth, Caroline Turner, Roger Johnson, Jack Gray, Tony Livesey and Graham Liver, who followed our story from day one and made sure it spread as far and wide as possible.

Michael Cheema, Ambreen Mirza and all the staff at Giddy Kippers for keeping the ship afloat and giving us precious time with Laura.

Barrowford Community Choir, the village school and the whole wonderful Barrowford community.

Jamie, Paul, Steph and Kerrie-Ann for getting 'Doing it for Laura' off the ground. Trawden AC (especially Jamie) and all the runners and running clubs of East Lancashire.

Bill Kenwright for his incredible generosity and the team at Everton FC for their hospitality.

Eddie, Captain Dave, Colin and the wonderful Leopardsong family for making us so welcome.

David Ross for the unforgettable family holidays in France; Candice and Steph for sharing their own little corners of heaven with us.

Rob Lockyer and HM Royal Navy for making Laura feel she belonged.

Jonathan Lane and the lovely pilots who got us to Germany when it seemed impossible.

The Lionesses, England Rugby League and the Birmingham Commonwealth Games organisers.

Reedy and GMP, Sophie and the Waiting family, Ainscough's Crane Hire, White Watch Bolton, The Clink HMP Brixton, Donna and Phil Guy, Heinz and Santus, Aardman Animation, Drew Steel, Trevor Sorbie Covent Garden, Scarlett and Richard Curtis, Dave and Nicky Fishwick, Jim Toms, Ron Haslam, Clive and Alex at TFL, Rachael and Sarah, Deborah Armstrong, Andy Redhead, Malala Yousafzai, Paul Whitehouse and Bob Mortimer, Aly, Ory and Johnny Marr, Drew Steel, Sajid Javid and MI5, Caitlin Moran, Ben Shaw, Angela and Neil Dickson, Sir John Royden and Sarah Bone, Christy and Dave Hughes, Owain Wyn Evans, Sonia Friedman, Ed and Lauren at Underbelly, Rosalind Wyatt, Ed Thomas, Jack Black (not that one), Vince Thirkettle, Midlife, Ben Robertson, Tom at Veselka, LadBible, Kate McKinnon, Richard and Cath Kenyon, Rachel Cox, Dany Robson, Mary Hall, Dennis Heritage, Abi Luccock, Sean Reddington, Chloe Kelly, The Red Arrows, Leisure Pursuits, Thornton Hall Farm, Donmar Warehouse, Margot Robbie, Yav Keogh, Sandra Bullock, Tina Fey and Diane Morgan.

Courtney, Louise and all at Birchall Food Service, Marks & Spencer for the fake Christmas.

Georgia and Ian for taking such good care of the girls in Cyprus.

Professor Jackie Carter and the support team at the University of Manchester. The staff and students at Skipton Girls High School.

The fabulous hotels … The Langham, The Claremont Victoria, The Waldorf Hilton, The Ritz, The Baglioni, Virgin Hotel Edinburgh, Hyatt Regency Manchester, Nobu Shoreditch, The Savoy and The Plaza NYC.

The charities working to make a difference: The Brain Tumour Charity, Brain Tumour Research, Brain Tumour Support, Brains Trust, The Institute of Cancer Research, Our Brain Bank, Rays of Sunshine, The Ellen McArthur Trust, Thumbs Up for Charlie, Teenage Cancer Trust, Mission Motorsport, Fly2Help, The Willow Foundation and Maggie's.

Thank you to my early readers for their honesty and generosity.

Mark and Gracie, Mum, Dad, Neil and Georgina. Shelley Welsh, Lorraine Dickinson, Debs Lloyd, Leo Pendlebury, Clare

Allan, Dr Mary Black, Deborah Stevenson, Lucy Boyle, Rachel Harvey, Victoria O'Dowd, Nicholas Lee, Olivia Sutcliffe, Erin Brown and Steph Taylor Bolshaw. Cathy Rentzenbrink, Raynor Winn and the Arvon 'posh candle' ladies.

I could fill a whole book with thank yous, so please forgive me if your kindness wasn't mentioned. Grief has messed with my memory, but we are so grateful to you.

In memory of

Charlie, Daniel, David 'Did', Grace, Matthew, Amani, Ria, Liam, Laurent, Shay, James, Mary, Emily, Andy, Oliver, Charlotte, George, Tom, Chris, Fifi, Abbie, Eva, Oscar, Atticus, Izzy, Cleo, Olivia, Logan, Stu, Jana, Jessica, Deb, Oli, Zoe, Con, Duncan, Tom, Charlie, Anthony, Owen, Emma, Archie, Lindsay, Dave, Judy, Bobby, Isla, Matt, Samantha, Grace, Victoria, Ethan, Dr Vicki, Rose, Isla, Lisa, Freya, Rachel, Ashley, Zara, Jason, Alfie, Connor, Harry, Renai, Susie, Evie, Matt, Jillie, Fred, Ruby, Tory, Jess and, of course, our Laura, who we miss every minute of every day.

More reading

Do No Harm by Henry Marsh
The Emperor of All Maladies by Siddhartha Mukherjee
When Breath Becomes Air by Paul Kalanithi
Surviving 'Terminal' Cancer by Ben Williams
Pear Shaped by Adam Blain
How to Starve Cancer by Jane McLelland
I Am Malala by Malala Yousafzai
More than a Woman by Caitlin Moran